# CONDOR

# The Stackpole Military History Series

## THE AMERICAN CIVIL WAR
Cavalry Raids of the Civil War
Ghost, Thunderbolt, and Wizard
Pickett's Charge
Witness to Gettysburg

## WORLD WAR I
Doughboy War

## WORLD WAR II
After D-Day
Armor Battles of the Waffen-SS, 1943–45
Armoured Guardsmen
Army of the West
Australian Commandos
The B-24 in China
Backwater War
The Battle of Sicily
Battle of the Bulge, Vol. 1
Battle of the Bulge, Vol. 2
Beyond the Beachhead
Beyond Stalingrad
Blitzkrieg Unleashed
Blossoming Silk against the Rising Sun
Bodenplatte
The Brandenburger Commandos
The Brigade
Bringing the Thunder
The Canadian Army and the Normandy Campaign
Coast Watching in World War II
Colossal Cracks
Condor
A Dangerous Assignment
D-Day Bombers
D-Day Deception
D-Day to Berlin
Destination Normandy
Dive Bomber!
A Drop Too Many
Eagles of the Third Reich
The Early Battles of Eighth Army
Eastern Front Combat
Exit Rommel
Fist from the Sky
Flying American Combat Aircraft of World War II
For Europe
Forging the Thunderbolt
For the Homeland
Fortress France
The German Defeat in the East, 1944–45
German Order of Battle, Vol. 1
German Order of Battle, Vol. 2
German Order of Battle, Vol. 3
The Germans in Normandy
Germany's Panzer Arm in World War II
GI Ingenuity
Goodwood
The Great Ships
Grenadiers
Hitler's Nemesis
Infantry Aces
In the Fire of the Eastern Front
Iron Arm
Iron Knights
Kampfgruppe Peiper at the Battle of the Bulge
The Key to the Bulge
Knight's Cross Panzers
Kursk
Luftwaffe Aces
Luftwaffe Fighter Ace
Luftwaffe Fighter-Bombers over Britain
Massacre at Tobruk
Mechanized Juggernaut or Military Anachronism?
Messerschmitts over Sicily
Michael Wittmann, Vol. 1
Michael Wittmann, Vol. 2
Mountain Warriors
The Nazi Rocketeers
No Holding Back
On the Canal
Operation Mercury
Packs On!
Panzer Aces
Panzer Aces II
Panzer Aces III
Panzer Commanders of the Western Front
Panzergrenadier Aces
Panzer Gunner
The Panzer Legions
Panzers in Normandy
Panzers in Winter
The Path to Blitzkrieg
Penalty Strike
Red Road from Stalingrad
Red Star under the Baltic
Retreat to the Reich
Rommel's Desert Commanders
Rommel's Desert War
Rommel's Lieutenants
The Savage Sky
Ship-Busters
The Siegfried Line
A Soldier in the Cockpit
Soviet Blitzkrieg
Stalin's Keys to Victory
Surviving Bataan and Beyond
T-34 in Action
Tank Tactics
Tigers in the Mud
Triumphant Fox
The 12th SS, Vol. 1
The 12th SS, Vol. 2
Twilight of the Gods
Typhoon Attack
The War against Rommel's Supply Lines
War in the Aegean
Wolfpack Warriors
Zhukov at the Oder

## THE COLD WAR / VIETNAM
Cyclops in the Jungle
Expendable Warriors
Flying American Combat Aircraft: The Cold War
Here There Are Tigers
Land with No Sun
MiGs over North Vietnam
Phantom Reflections
Street without Joy
Through the Valley

## WARS OF AFRICA AND THE MIDDLE EAST
Never-Ending Conflict
The Rhodesian War

## GENERAL MILITARY HISTORY
Carriers in Combat
Cavalry from Hoof to Track
Desert Battles
Guerrilla Warfare
Ranger Dawn
Sieges

# CONDOR

The Luftwaffe in Spain, 1936–39

Patrick Laureau

STACKPOLE
BOOKS

Copyright © 2000 by Hikoki Publications

Published in paperback in the United States in 2010 by
STACKPOLE BOOKS
5067 Ritter Road
Mechanicsburg, PA 17055
www.stackpolebooks.com

First published in Great Britain in 2000 by Hikoki Publications Limited. This edition published by arrangement with Creçy Publishing Limited. All rights reserved, including the right to reproduce this book or portions thereof in any form or by any means, electronic or mechanical, including photocopying, recording, or by any information storage and retrieval system, without permission in writing from the publisher. All inquiries should be addressed to Creçy Publishing Limited, 1a Ringway Trading Estate, Shadowmoss Road, Manchester M22 5LH.

*Cover design by Tracy Patterson*

Printed in the United States of America

10 9 8 7 6 5 4 3 2 1

**Library of Congress Cataloging-in-Publication Data**

Laureau, Patrick, 1951–
 [Legion Condor]
 Condor : the Luftwaffe in Spain, 1936–39 / Patrick Laureau.
  p. cm. — (Stackpole military history series)
 Originally published as: Legion Condor. Ottringham : Hikoki, 2000.
 ISBN 978-0-8117-0688-9 (pbk.)
 1. Germany. Luftwaffe. Legisn Csndor.  2. Spain—History—Civil War, 1936–1939—Participation, German.  3. Spain—History—Civil War, 1936–1939—Aerial operations, German.  4. Spain—History—Civil War, 1936–1939—Regimental histories.  I. Laureau, Patrick, 1951– Legion Condor. II. Title.
 DP269.47.G3L38 2010
 940.54'4943—dc22
                    2010020724

# Contents

*Introduction: The Place of the Legion Condor in History* ........ vii

Operation "Magic Fire" ........................................... 1
The Legion Condor ............................................... 21
Aufklärungsgruppe A/88 .......................................... 31
The Dornier Do 17 in Spain ...................................... 41
The Heinkel He 45 in Spain ...................................... 55
The Heinkel He 46 in Spain ...................................... 63
The Heinkel He 70 in Spain ...................................... 73
The Henschel Hs 126 in Spain .................................... 83
Seefliegerstaffel AS/88 ......................................... 87
The Heinkel He 59 in Spain ...................................... 97
The Heinkel He 60 in Spain ..................................... 103
Jagdgruppe J/88 ................................................ 107
The Heinkel He 51 in Spain ..................................... 143
The Messerschmitt Bf 109 in Spain .............................. 163
The Arado Ar 68E in Spain ...................................... 195
Kampfgruppe K/88 ............................................... 197
The Junkers Ju 52/3M in Spain .................................. 231
The Heinkel He 111 in Spain .................................... 259
The Stuka Adventure in Spain ................................... 301
The Henschel Hs 123 in Spain ................................... 307
The Junkers Ju 87 in Spain ..................................... 313
Versuchsbombengruppe VB/88 ..................................... 325
The Junkers Ju 86D in Spain .................................... 341
Versuchsjagdgruppe VJ/88 ....................................... 345
Stab/88 ........................................................ 351
They Also Served ............................................... 361
In Spanish Service ............................................. 367

*Captions to Color Artwork* .................................... 375
*Notes* ........................................................ 381

# Introduction: The Place of the Legion Condor in History

The story of the Legion Condor[1] is remarkable. It is, in fact, proper to emphasize, before going into details, to what extent this corps was out of the ordinary. There was never any question, at the departure of the first German volunteers, of forming an expeditionary corps so complete and so costly. For the first Heinkel 51 squadron and the quasi-independent force whose image is retained in the world, the path was not so obvious, and the growing importance of the Legion Condor in Spain was many times put in question by the Nazi leaders themselves.

This diplomatic game of "give-give" was not, in the course of the Spanish War, a German speciality. The Soviet Union was also up to imposing its cadres and political concepts, as well as consignments of indispensable matériel. The difference resides in the fact that Germany at that time was playing a game that was much more dangerous for its economy than it was for that of the USSR of the 1930s. When the Legion Condor had to be replenished, at the beginning of 1937 and then in 1938, in order to regain its effectiveness, the Nazi regime had a high price to pay for the political influence that it wished to preserve in Spain.

Unknown facts remain numerous, and oral history, sadly practiced too late, has allowed many actors to take their role into infinity. Happily, others have been left to eliminate a good number of myths and to bring some reality out of the shadows.

Leaving aside the uncertainties of the "hunting scenes" painted by the German pilots (and by the Italians and Franco Spaniards also), the importance that the Legion Condor has had on the Spanish conflict cannot be denied. It would be too much to argue that it won the war by itself; that would cheapen the enormous quantity of Italian matériel, and also the courage and the willingness of the other men. One can however note that the Legion Condor was, from March 1937, at the base of actions which led to the progressive military collapse of the Republicans. As regards aviation, these last mentioned are unanimous: those feared, in the air, were the Germans. And it is probable that this fact contains, in its simplicity, more reason than passion.

As the exotic venture of German Fascism transformed itself into a real campaign of experimentation, it is the history of military aviation itself that is found to be changed. New material, of course, but also new tactics and new techniques—the Legion Condor rethought it all in Spain. Clearly overtaken by Soviet products at the time of the first encounters, German technology, galvanized by a militarist and vengeful regime, was able to go farther than the Nazi cadres thought in 1936, while their great Eastern rival became mired in the purges and did nothing less than cut off its right arm. Germany was at the time united and efficient, and its best travelling salesman was called the Legion Condor.

By its undeniable successes, by technological advances which it encouraged directly, the Legion Condor contributed greatly to launching the Nazi regime into the great territorial adventure of the Polish campaign and the Second World War. But one can today put the question of knowing whether the qualitative advantage obtained in the course of the "Spanish campaign" was not in the end deceptive. In fact, it may well be that it was in too short a term, for the strategy applicable to a medium-sized and divided country like Spain did not have much to do with the conditions imposed by the great spaces of the Eastern plains, or with the too-long operational distances to which Germany would soon be condemned, against England for example.

Nonetheless, the Legion Condor, an exceptional unit formed with unexceptional men, should undeniably remain in the history of aviation and in history in general as a chapter and part and parcel of a paradox to be given thought: a unit very near to operational perfection, but the foundations of which were only viable in the short term and in a relatively precise environment.

# Operation "Magic Fire"

## Unternehmen "Feuerzauber"

**FIRST CONTACTS AND PRELIMINARY AID**
Hardly two or three days after the "pronuncimiento"[2] of the rebel Generals Sanjurjo, Mola and Franco, there was no doubt that the rapid and almost painless coup d'état, at first awaited, was going to be transformed into a longer, and also more difficult, struggle to the point where the Republican government was able to regain the initiative. Indeed, the latter had at their disposal the majority of the Spanish troops, three quarters of the air force, and all of the navy. There reigned, certainly, at the heart of high Republican circles, an astonishing incompetence, very close to what is commonly called a "shambles"; in any case, the name eventually stuck to it. The best troops of the rebel generals were to be found in Spanish Morocco and could not, it seemed, risk the passage of the narrow Straits of Gibraltar under the guns of the fleet, which remained loyal after the massacre of the majority of traditionalist officers.

On 22 July 1936, General Franco sent a first message to Germany. This, conveyed by Colonel Juan Beigbeder Atienza to *General* Kühlenthal, German military attaché in Paris, called as principal aid for the sending of "ten heavy transport planes, able to carry a maximum number of passengers"; these planes would of course be bought by civil companies. To insist to the maximum extent, Franco also decided to send a messenger to Berlin, Captain Francisco Arranz, and two notable Germans installed in Morocco, Adolf Langenheim and Johannes Bernhardt. The journey was made in a civil Junkers 52 aircraft of Lufthansa, piloted by Captain Henke and requisitioned in Las Palmas in the Canary Islands. These emissaries only arrived at their destination on the 24th, after an unforeseen technical stop at Seville and another at Stuttgart.

On the same day, the German Minister of Foreign Affairs replied to General Beigbeder's despatch in the negative, and the three men were greeted in Berlin with the minimum enthusiasm. The political professionals in the Wilhelmstrasse, although sympathizing in all logic with a movement rebelling against communist influence, were not about to risk entering such a venture, and wanted above all to protect their interests and their residents in Morocco, and also, of course, their relations with the eventual victor in this confrontation, whichever it may be. Finally, it should not be lost to view that the Nazi regime of 1936 was not yet what it was later to become, and that Germany in full economic resurgence had hardly made a start on its policy of rearmament. In these circumstances, any sending abroad of heavy matériel from Germany represented a considerable sacrifice, too important in fact, in the eyes of Wilhelmstrasse.

The rebel leader, General Francisco Franco y Bahamonde, in the dark jacket, during a rare visit to the Legion Condor in front of the Fieseler Storch (46-1 or 46-2) in which he, *Generalleutnant* Helmuth Volkmann (in peaked cap), and the crafty Spanish General Antonio Aranda (in glasses) had arrived.

This negative reply sold short the ambitions of the new politicians of the *Auslandorganization*,[3] and through it, of the National-Socialist Party itself. For their part, Bernhardt, and above all Langenheim, who was *Ortsgruppenleiter*[4] for Morocco, took it upon themselves to discuss the rebels' appeal with *Gauleiter*[5] Bühle, who organized a meeting with Rudolf Hess. When Hess decided to send the envoys of Franco directly to Chancellor Adolf Hitler, in the middle of the Bayreuth festival, the initiative and power of decision no longer rested with the "timorous" people of the Wilhelmstrasse, but with the Party.

The "Council," hastily organized in situ, also comprised *General* von Blomberg (then Minister of War), Hermann Göring (then Reich Minis-

# Operation "Magic Fire"

ter of Aviation), and *Admiral* Canaris. This last named, who finally overcame the hesitations of Hitler and von Blomberg, was now Chief of the *Abwehr*,[6] and Canaris was a friend of Franco and also a great psychologist. It was decided that aid would be immediate and secret. A legal cover would be ensured for the exchange of materials through "private" organizations.

In passing, Hitler's strategy in the event should be underlined. Beyond ideology, with which one can take liberties in politics, it is longterm strategy that imposed this option. Rather than see the Nazi Reich framed in the East by the USSR, a growing power, and in the West by the French Popular Front and an obedient communist Spanish Republic, it was more reassuring to install in Spain a regime similar to Italian fascism. It was then France that found herself in a bad posture, or at least neutralised, being obliged to guard three potential fronts at the same time. Finally, a corollary impossible to ignore, and which had to weigh heavily in the decision, German industry and the new army being formed could only benefit, the one from Iberian minerals, and the other, later, by an opportunity to put to the test of actual combat experimental and new materials and tactics recently developed by the young chiefs of the *Wehrmacht* and *Luftwaffe*.

In the the evening of 26 July, the ways and means of German aid were fixed. Present at this working meeting were General Keitel (representing von Blomberg), Hermann Goering, *Admiral* Canaris of course, and *General* Milch, representing the RLM.[7] Operation *Feuerzauber* was now already on the march.

With the aid of Teutonic efficiency, it needed less than one week to put the business in motion. *General* Helmuth Wilberg, codenamed "Wild" on this occasion, was charged with the formation of *Sonderstab W*. This "Special Staff W" would centralize the transfer to Spain of the volunteers and matériel.

In parallel, two commercial companies were to follow soon afterwards to carry out the consequent administrative tasks, imposed by this juggling. The "Spanish" HISMA, the director of which in Seville was none other than Johannes Bernhardt, was to take charge of the resupply, lodging and wages of the German volunteers, and drawing up the indispensable link between the Franco Headquarters and *Sonderstab W*, in order to facilitate the creation of the necessary military organisation and an effective General Staff. Soon after HISMA, the German ROWAK emerged from the imagination of the NSDAP, set up to deal with the German end of the economic cooperation with Franco. Among its principal directors was to be found a certain Hermann Göring. It is known that the Wilhelmstrasse services were not immediately made aware of the establishment of these companies; on the other hand the Ministry of Finance quickly came into the conspiracy, presenting the ROWAK, from the date of its creation, with a credit of three million Reichsmarks.

The first aid consigned considerably exceeded what was raised by the despatch of Beigbeder, since instead of ten aircraft, Germany sent twenty Ju 52 three-engined transport aircraft, piloted by Deutsche Lufthansa crews, under the command of Rudolf von Moreau, one of the most celebrated German pilots of the time on account of his flights and records. The first aircraft took off from Berlin-Tempelhof on 27 July with Flugkapitän Henke at the controls, and landed at Ceuta on the twenty-eighth to immediately undertake the crossing between Morocco and Seville.

Thereafter, from the twenty-seventh, the Party operated a discreet but effective recruitment campaign among the *Jagdgruppen* of Dortmund and Düberitz, and the *Kampfgruppen* of Gotha, Mersburg and Anspach. It is evident that these young aviators, brought up in a country rising from an unprecedented economic crisis, and who were still quite dazzled by a Nazi future, could do no other than come forward en masse as volunteers. Two days later, after selection, a first contingent of eighty-six men was ready to depart and placed under the command of *Major* Alexander von Scheele, a veteran pilot of the First World War, who had the advantage of speaking fluent Spanish. It therefore fell to von Scheele to direct this first party from the *Reisegesellschaft Union*—"Union Travel Society"— the cover organisation which would give a veneer of normality, if not respectability, to these journeys.

On 31 July, *General* Milch took leave of these volunteers, who embarked that evening at Hamburg at the Petersen Quay, on the steamer *Usaramo* of the Wehrman Company, under *Kapitän* Heinz Stammer. The ship also carried in its holds six Heinkel He 51 biplane fighter aircraft, twenty 20-millimeter antiaircraft guns, and about one hundred tons of miscellaneous war matériel. This service was to function throughout the entire war at the frequency of one ship every five days. In all, there were around 170 shiploads which made up the Spanish shuttle service, generally departing from Hamburg.

*Vize-Admiral* Karls, commanding the German forces cruising in Spanish waters, had the task of escorting the steamer from the coast of Portugal until Cadiz. The cruiser *Deutschland* and the destroyers *Leopard* and *Luchs* took over from 5 to 6 August. Once the matériel was disembarked, the whole group continued with their agreeable journey next day in a special train to Seville.

The six fighters had to be assembled in situ, then tested by Eberhardt, Knüppel, Trautloft, von Houwald, Hefter and Klein. The task was covered by experts from Heinkel under the orders of Chief Mechanic Winkler, who himself had to lend a hand. The Heinkel 51 being the second type of fighter to fly in the ranks of the rebels after the Hispano-Nieuport 52, it was decided to allocate the type code "2." Perhaps by osmosis, the Junkers 52 then took on the number "22."

**FIRST EXPLOITS, FIRST SETBACKS**
The air bridge, which the rebels started to throw over the straits with some miscellaneous aircraft (Savoia-Marchetti SM.81 brought in by the Italian Air Legion, Savoia S.62, Dornier Wal and Breguet XIX), was to be the first important operation of the German detachment in Spain. Of the first twenty Junkers Ju 52s accorded to Franco by the Third Reich, ten were in the first instance brought to Seville by the Lufthansa pilots. *Leutnant* von Moreau and his forty-two men then harnessed themselves to the job. They were, like the Spanish pilots in Africa, to do three to four round trips daily to transport the troops who were to open the insurgents' road to Madrid. Their "cargo" of very local color gave rise to some astonishment on the part of the German pilots: the Moorish soldiers were unable to depart on campaign without their traditional impedimenta; loaded with them in the Junkers were copper dishes and tea sets, teapots, guitars, packets of sugar, sacks of flour, multicolored blankets and quite a number of live sheep. The German planes were soon to carry the daily "capacity" of the air bridge of 240 to 500 men, supported by the Italian three-engined aircraft, already disappointing due to their unreliability.

The Junkers started the shuttle on 29 July. These were piloted by the Germans carrying out their first service on 28 August, taking on board 40 men (and their luggage) instead of the 17 passengers normally expected. On the basis of three or four round trips per aircraft per day, the air bridge in this fashion transferred 6,453 men in August (against 897 in ten days in July), 5,455 in September and 1,137 in October.

The German three-engined aircraft were soon in need of a second wind, and their legendary reliability suffered from loading and flight conditions; the heavy air obliged the pilots to maintain maximum power constantly, and maintenance was done too quickly. The most urgent difficulties were dealt with first, following the orders of the Spanish commanders, and the result was left to chance. At the end of a week of continual service, there were only seven Junkers in a condition to fly. At the end of fifteen days, there were only five, and four at the end of one

A rifle section of North African rebel troops climbs aboard an already camouflaged Ju 52. The obvious calm and discipline of these tough professional soldiers is readily apparent and contrasts with many pictures of the same kind we know from the Republican side.

month of operations. In particular, it was the sand which consumed the engines. The Germans would not forget this lesson when they were to return to North Africa some time afterwards.

The rhythm of the shuttles was to wear out not only the matériel. On 15 August, a Ju 52 crashed at Jerez de la Frontera. Fortunately, it was empty, but *Unteroffizier* Helmut Schultze and his mechanic, Herbert Zech, were killed instantly.

From there on, the German volunteers were only involved on the logistics side. The orders issued by *General* Milch were precise: "Volunteers must transport Franco troops and protect them. It is forbidden to look for combat, they must only fight in the event of an attack on transport aircraft." Things, however, evolved very quickly. The cruiser *Jaime 1*, which had remained in the hands of the Republicans after the rapid elimination of the majority of the officers, was moored fore and aft in the roads of Málaga and prevented by her presence alone all transit of rebel troops by sea. Moreover, even deprived of her officers, there remained a redoubtable floating battery, and her antiaircraft guns drove off the planes at each passage, because these, overloaded, could not climb above 3,000 meters. Even though the Spanish seamen were very poor shots, they eventually had to shoot down something.

# Operation "Magic Fire"

On 10 August, the German crews received the DSAC 250-8 bomb racks which enabled them to carry six 250-kilogram projectiles in their three double holds. On the orders of von Moreau, two Ju 52s were thus immediately converted, and took off on 13 August at 16.10 and 16.15 hours, the pilots respectively being von Moreau and Hencke. After fifty minutes of flight at 2,000 meters, the latter decided to descend under the cloud cover; he broke cloud at almost 500 meters. At this altitude, the Goertz-Beukohf Type FL 219B bomb sight was unusable. The bomb aimer, Graf von Hoyos, succeeded anyway in placing two bombs on the moored battleship by guesswork. Immobilized, the flagship of the Government fleet had then to be towed the Cartagena with about fifty dead on board. For his part, von Moreau was lost in the clouds and finally resigned himself to putting down at Ceuta, with his bombs, which were still too precious to be sacrificed in vain.

In view of the unforeseen success of the operation, four other Ju 52s were then hastily transformed into bombers. One of them was taken from the transport group, and the three others were new aircraft which had just arrived from Germany. These six aircraft formed one of the first Ju 52 bomber "squadrons," respectively christened *Pedro I* to *Pedro III* and

In Tetuán, Morocco, some of the first tabors of the Spanish Moroccan troops wait for what will probably be their first air trip, to Andalucía. The aircraft are straight from Lufthansa service, the only difference being the removal of civilian registrations and the painting of rebel markings. Aircraft 22-79, in the background, was later assigned to K/88 as a Stab aircraft.

*Pablo I* to *Pablo III*. Rudolf von Moreau of course took command of the first of these units, the other being entrusted to *Oberstleutnant* Rudolf Jüster; from among the pilots present, Josef Schmitz, Hans Hemmel, Hencke and Hajo Hermann were chosen to pass from transport to combat role.

It should be made clear that the air bridge was not the only means of transporting the African troops to the mainland. The 13,942 men carried by air were also joined by troops and heavy matériel which made the crossing on various ships. (On 5 August, a first convoy took over by this means 2,000 men, guns and vehicles, after a savage skirmish against the Republican units, which was ineffective because the Republicans had no real command structure.) It nevertheless constituted a great first and an audacious logistical improvisation, which formed a milestone and was later to be perfected beyond all expectation. But what would have happened if Republican fighters from Andalusia, very superior in numbers, had brought down one or more transports?

This German participation in a conflict that was still internal did not of course go unnoticed, and the Republican government was not deceived. The situation was all the more delicate because in Madrid there was still a German mission. And Lufthansa continued to make a stop in the Spanish capital, at the same time for its last commercial flights and for the conveyance of military Ju 52s, disguised occasionally under civil registration. So it was that on 9 August, D-AMYM, piloted by von Bastian, head pilot of the company, landed at Barajas while the relationship between the German chargé d'affaires, incapable of justifying the activities of his compatriots, and the Republican authorities was quite degraded. After a brief exchange of words with the representative of Lufthansa in Madrid, Georg von Winterfeld, the plane straight away took off again towards the south. But von Bastian had deviated from his route before landing in Madrid, and he soon had to land for lack of fuel 400 kilometers from there, at Badajoz, in Extramadura.

The crew was immediately apprehended by the militia, and the aircraft was confiscated, refuelled and sent back under close guard to Barajas. The measure was matched by a refusal of clearance to take off for the company's six aircraft then present in Spain. This was lifted several days later after a vigorous protest to the chargé d'affaires, and von Bastian's crew was released at the same time, but D-AMYM, repainted in the Republican colors, stayed at Barajas under guard; the presence on board of documents of a military nature also explains the Republican reaction very well. The aircraft was finally destroyed in its hangar in the course of a bombardment on its sister aircraft, without it being possible to indicate or confirm its use by the Republican air force.

The definitive cutting of the regular line in one respect did not have great importance, for the "moustachioed" pilots of *Sonderstab W* hardly had a problem in replacing it by a slightly longer route. From November, they regularly followed their weekly connections, only losing three aircraft throughout the entire war.

On 20 August, 1939, the fierce—and unpredicted—resistance at the Alcazar at Toledo excited almost general admiration. This strong center of traditionalism, which was thought at first to be condemned to fall like a ripe fruit into the hands of the militias, suddenly crystallized the hope of having a firm base in the proximity of Madrid. A symbol was born; glory could not, must not, escape the German aviators.

In the night of the twentieth and twenty-first, von Moreau then loaded his aircraft with supplies and munitions, packed in double canvas bags. Leaving Tablada at dawn, he soon approached Toledo at 4,000 meters altitude, with engines off. To make a Ju 52 glide is not an easy business, and the fresh supplies, dropped all at once, fell outside the ruins. Returning to Seville, von Moreau reloaded his aircraft. This time, he took the aid in large metal cans, of more predictable ballistic shape. In mid-afternoon, he took off for Toledo. Climbing first towards the east, he succeeded in deceiving the Republican look-outs, who certainly were not expecting a Junkers to arrive in the government zone, and were probably thinking that it was one of their bombers. The drop was made this time with precision, from 500 meters altitude. The load fell completely into the courtyard of the besieged Academy. It measures 60 by 70 meters. It only remained for von Moreau to come back to Seville with an aircraft drilled like a sieve.

After this demonstration of heroism, very romantic and lasting, the German volunteers were soon viewed in a favorable light. Nor was their presence in the ranks of the insurgents any longer a secret, because after a first period of "camouflage" they distributed to the blond Aryans some of the uniforms and headgear of the same model as those worn by the forces of order at the Olympic Games, which had just closed down at Berlin. There were not enough of these white outfits to dress everyone, however, and those who were left out were soon called the lucky "Soap Salesmen."

For their part, the two Ju 52 detachments, somewhat grandiosely called "squadrons," had already been thrown into the conflict, passing outside the control of *General* Milch. In this first period of almost permanent improvisation, the three first *Pedro*s and *Pablo*s had to cover almost

Republican soldiers and militiamen seem to enjoy the moment; D-AMYM was soon be repainted in Republican colors, but was later destroyed on the ground without ever having had an opportunity to fly for its new masters.

everywhere: on the Toledo front from Salamanca, up to Cartagena from Granada, up to Bilbao, even from Léon, in order to disturb the unloading of matériel being sent by sea to the Republic. So, on 18 August, Hencke attacked the Republican command posts around Badajoz. On the twenty-third, it was von Moreau who carried out the first German bombing raid on Madrid. The War Ministry was targeted, but the results were rather mediocre. The operation was repeated with three aircraft with such a success, however, that Hans Voelckers had to protest, and requested his government to withdraw the Ju 52s from offensive operations, at least while the regular Lufthansa service continued.

The next day in Berlin, *Admiral* Canaris met Count Ciano, who insisted on the freedom of action that the Italian government gave its pilots. That same evening, the consignments for Milch were cancelled by the Nazi officials, at the time very impressed by the Italian fascists. The German volunteers again found themselves to be the abandoned bride. This order was, however, only for the purpose of legalizing a *de facto* situation, the fighter pilots in particular becoming ever more active—and effective, as we will see.

Perhaps to celebrate that, the German bombers came back to the capital on the twenty-ninth. This time, deaths were numerous and public opinion turned unanimously against the Germans. This did not prevent the

*Pedros* and *Pablos* from carrying out almost all the bombing done by the insurgents in the course of the month of September. Among the most outstanding operations, one notes the attack on the Four Winds aerodrome on the seventh, which left three Dewoitine and three Nieuport fighters completely out of action; on the twenty-fourth, the Ju 52s, all together, attacked the aircraft of the Republican naval air arm located at Bilbao.

*Feuerzauber* then came to a close, and the German volunteers were soon to find themselves integrated in the Legion Condor, as will be seen further on. From the twentieth, the *Pedros* and *Pablos* were based at Ávila, to the northwest of Madrid.

For their part, the Heinkel He 51 biplanes had been assembled, with some difficulties; certain parts were missing, which had to be forged on site. All came together thanks to the talent for improvisation of *Leutnant* Kraft Eberhardt, but the delay ensuing from this unforeseen shortage was at the origin of the first friction between the Germans and the Spaniards. *Leutnant* von Houwald reacted rather strongly against the constant surveillance (or curiosity) exercised in the course of the assembly by certain Spanish pilots, eager to touch their new mounts. The incessant questions about this machine, very superior to the Nieuport 52 fighters known by the Spaniards, and especially the calls about the urgency of the situation, greatly irritated von Houwald, who contented himself with taking charge of the acceptance tests of the aircraft that were finally assembled.

On 15 August, Eberhardt officially handed over the six brand-new He 51s to the Spanish pilots Rambaud, García Morato, García Pardo, Salvador and Ramiro Pascual. The task of the German pilots was practically finished—in theory. In fact it is probable that the ebullient young men did not intend to stay on the sidelines for very very long. Considering moreover their Iberian colleagues, certainly still inexperienced, as "technically underdeveloped," they were probably ready to grasp the first opportunity to recover "their" machines. They did not have to wait long. On 18 August, Morato counted two victories in combat against a Potez 54 and a Nieuport 52, and Salvador three, over two Breguet XIXs and a second Nieuport, on the Granada and Mérida sectors. On the other hand, two of the other pilots made such hard landings that their machines were immobilized, one of them with a broken propeller, a particularly grave breakdown, in view of the lack of spares. Given this situation, Eberhardt went to obtain permission from General Kindelán for the German pilots to take part in war missions. This soon widened the breach, in spite of the brilliant repair job carried out on the broken propeller by the "underdeveloped" mechanics, who had seen others of the same kind with the catastrophic Hispano-Nieuport 52.

On 22 August, the five He 51s, piloted by their German "masters," took off in good order for Escalona del Prado, between Cuellar and Segovia. The Nationalist staff were planning a heavy bombing raid on the Getafe airfield, to the south of Madrid. On the twenty-fourth, three machines therefore escorted the Spanish Ju 52s onto the target. They were piloted by Rambaud, García Morato and Ramiro Pascual. Although the bombing went well, the return was less glorious. Rambaud's Heinkel was hit by the flak at Getafe, and its landing gear collapsed; Ramiro Pascual for his part again undershot on landing, his second such landing in a week.

That was enough. The German pilots, indignant and quite refreshed, got together and went to express their resentment to "Papa" von Scheele, who insisted to General Franco on the return of the three remaining He 51s exclusively to the German volunteers who had brought them. They were then attributed nominally to Eberhardt, Trautloft and Knüppel, who called themselves the "Guadarrama Fighters." On the twenty-fifth, the patrol fell upon three Republican Breguet XIXs in the Madrid sector and Trautloft obtained the first air victory of what was to be the Legion Condor. The following day, it was Knüppel who recorded his first success, and Eberhardt his second, again against Breguet XIXs. On the twenty-seventh, Knüppel downed the first Republican fighter reported to the credit of the German volunteers; an Hispano-Nieuport 52 piloted by a young British volunteer.[8]

It was a blessed time for the German fighter pilots. The only Republican aircraft capable of out-performing the He 51s were the Loire 46s and high-wing Dewoitine 371s and 372, which operated under Malreaux's "Spain" Squadron and the Martin Luna International Squadron, officially dubbed the "2-Lafayette Squadron" because of the Anglo-Saxon pilots gathered in it. But there were very few of these modern aircraft, and they were often badly flown by foreign pilots who remarkably were not very aggressive or were incapable, as on the twenty-sixth, when Knüppel tore apart a Dewoitine although it was clearly more rapid and more manoeuvrable, and particularly well placed behind him. All that had the air of being a pheasant shoot. At this time also, one could picnic at the Escalona airfield, where the He 51s were in the open air, and where the ammunition boxes and fuel were lined up under the trees bordering the track, hardly covered.

The German pilots, or the propaganda system, tended to exaggerate their exploits somewhat, as when, on 28 August, the Eberhardt flight surprised two Potez 54s in the Guadarrama sector. The bombers flew at 100 meters altitude, thus delivering themselves tied hand and foot to the

### Operation "Magic Fire"

opposing fighters, since their engines were set to gain their maximum nominal power at 4,000 meters (presumably these were planes from the Martin Luna unit, because the French pilots of the Spain Squadron were unlikely to have made the same mistake). The three fighters emptied their ammunition boxes into the second machine, which went off spitting oil. The next day, same scene, same actors; there was one Potez and an additional Heinkel, but the scenario was identical. The German pilots, at full throttle, finally saw the three twin-engined Potez pull away. Trautloft did not succeed in placing himself for a frontal pass, the Potez being too quick. The aircraft "downed" on the twenty-ninth was credited to Eberhardt, "that" of the thirtieth tripled, one for each of the three usual members of the flight, which all the same doubles the theoretical maximum result which was very probably obtained.[9]

The wind turns quickly in the matter of aerial combat, and glory is ephemeral. Earlier, on the twenty-seventh, one of the German pilots, unnamed for obvious reasons, had been the precipitate author of one of those regrettable errors which may be elegantly called "bravura," when downing a De Havilland D.H. 89 Dragon Rapide which he was detailed to protect. But on 30 August, the "Guadarrama fighters" suffered their first grave reverse when Trautloft was surprised by a Dewoitine and shot down. With the right wing riddled and the controls cut, he could only take to his parachute while the He 51 plunged to the ground. He took his revenge the next day, marking up a new victory over a Nieuport.

On 1 September, the unit moved again, Escalona being decidedly too near the front, and it installed itself in greater safety at Cáceres. The new deliveries of matériel which were then made comprised nine totally new He 51s, which enabled the setting up of one complete squadron comprising the German volunteers, and occasionally, Morato and Salvador. These, soon disgusted with the (at best) paternalistic attitude of the Germans, again flew on 2 September on this model on the Talavera front, where Morato marked up a victory against a Nieuport. It was at this time that he started to contact the Italians to fly the Fiat CR.32, and he even put off some of his Spanish comrades from flying with the Germans.

Von Houwald was then entrusted with a *Schwarm* (patrol of four aircraft) which had to ensure mastery in the first half of the month of the air space over a Republican air force that was becoming more and more weakened. So on the fifth, von Houwald marked up the destruction of a Nieuport and a Breguet, and Knüppel that of a Loire 46; the next day, the latter shot down a Potez 54 to the east of Talavera, imitated at Navalmoral by Kraft Eberhardt.

Apart from this free-ranging flight, the other He 51s assured protection, from Navalmoral to Talavera, of the Ju 52s which participated in the offensive on the Tago. At this time, the Nationalists thought, logically, that the business was concluded and that Madrid would soon fall. Also, the flak had moved from Seville-Tablada, which was not really threatened, in favor of the airfields at the front. The German Headquarters then followed their Spanish counterpart to Cáceres, "Papa" Scheele at the head: Major Deichmann was put in charge of the offices at Seville, the management of which occupied a good part of the Hotel Cristina.

Things did not happen by themselves alone, however, when the German pilots had to confront the best Republican pilots on the few surviving Dewoitines and Furies. Thus, on the seventeenth, the "Guadarrama fighters" had a bad time in the face of a flight composed of each of these two types.[10] Everyone returned home empty handed, but happy to have got out of it. In the afternoon, Knüppel forced a Nieuport to land behind Nationalist lines, but he was unable to draw the Ptas 40,000 reward for the "release" of a Republican aircraft in good condition, because the downed pilot set fire to his machine before making good his escape to his own lines.

After a short stay on the Ávila base, the He 51s moved on 23 September to the base at Vitoria, to support General Mola's campaign against the Republican provinces in the north. On the twenty-sixth, a flight composed of von Houwald, Hefter and Klein encountered a Republican formation composed of a Vickers Vildebeest of the naval aviation, a Breguet XIX and a protective Nieuport fighter. The German fighters had no problem about putting themselves in a position to fire, but the three opposing pilots were not novices; after some fruitless aerobatics and some bursts of fire, the three "Reds" spun towards the ground, each to their own side. On their return to their base, each of the German pilots claimed one aircraft. In fact, all three Republican machines returned home, the most badly hit being the Breguet, which recorded twenty-one impacts in the wings.

Having, it seems, copiously celebrated his victory the previous evening, Hefter botched his take-off from Vitoria on the twenty-eighth, and crashed on the Town Hall Square, killing himself immediately. Discreetly, at the official level, the cause was attributed to an engine failure.

The squadron returned on 29 September and on the thirtieth Eberhardt and Trautloft each shot down a Potez 54 on the Madrid front. In fact, there was only one ("E"), alone, flown by the Frenchman Deshuis, who overturned behind his own lines, with three wounded and two dead on board. At the end of September, the main event for the German fighter pilots was the arrival of fresh blood when on the twenty-seventh the detachment received reinforcement by six planes and six pilots: *Unteroffizier* Willi Gödecke, *Oberleutnant* Oskar Henrici, *Unteroffizier* Kowalski, *Unteroffizier* Ernst Mratzek, *Oberleutnant* Günther Radusch, *Leutnant* Paul Rehahn, *Unteroffizier* Erwin Saw-allisch, *Leutnant* Kurt Strümpell, *Oberleutnant* Dietrich von Bothmer and *Leutnant* Kurt von Gilsa. The squadron had become overcrowded, with fifteen pilots and seventeen aircraft. It was therefore divided into two small units placed under the commands, respectively, of Eberhardt, who was to be based near Barahona, and of Trautloft, who found himself at Léon with the mission of escorting the resupply and bombing flights on Oviedo. The Spaniards finally received the three machines remaining from the first delivery, and which were now rather worn out. They served some time with Morato, Salvador and Salas, where they had plenty of leisure to compare them against the Fiat CR.32 in a series of mock combats. The result was very clearly in favor of the Italian type, and from 2 October, the Spaniards only flew in the biplane designed by Celestino Rosatelli.

In the month of December, the position of the Republicans became almost untenable. Their air force became nonexistent, while the numbers of the Ju 52s, He 51s and He 46s, Fiat CR.32s, Romeo Ro 37s and Savoia-Marchetti SM.81s were on the increase. All was going badly everywhere for the Government forces, even in Aragon, where the militias nevertheless since the end of July were besieging Saragossa, which seemed less and less disposed to fall. In addition, in the air, the hegemony of the "Red Wings" squadron was no more than a distant memory. On 19 October, Knüppel and the flight based at Saragossa intercepted a dozen aircraft. After a short fight, Henrici announced that he had shot down a three-engined Fokker, a Breguet and a Nieuport, to which must be added two other Nieuports for the account of von Houwald and Stempell. Henrici later reduced his claim, for it seems that "his" Breguet went into the ground following an aerial collision.

The air bridge was finished on 11 October, and all the aircraft massed before Madrid, yet Madrid still held out. In the morning of the twenty-fifth, the rebel air force paraded above the capital with forty-eight bombers and thirty-two fighters. In the afternoon, the parade started again with 100 machines, all that could be found apart from seaplanes and some fighters "on guard" in the north and in Aragon. The heavy transports dropped leaflets inviting surrender while the fighters competed in a display of aerobatics. Even so, on the ground, the Front held, in the country and the University City. Graver still, the Russians were there, it was known. New fighters, new bombers, soon came to defend Madrid. On 28 October, the first Tupolev SB-2s carried out a bombing raid on the Seville-Tablada airfield. They were clearly faster than the Italian fighters. What would the He 51 biplanes be able to do?

The same difficulties afflicted the Ju 52s. On 4 December, *Leutnant* Oskar Kolbitz's plane was intercepted above the University City by the Russian I-15s, and shot down at Esquivias. The crew had time to get out with parachutes, but not the pilot who was killed at the controls. Two days later, it was von Moreau who was severely hit above Madrid and had to make an emergency landing. The German crews understood; on a very active front, the Ju 52s could no longer operate unescorted by day.

The Ju 52s and He 51s were no longer the only German aircraft in Spain. In September, cargoes departing from Hamburg brought about twenty Heinkel He 46 support planes, with performances unworthy of a combat front. They were ceded rapidly to the Spanish, who did not rush to take them up. On the other hand, the six He 45B biplanes that arrived in October had already formed the kernel of a future German reconnaissance group. In the south, two He 60 flying boats also made their appearance, commanded by *Leutnant* Karl-Heinz Wolff and *Leutnant* Siegmund Storp. Finally, doubtless on the recommendation of Ernst Udet, an Heinkel He 50 and two Henschel Hs 123s were based at Jerez de la Frontera, for comparative dive-bombing trials. The former did not stay very long in Spain, totally eclipsed by the first true operational "Stuka" in history. Five old Junkers W34 transport aircraft also appeared. They served first as couriers, before being used as weather reconnaissance machines and as general maids of all work.

It is often forgotten that there was at that time in Spain a German contingent other than the flyers. On their arrival, certain officers were put in charge of training Spanish specialists in various fields. So on 30 August there arrived the ground radio stations which could replace the low-powered radios brought on the Ju 52s of Lufthansa. At Seville, Pfleiflugleiter Fläschendränger was soon also to open a school to train specialists in communications.

Also, *Leutnant* Hajo Herrmann, whose name would become well known during the Second World War, was put in charge, in between operations with the air bridge, to set up detailed instructions on the use of 20-millimeter antiaircraft flak guns and to explain them to the future leaders of the batteries. He soon remained in position as the Inspector of Flak. Herrmann was not long in forming an instruction team which, under the command of *Wachtmeister* Hackenholt, split up into three elements which travelled up and down the front bringing the good word, thanks to the interpreters kindly furnished by the German consulate at Madrid. In October, the most effective weapon to be seen in its genera-

# Operation "Magic Fire"

tion in this field was unloaded—the 88-millimeter Flak 36 gun, a battery of which was set up shortly thereafter at Tablada under the command of *Leutnant* Aldinger, while the light antiaircaft artillery was at the same time reinforced by twenty-eight supplementary 20-millimeter guns.

On the technical side, *Hauptmann* Deichmann had arrived in Spain with an aeronautical engineer and two specialist officers, charged with supplying technical aid and invaluable advice to the Nationalist naval shipyards.

At the end of September, the first detachments of the *Wehrmacht* had finally disembarked: 122 men from the 4th Schweinfurt and 6th Neuruppin Regiments forming two companies with forty-one Panzer I tanks and a transport company and an antitank group armed with twenty PaK field guns. In October there arrived in support another armored company, a reconnaissance and repair group, and some supplementary guns. *Oberstleutnant* Ritter von Thoma, commander of the II/Panzer Regiment 4, had on 20 September taken up his appointment as commander of this light tank battalion. The activity of these soldiers was far from being negligible during the course of the war. They trained the officer-students of many Spanish schools, notably that of Ávila, and were free to carry out all the operational experiments evoked by the theoretician geniuses Guderian[11] and Tukhachevskiy[12]; they thus enabled the *Werhmacht* to overcome the mediocre quality of its tanks (compared with the Soviet T-26s), thanks to the excellence of new tactics. Until the end of the war, it was *Oberst* von Funck who would remain at the head of all the German land forces in Spain.

Spain held a place that rose higher and higher in German politics, economics and concerns. In October, the personnel and premises assigned to Spanish affairs had been, on the orders of Göring, greatly increased, thereby adding numerous offices and a good number of services of the Ministries of Economy and Foreign Relations, without counting that emanation of the Party, the *Auslandorganization*.

There were also on the ground in the Peninsular special envoys with darting eyes. *Oberstleutnant* Warlimont ("Volkersdorf")[13] went there to make a tour on the ground and take notes. His dominant impression was not very flattering. It was even less so after *Admiral* Canaris's journey under the pseudonym of "William." The latter commented on and was anxious about the immobility of the situation before Madrid. With the arrival of Soviet arms and Soviet-style units, all hope of an early victory would have to be abandoned. The opportunity had passed in October. What was to be done? Abandon everything, after having consented to all these efforts being financed? The decision was made.

On 30 October, Canaris was entrusted with a delicate mission from the German Minister of Foreign Affairs, Constantin von Neurath. This was to tell *Generalissimo* Franco that the methods of "white" Spain did not exactly meet with the enthusiasm of the German Chiefs of Staff. Germany wished to send more important reinforcements, on condition that these would be perfectly independent and responsible solely to General Franco himself; furthermore, the latter had to be committed to carrying out the war more energetically. These conditions were totally humiliating for the Spanish officers, as it thus laid bare their inability. Only Canaris, based on his friendship with Franco, was able to make the bitter pill go down. This was undoubtedly difficult, but the situation of the rebels, without Germany, would soon become desperate. Franco had no choice; he accepted. So the Legion Condor was born and would soon make its entrance on the scene.

A pristine Heinkel He 51 in its original German RLM 63 paint but with newly applied early-style Nationalist markings and a long-range fuel tank. 2-24 served with 2.J/88 and is probably seen early in 1937. The aircraft carried double black discs and stripes on the upperwing.

For much of the war, the mainstay of the Republican fighters was the Soviet-designed Polikarpov I-15, known as the Chato. Well over 200 were built under licence by the Republicans, who found the type's agility greatly superior to the He 51s and on a par with the C.R.32. This one was flown by the defecting Republican pilot Sargento Arranz on 2 November 1938 to La Cenia, where it is clearly the subject of much curiosity. The red Republican markings have already been partly overpainted.

The bomber equivalent of the I-15 was the Tupolev-designed SB, a captured example of which is seen here in Nationalist camouflage and markings. Generally known to both sides as the Martin bomber, it could show a clean pair of heels to the Nationalist biplane fighters. At the time of its combat debut, it was probably the most advanced aircraft of its type in the world but was dismissed by the Western powers as a copy of U.S. types, to the satisfaction of the secretive Russians.

A battlefield discussion between *Oberst* Hans Seidemann (center), Chief of Staff of the Legion, and, with back to camera, a man who resembles the newly arrived commander of the Legion, *Generalmajor* Wolfram von Richthofen. The Spanish major on the right is the commander of the Navarre Brigade. As the war was clearly in its final stages, there was good reason for Seidemann to look cheerful.

# The Legion Condor

## Organization

Throughout the whole of the Spanish Civil War, the Legion Condor remained essentially an air force unit that was always commanded by flyers: *Generalmajor* Hugo von Sperrle up to November 1937, then *Generalleutnant* Volkmann up to November 1938 and, finally, *Generalmajor* Wolfram von Richthofen, cousin of the great Manfred and second chief of staff of the Legion under von Sperrle, a post in which he succeeded *Major* Alexander Holle. As a general rule, the total personnel strength of the Legion regularly available, including support staff, was about 6,000 men.

The first part of the Legion left Stettin on 7 November 1936 on board the *Fulda* (which even at this early date was already the twenty-first special steamer destined for Spain) and quickly found itself reassembled in Seville with 100 vehicles of its own. Twenty-five other cargo ships followed in the period up to 29 November, discharging men and matériel at Cadiz which were always reunited afterwards at Seville. Among others, the vessels *Berlin* and *St. Louis*, right at the start of the campaign, brought the first large contingent of fighter pilots and sixteen He 51s.

The Legion was a revolutionary unit due to its organization, encompassing all the arms and services necessary, not only for its offensive function, but also for its defense, provisionment and administration. It was thus described by *Admiral* Canaris as perfectly self-sufficient. For the General Staff of "Unit 88," mobility and independence had to be the keys to efficacy; for the first time, real combat operations were going to be carried out by a completely autonomous unit.

Each task was well defined within the Legion Condor, and a variably sized *Gruppe*—unit—existed for each specialty:

**A/88**: *Aufklärungsgruppe 88*—Reconnaissance Group. This unit successively used He 45Bs; He 70Es and Fs; Do 17Es, Fs, and Ps; and finally Hs 126As.

**AS/88**: *Aufklärungsgruppe am See 88*—Maritime Reconnaissance Group, using principally biplane, twin-motor He 59Bs and a few He 60Es.

**B/88**: *Betriebskompanie 88*—Maintenance Company, responsible for the aircraft park.

**F/88**: *Flakabteilung 88*—Antiaircraft artillery unit or detachment. Of increasing importance as the conflict became "professional," F/88 introduced into Spain the much-celebrated Flak 36 88-millimeter gun. There, by chance, they discovered its ability against tanks.

**J/88**: *Jadgruppe 88*—Fighter Group. It comprised between three and four squadrons flying first He 51Bs, then Messerschmitt Bf109s of types B, C, D, and E. It also tested the He 112 and the Ar 68 night fighter under service conditions.

**K/88**: *Kampfgruppe 88*—Bomber (literally Battle) Group. It was comprised of three to four *Staffeln*—squadrons—depending on the period in question, flying first Ju 52/3m3e's and 3mg4e's, then He 111Bs, and finally He 111Es.

**Laz/88**: *Lazaret 88*—field hospital.

**Ln/88**: *Luftnachrichtenabteilung 88*—Communications Group, divided into radio, telephone, aerial communications, and runway lighting.

**MA/88**: *Munitions-Anstalt 88*—Munitions supply.

**P/88**: *Park und Luftfahrzeuggruppe 88*—Aircraft Park Vehicles. The functions of the unit often necessitated going to examine recoverable or nonrecoverable wreckage on the ground. Eventually, it received two of the six Fi 156 Storchs, which arrived in 1938.

**S/88**: *Sondersstab 88*—General Staff. As one would expect, S/88 disposed of different types of transport for liaison, among which there were Junkers W34hi's, Fi 156As, and three Klemm Kl 32aXIV three-seaters, which arrived during 1937.

**VB/88**: *Versuchsbomber 88*—Experimental Bomber Group, which tried out the first Do17s and He111s, eventually forming a fourth operational bomber squadron in 1937.

**VJ/88**: *Versuchsjagdstaffel 88*—Experimental Fighter Group, which did so much with the Bf 109s, He 112s, and Ju 87As before being integrated with J/88.

**VS/88**: *Verbindungsstab 88*—Liaison Group with the Spanish and Italian general staffs.

**W/88**: *Wetterstelle 88*—Weather Office.

**Büro Grau**: "Grey Office"—Office of the air attachés.

Finally, the diverse services of assistance and instruction for the preceding detachments were integrated into:

**Büro Anker**: "Anchor Office"—Office of the marine attachés.

**Büro Nordsee**: "North Sea Office"—Office of marine operations.

"Happy Easter 1939—the war is over" is the message on these SC250 and 500 bombs in the well-stocked Legion Condor bomb dump. Stacked in neat rows and totally uncamouflaged, they would have made an excellent target for the Republican air force, had that organization been in a position to mount serious attacks.

**Imker Ausbilder Gruppe**: "Beekeeper Instruction Group"—*Imker* was the overall code name for the German army units tasked with training Spanish Nationalist troops.

**Imker Drohne**: "Beekeeper Drone Company." There is a degree of Germanic humor in the cover name of this supposedly nonoperational training unit that was tasked with teaching the Spanish the use of tanks and armored warfare.

**Imker Horch**: "Beekeeper Listening Company"—Signals Company.

It is noteworthy that the independence of the Legion Condor was reflected in its relations with the Italian and Spanish general staffs, which were not always the most cordial and were frequently marked with a certain self-conceit. The Germans would accuse their Mediterranean comrades of systematically glorifying themselves by the use of propaganda, whereas the Legion Condor was content to get on with the job. It is certain that the Latins had an ambivalent attitude towards their northern allies, and it was not one of sympathy.

More specific allegations were put into writing in the memoirs of certain pilots of the Legion such as Galland and Harder. These called into doubt the aerial victory list, which was somewhat flattering to the Italian pilots, and noted the incompetence of the Spanish fliers. These two accusations were without doubt at the time well-founded, but not too much importance should be attached to them. In any case the pilots of J/88 also had a tendency to inflate their exploits. This was to a certain measure inevitable in the framework of the system of attribution of victories practiced by the Nationalist side.

Rather than treat the history of the Legion Condor in exclusively chronological order, mixing all the units, the author has chosen to talk independently of each air group in alphabetic order. On the other hand, the listings of the types of aircraft used throughout the war are presented more logically at the end of each chapter rather than in less readily accessible appendices.

The color party of the Legion on parade at Léon on 1 April 1939 immediately afer the cessation of hostilities. In the German forces, the standard bearer was usually an NCO with an escort of junior officers. The bandolier he is wearing here is entirely Spanish in style; in the *Wehrmacht*, his status would be indicated by a gorget. The flag combined a German design with Spanish colors of red and gold.

The Hotel Cristina was the headquarters of the Legion in Seville, all its facilities being reserved for the administrative duties and the lodging of resident and nonresident Condor officers.

Seville in 1936 was certainly a quiet place to be—the only traffic appears to be a couple of trams.

Looking very relaxed is *Major* Hans Wilhelm Deichmann, deputy for *Major* Alexander Scheele, who was the commander of the very first *Luftwaffe* contingent sent to Spain in July 1936. The headquarters staff was based in the Hotel Christina, Seville, from early August.

One of the main stars of the Legion Condor never flew: the 88-millimeter Flak 18 gun was revealed in Spain not only as an excellent antiaircraft gun (a duty for which it had been designed), but also, quite fortuitously in a moment of high pressure, as an outstanding antitank weapon. It is here in action in the latter duty. Note the loader racing into position with another shell; the standard armor-piercing round weighed ten kilograms. The level of work involved in man-handling large numbers of these in combat conditions under the Spanish sun can be imagined.

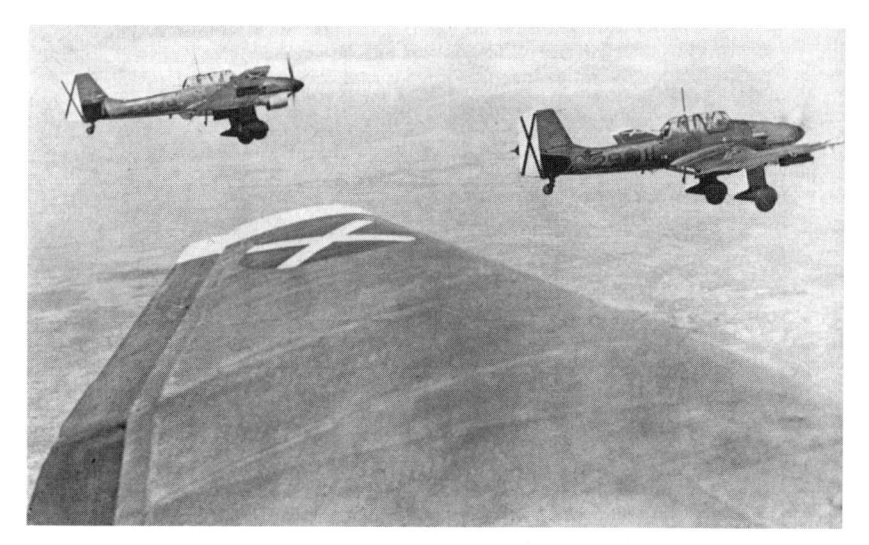

What would prove to be the combat companion to the 88 millimeter was the aerial artillery, the ubiquitous Ju 87. These three Ju 87Bs—29-8, 29-11, and the camera ship—are heading out to a target somewhere in Spain (note the underwing bombs) at some time between October 1938 and early March 1939 when 29-11 was seriously damaged by enemy ground fire. They were respectively the first and the last of the batch delivered for trials to Spain.

This is *Generalmajor* Wolfram von Richthofen and his staff and Spanish officers during his tour of inspection in November 1938. The location is most probably the trenches near Toledo.

This is a Krupp L3H163 radio truck in service with the Legion. It wears a complex four-tone camouflage scheme which was superseded by the outbreak of World War II in favor of a single overall color. Experience in Spain meant that the *Wehrmacht* had developed some of the most sophisticated inter-arm military communications systems in the world by 1940, a factor which gave them a great advantage over both the French and British armies, whose ramshackle communications did little to help them during the critical periods of May 1940.

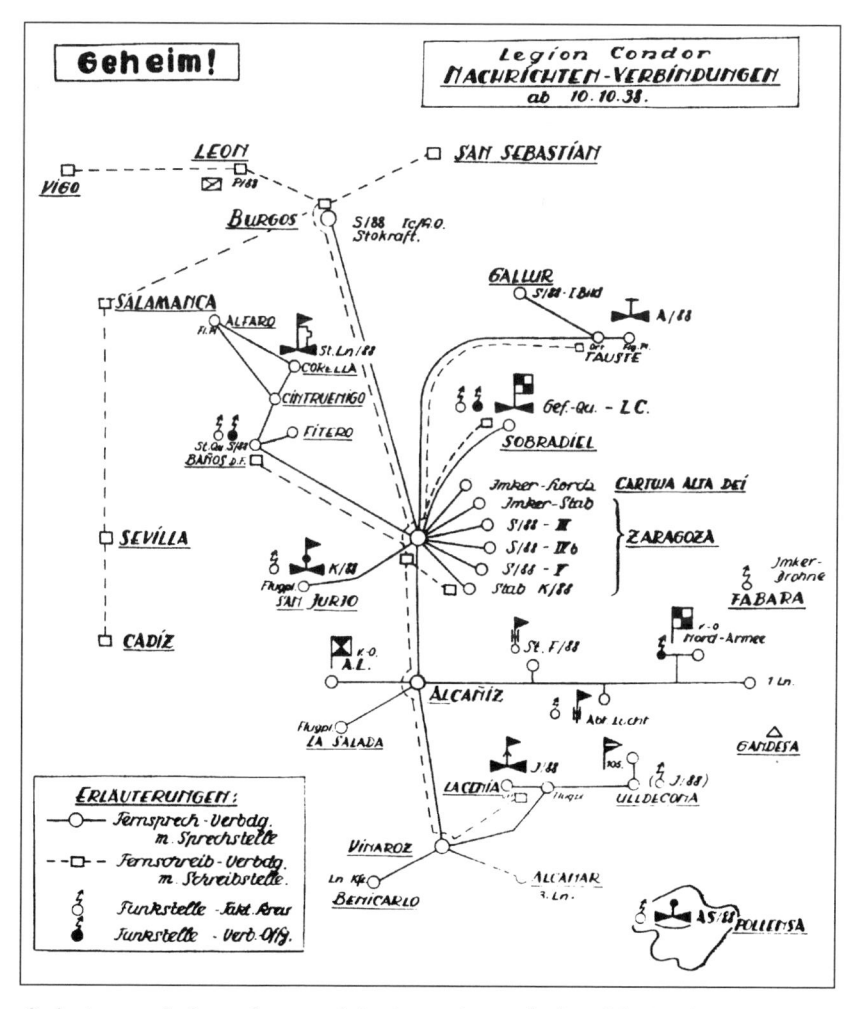

Only six months later, the growth in size and complexity of the Legion is immediately apparent from this secret signals links diagram dating from 10 October 1938. There is now a teleprinter link all the way from the port of Vigo, where most Legion matériel arrived, via the aircraft park at Léon and the *Stab 1c* at Burgos to the Imker Stab at Saragossa. All the operational *Gruppen* are based at the same locations as previously, except A/88, which has moved to Tauste, and the HQ, which is now at Sobradiel. It can be seen that the focus of operations has moved north and west. The same set of symbols to denote military units and their functions, such as the checkered flags showing an army HQ, were retained into World War II. Not as glamourous or visible in the same way as aircraft or tanks, the experience and techniques developed in Spain, particularly in the field of ground-to-air communications between the frontline troops and the ground-attack units were of vital importance to the later successes of the *Wehrmacht*. Spain was probably the first war where there was real integration between air and ground operations at the tactical level. The links between the Spanish and the Legion were probably another matter.

# Aufklärungsgruppe A/88

## Organization and Operations

After the Bomber Group, A/88 was the second unit of the Legion Condor ready for action in Spain. The first reconnaissance aircraft in fact arrived at Avila before mid October 1936 and, at the beginning of November, *Hauptmann* Heinsius was able to line up a dozen Heinkel He 70Fs lifted from units of the young *Luftwaffe*, and six Heinkel He 45Bs. On the first mentioned type were *Leutnant* Kurt Strümpell (pilot and brother of Hennig Strümpell, who flew an He 51), *Leutnant* Bernetzeder, *Leutnant* Wilhelm Balthasar, and *Leutnant* Rolf Kaldrack (observers). These last two became celebrated in Spain, firstly on account of their service with the General Staff of K/88 as observers, then later as fighter pilots during the war itself. The first three He 45Bs were entrusted to pilots Michelos, Schirrtelo and Blecher, who had the above-mentioned observers with them.

The six He 46s present at Avila in mid-October were numbered 11-171 to 11-176, and were piloted by Gerster, Datz, Kowollisch, Sicking, Bombach, and Lampe. The observers were von Recken, Stage, Meier, Cherubin, Bertram, Flug, Ciekert, Loytved, and Wein. Some reports mention the presence of twenty He 46s at Seville on the nineteenth of the month, but it appears that this figure includes all three types of aircraft then in use. They were mentioned again on 6 November, and on the eleventh, a Republican attack damaged several of them on the ground at this location.

The first days quickly passed in operational testing. While the Legion was well pleased with its He 70s, with their remarkable turn of speed for the times, there was less certainty over the most suitable roles for the other two Heinkel types, the He 45 and He 46. Were they to be used for artillery cooperation and gunnery direction or low-level reconnaissance? The hesitation did not last long, thanks above all to *Leutnant* Balthasar, who, after several missions on the Madrid front, declared himself violently against the latter. In particular, during a mission on 13 November, when he was leading[14] a patrol of three aircraft against positions on the west bank of the River Manzanares, he was far from being convinced. It seems that from then on the Legion may not have had full confidence in its equipment. This disaffection may be the reason for the surprisingly high numbers given to the He 46s, which began at 150, while the He 45s were numbered from 1 to at least 38 and the He 70s from 30. The He 46s were soon passed into the hands of the Spanish, who did not want them either. Consequently A/88 was left to wage war with two types of very different aircraft, but which none the less responded quite well to its needs.

As is quite usual in just about all air forces, there is very little evidence of the work of pure reconnaissance; quick sorties, quickly forgotten, the results are still indispensable. A/88, however, got itself noticed in the first months of the war in Spain by incessant activity on all fronts. In this it was the He 70's which were the undoubted stars; they were used much more as light bomber aircraft than in their primary role. The aggressive tendency of the group was accentuated by the arrival in January 1937 of a new group leader, *Oberleutnant* Hans-Dettler von Kessel. Attacking particularly strategic and pinpoint objectives, A/88 at this time gave the impression of being everywhere and earned the nickname of "Universal."

So, in this way, on 8 February, 1937, a patrol of three He 70s, under the command of *Leutnant* Runze, bombed the training camps of the International Brigades at Albacete. The following day the operation was repeated against Alcazar de San Juan, to the south of Madrid. One of the

27-20 is a Dornier Do 17E bomber of A/88. Behind is 27-27, a reconnaissance variant. The location is either Sanjurjo or Saragossa, the time is probably sometime soon after July 1938 when these machines first arrived.

He 70s, chased by a Republican fighter, succeeded in shaking it off by doing a low-altitude "slalom" at platform level over the station at Linares. On 16 February, the same patrol leader led a very successful strategic mini-bombardment against the electrical power stations of Seira and Capdella in the Pyrenees.

This showmanship ended about the month of March, 1937; the Republican fighter group was reinforced, and the speed of the He 70s was not able to put them outside the reach of the Soviet-built Polikarpov I-16s. At the end of this month, most of the unit remained at Seville-Tablada while six He 70s and two He 45s were based respectively at Salamanca and Vittoria to prepare and sustain the offensive against Bilbao. In the course of the month the unit received reinforcements in the shape of three new He 45s in order to compensate for the losses of the first months of the war. On 16 March, Balthasar succeeded in flying back in an He 70 which had been riddled by enemy fire, (two other aircraft suffered the same sort of damage within a few days). The problem occurred over the area of Almorox, where he was forced to land. By subterfuge, he involved himself in "testing" the prototype Heinkel He 112V-4 fighter before being officially promoted to pilot. At the end of these personal exploits, he went north to command a mixed flight formed from two He 45s and the prototype in question, a first step towards the glory of the fighter group J/88.

On the Bilbao front, there was little respite for A/88, which lost little by little a good part of its equipment, and more seriously, a part of its crews. The Basque fighters and flak were deadly serious. The northern campaign drew to an end when the group lost its first crew in combat over Miravalles on 15 June. *Leutnant* Siegfried Gottanka and *Leutnant* Helmut Hildemann and *Unteroffizier* Fritz Heerschlag were killed in action. During this time, Kaldrack had become the "ace" of close reconnaissance in He 45s and was called the "Eyes of the General Staff."

The year 1937 was when the Republican air force was the most dangerous and this was most notably felt during the course of the campaign at Brunete. On 7 July, A/88 was based at Valdemorillo with eight He 70s in the company of German fighters and VB/88. Three days later, one of the He 70s was shot down by Republican fighters over Cuatro Vientos; one of the crew parachuted, but *Leutnant* Hans von Posser and *Obergefreiter* Roland Reinhold were killed. A/88 was to be in the vanguard of the creation of a large bridgehead against the efforts of the Republicans. The objective was to be achieved with such losses that, for the participants, Brunete would always be the hardest campaign of the war: "a real slaughterhouse."

Calm had only just returned to the region of Madrid when A/88 returned to the fray for the push towards the north against Gijon with six He 70s and three Do 17s which were based at Villarcayo. The Republican air force exacted a heavy tribute. On 23 August, an He 70 was shot down over the port of El Musel and Gijon, the crew parachuting. On 4 September, A/88 lost an He 70 and VB/88 lost a Do 17 with both crews, shot down by antiaircraft artillery over Lanes (*Oberleutnant* von Kessel, the commander of A/88, *Unteroffizier* Ernst Hein, *Unteroffizier* Waldemar Schnell, *Leutnant* Gerhard Krocker, *Unteroffizier* Hermann Heil, and *Obergefreiter* Waldemar Kruger). The loss of von Kessel was appreciable; he was replaced by *Hauptmann* Joachim Gerndt, more technician than leader. The losses did not stop there, however, as on 11 September, *Gefreiter* Stanislau Leske killed himself while landing at Burgos with an He 45 which had been badly hit by flak. On the twenty-second, another biplane was shot down over Santander and resulted in the death of *Leutnant* Hans Kemper (certain sources indicate a collision on take-off with an He 70). Happily the group received its first allocation of four Do 17Es taken from the resources of VB/88, which had received them from *Aufklärungsgruppe (F) 122* at Prenzlau. These were replacements for three He 70s which had been grounded due to structural fatigue and damage. The Dornier was a fast, well-armed twin-engined machine and quickly became the essential flying equipment of A/88. Equipment, however, still has to be used and this does not happen without things getting damaged. On 15 September, 27-11 crashed soon after take-off. The crew were unhurt, but the aeroplane was destroyed. The remaining Do 17s—27-1, 27-7, and 27-9—stayed with A/88. A little later, the unit received 27-6 as a replacement and then the rest of the Do 17s still in service with the VB. This was the period when *Leutnant* Kurt Strümpell left the *Gruppe*.

At the beginning of October 1937, A/88 was based at Santander. Here it was that the principal change occurred to the unit's operational life in Spain. In November, four of the aged He 70s were finally abandoned and passed on to the Spanish. A little before a last He 70 had been lost during a forced landing by *Leutnant* Runze. The rest and recreation periods of the group were very short for on 22 October a new He 45 was shot down over Avilés by Republican ground fire, *Leutnant* Friedrich Schwanengel being killed.

A/88 went to rest at Santander-Est until mid-November, two Do 17s going to Burgos and three others leaving at the end of the month to Burgos de Osma in the region of La Rasa, accompanied by the sole remaining He 45 able to fly. There is no trace of this latter aircraft after 1 December.

The year 1938 started very badly for A/88 when *Leutnant* Runze was shot down in an He 45 by 20-millimeter antiaircraft guns that the Republican gunners had started to master all too well. The battle of Teruel saw intense activity by A/88's Do 17s, first of all on the Madrid front (Villa de los Navarros, Aranjuez and its railway station, Tajuña), then against Teruel, dropping four tons of bombs daily between 27 December and 6 January, alternating with reconnaissance flights over the central sector (the railway lines between Cifuentes-Brihuega-Saelices on the fifth, Guadalajara on the sixth). On the tenth, during an attack against a road complex to the northeast of Teruel, one of the Do 17s was hit by Republican flak but got back to base. On 13 January, the Do 17s attacked Venta del Puente then, on the sixteenth and seventeenth, Villel and Guadalajara.

It was in mid-January that the group eventually received a handful of He 45s recently erected at Léon and several brand-new Dorniers. On the nineteenth, a pair of the biplanes was sent to Masegoso, while the Do 17s bombed Perales, Peralejos and Alfambra. On the twenty-first, Argenta and Visiedo, where large concentrations of enemy troops were situated, were attacked; at the same time the four Do 17Fs carried out four reconnaissance flights on the fronts of Huesca, Teruel and Guadalajara. On the twenty-second, all nine available Do 17E bombers attacked Villalba Baja, an operation repeated the following day against Canredondo and Cifuentes. The reports of the Legion talk of a bombing precision of 80 percent—very superior figures, to be sure, to those figures recorded by the units of K/88. At the end of the month, A/88 was based at Buñuel, from which, on the twenty-fifth, it reconnoitered the sector of Singra prior to bombing it on the twenty-seventh, having, in the meantime on the twenty-sixth, attacked enemy reserve troops at Alfambra.

On 1 February, the Do 17Fs gathered a complete mosaic photograph of the Teruel front, reconnoitering the following day over the lines at Guadalajara and Teruel. On 5 February, there was a change of command as, at the time of releasing the bombs onto the objective, one of them exploded as it left the bomb bay of 27-1, which then, seriously damaged, made a crash landing at the base with two wounded on board: *Obergefreiter* Meix and *Hauptmann* Gerndt, the commanding officer who, because of his injuries, passed command to *Hauptmann* Hentschel. Some reports refer to a real stroke of luck that day as the explosion of the bomb could have been caused by a direct flak hit, which in the event saved the crew from more serious injuries. The fifth, sixth, and seventh of February were crucial for the outcome of the battle, with A/88 carrying out intensive operations against troop concentrations, roads and enemy reserves, otherwise reconnoitering the river valley of Alfambra. After a pause of several days the unit successfully pushed on with operations during the reconquest of Teruel, despite the bitter weather between the fourteenth and twenty-second of February, particularly on the sectors Valdecebro, Vivel del Río, Corbalán, Villastar, Cedrillas and Cubla. Even when the battle was finished there was still a need for several pinpoint attacks, such as that on a supply convoy of trucks at Hijar on 6 March. On 9 March, the offensive against Aragon started.

For several months, the Do 17s of the group were put to all manner of tasks: routine reconnaissance twice a day; weather reconnaissance at heights which the Ju W34s were not able to climb to; above all precision attacks on targets such as railway stations, bridges, groups of vehicles, munitions factories, road complexes, Republican command posts and so on. On 10 March, A/88 bombed Bujaraloz and the railway station of Escatron, where the train housing the general staff of the Republican air force was stationed. The following day seven reconnaissance flights were carried out on the two banks of the Ebre, pushing up to Alcañiz, Caspe, Candasnos and Cariñena. The operations soon developed into a rythmical tempo: Montalbán, Alcaníz and Caspe on the thirteenth, Bujaraloz the fourteenth, Ebre the fifteenth, La Zaida and Escatron on the seventeenth. For the second phase of the offensive, between 19 and 24 March, bearings of the sector to the north of the Ebre were taken, bombing Arascues (to the north of Huesca) on the twenty-second, Granen and Sesa and the railway lines towards Sariñena on the twenty-fourth, Poleñino and Lanaja on the twenty-fifth. Reconnaissance followed: four missions on the roads to the east of Saragosse and Huesca on the twenty-fifth, Albalete on the twenty-sixth, the road from Frega to Monzon and the fortifications of Monzon on the twenty-seventh. On the twenty-eighth, the Do 17s attacked road traffic between Monzon, Frega and Lerida, the operation being extended the following day to the roads between the rivers Cinca and Segre. The sector of operations of the Do 17s thus arrived at Lerida on 1 April, Balaguer and Artesa de Segre on the fifth and Tremp on the sixth.

The Do 17 was a quick aeroplane, difficult to intercept. Nonetheless, things did not always go its way. On 15 March 1938, the aircraft of A/88, which were attacking troop concentrations in the sector of Maella, were obliged to jettison their bombs in all haste to escape from the attentions of the I-15 and I-16 fighters. On 7 April, the *Gruppe* lost one of its machines shot down over Cubells. Receiving a direct hit by flak, it disintegrated and left no chance for the crew, killing *Leutnant* Max Kendel, *Unteroffizier* Paul Birkhoffen, *Unteroffizier* Willi von der Driesch, and *Obergefreiter* Erich Fiedler.

The breakthrough towards the Mediterranean was such a success that it imperilled the liaison of the Nationalist forces. In these conditions, the Do 17s had to go on making supplementary missions to assure continuous reconnaissance of enemy capability. In May, most of A/88 stayed at Buñuel and Tauste but one flight of two He 45s was detached to La Cenia in order to get closer to the combat zone. Several days later the whole unit moved to a base at Vinaroz on the western coast which had been recently occupied. By this move the Do 17s ensured all the reconnaissance flights and bombing support missions for K/88 until mid-August and proved themselves indispensable. The general staff of the Legion profited by the experience gained from experimenting with bombing altitudes between 2,500 meters to 4,500 meters with an average precision superior to that obtained by the He 111s; the Dorniers could even strafe underneath bridges and key offensive Republican locations.

On 18 May, A/88 heavily bombed Cabanes, Oroposa, and Benicasim. Then, between the twenty-third and twenty-sixth, it attacked Lucena del Cid and Vistabella, all close to the front, and Castellón and Almazora to the rear. On the twenty-eighth, Ares de Maestre and the railway station of Castellón were attacked, in all four missions. The *Gruppe* spent the following four days in harassing operations on the eastern flank of the offensive until, on 2 June, the new Do 17s encountered strong ground fire which hit two aircraft. One of these crashed on the way back to base, killing its pilot. On 7, 8, and 9 June, the Dorniers were principally occupied with the enemy rearguard. A/88 had to use maximum effort on 25 June on the fortified line between Onda and Bechi. The road between Artesa and Eslida which traverses the Sierra de Espadan was attacked on 2 July. The unit returned to the Sierra on the fourth and attacked Vall de Uxo the next day, then bombed the road from Sagunto on the eighth and the railway station in the same area on the following day. 18 June was a day crammed with three bombings of Vall de Almonacid–Algimia de Almonacid, Segorbe Algimia and la Sierra de Espadan, plus a dozen photographic reconnaissance missions.

The tempo of these operations could have been continued up to a partial victory if the Republicans had not launched their own great offensive against the River Ebro on the night of 25 July. The battle of the Ebro was going to exhaust a large part of the Legion Condor and, in particular, A/88, who carried out up to four bombing sorties per day in addition to its reconnaissance flights. Out of the new aircraft available at the start of the campaign, the squadron of Do 17s had diminished to four machines by mid-August, one of the reasons being the shortage of spare parts (some as critical as tail wheels). Some days were particularly tiresome, like 11 August with four missions, and the third, fifth, ninth, tenth, twelfth, and thirteenth with three sorties in formation. The end of this battle and the immediate consequences were extremely trying and difficult for the *Gruppe*. One Dornier (27-16) was shot down by ground fire over Flix on 5 August and fell in flames into the Ebro. *Oberleutnant* Wolf Fach and *Oberfeldwebel* Friedrich Mende parachuted out and were made prisoners, but *Unteroffizier* Otto Lehmann died in the action.

During the month of July, A/88 gave up five of its tired Do17's to Spanish units (27-3, 27-13, 27-17, 27-19, and 27-21), in return receiving from Germany nine new aeroplanes. At the end of August, there were seventeen Do 17s in service with A/88 which maintained one Staffel of nine bombers and a Schwarm of four reconnaissance aircraft. At the same time, the He 45s provided the same range of mixed operations even though on an evidently reduced scale, as on 20 July against the railway station of Ampolla. In contrast to the Do 17s, who used the tactic of covering each other in very active combat zones, the pilots of the biplanes often used *Freijagd*[15] tactics, working alone trying to mark and log artillery batteries, troop concentrations, vehicle parks and so on in order to attack them later with the several anti-personnel bombs that they habitually carried. They continued to operate daily, surprisingly without loss, whereas the unit of Do 17s had to reform its personnel. From 15 August A/88 abandoned its offensive operations and was integrated for a while with K/88, leaving a Spanish group, 8-G-27, the responsibility for combat with its own Do 17s. From then on the *Gruppe* lived up to its name and occupied itself solely with reconnaissance.

On 1 September, another Do 17F, 27-25, narrowly missed being shot down and just managed to return to its base after having taken a direct hit by a 37-millimeter shell in the port wing. By sheer chance the shell did not explode but the damage was such that it kept the aircraft on the ground for several months. During the same month a pilot of the unit attempted to land on the small strip of Llanes and completely destroyed his machine by mishandling the operation of the undercarriage.

For their part the He 45s were reduced to three by the storm that devastated La Cenia during the night of 29–30 August, which sent one of them crashing into some olive trees. On 20 September, another He 45 was completely destroyed when landing at Vinaroz at about 12.00 hours after an unequal combat against Republican fighters between Camposines and Fatarella. *Leutnant* von Kugelgen was seriously wounded. The next day another of the biplanes miraculously escaped destruction after having also been intercepted, but the damage was less, and *Leutnant* Wagmann was only slightly wounded by the shattered windscreen.

By 17 November 1938, A/88 was at the end of the road and had only one out of nine Do 17s in flying condition, and one He 45 out of three. Moreover this was the overall state of the Legion at this time. The *Gruppe* therefore rested at Tauste to recuperate from its losses and mend its various wounds. The unit was, however, to receive four new Do 17Ps with radial engines, considered to be the definitive version of the type. On 8 December, the group returned to duty after the transfer of its adjutant to Estacion de Tamarite to the northwest of Lérida.

The campaign of Catalonia was where the Nationalist forces chose to "drive home the nail" by taking on the Republican forces, demoralized and exhausted after a gigantic operation which had proven fruitless. On 23 December, the Legion based eleven of its Do 17s at Buñuel, with only 27-29 remaining in the park at Léon (which it seems never to have left). The advance was relatively easy and it was sensed that the end was close. On 9 January, A/88 kept seven Do 17s at Buñuel, three at Tauste and one at Sanjurjo. After nine months some Dorniers were to be based at Sabadell in Catalonia in the company of three He 45s and the first Hs 126 which had arrived from Germany. On 31 January 1939, the unit took up quarters at Sabadell. The crews quickly protested about the cramped area and the meager installations without discussing other requirements; it was from there, however, that the Republicans had carried on a long campaign. The same day the He 111s of K/88 were bogged down at take-off and only the lighter Do 17s were able to get into the air.

At this time, A/88 received its last commander, *Major* Matussek. It was the reconnaissance group that was tasked with preparing the mopping up of all the Republican aerodromes, which was effected on 5 February. The night before the Do 17s had spotted fifteen Republican aircraft at Vilajuiga, ten others at Rosas, a hundred vehicles at Figueras and four ships at La Selva. The clean-up was total; several Government aircraft escaped destruction on the ground by flying over the French frontier, only to be impounded, which amounted to the same thing for the Nationalists.

The debut of the new Henschel with the parasol wing was not very encouraging and, on 6 February, the first Hs 126 (19-1) crashed due to an engine failure and was completely destroyed six kilometers south of Gerone. By now, however, the whole unit did occupy much space. On 10 February 1939, the available aircraft at Sabadell were one Do 17 (27-30), two Do 17Es (27-14 and 27-25), three He 45s and one Hs 126 (19-2). On the thirteenth, the He 45s still airworthy were reduced to 15-34 and 15-36. At the end of the month the last He 45s were passed to a Spanish army cooperation group upon the arrival of four new Hs 126s. At the same time, the Do 17s numbered 27-4, 27-9, and 27-18 were handed over to the Spanish group 8-G-27. A/88 had available two Do 17Es and one Do 17P at its base at Sanjuro-Saragosse and two other Dorniers which were under repair there and at Léon. The *Gruppe* continued to function as normal whereas J/88 and K/88 were almost comatose.

On 4 March, the group had six Hs 126s in service (19-2 to 19-7 inclusive) of which five were in flying condition, 19-3 being in the park at Léon with an engine problem. It should be noted that without any doubt the unit also had available a Ju 52 (22-73) which had been under repair for some considerable time.

Reviewing their activities during the course of the conflict in Spain, the He 45 gives the appearance of being a champion in all categories, *Feldwebel* Hans König, for example, carried out ninety-five missions in one during a single tour of operations. Of the Do 17 crews, *Oberfeldwebel* Ernst Sorge (pilot), *Leutnant* Philips, and *Unteroffizier* Wawrock knocked up a record by carrying out fifty-seven missions together.

By now the direction of operations had changed; the twin-engined aircraft now did reconnaissance to the south, more precisely towards Cartagena, while the rest of the *Gruppe* started a complete photographic coverage of the region from Madrid to Toledo in preparation for a last great offensive that never came. On 19 March, the Do 17Ps completed a large photographic reconnaissance of Republican aerodromes situated inside the line Toledo-Navahermosa-Madridejos-Tarancon-Madrid. By 23 March there were three Do 17Ps and four Hs 126s at Barciencia. The last days of the war brought no changes to the composition of the unit. At the victory parade, A/88 participated with its four airworthy Do 17Ps.

A/88 was particularly effective in aerial photographic reconnaissance, which neither the Italians nor the Spanish truly mastered, and showed itself to be indispensable in this role. Besides this, however, its offensive operations, first under the command of von Kessel, and then that of Gerndt and Hentschel, ought not to be minimized; the small number of aircraft available for each mission often was compensated for by great bombing precision.

# The Dornier Do 17 in Spain

## Type code 27
## Nickname *Bacalao*—"Codfish"

| Code | Type | Unit | Arrived | Crew | Aircraft Name | Fate | Cause |
|---|---|---|---|---|---|---|---|
| 27-1 | | VB/88 | 03.37 | | | | |
| | | A/88 | 08.37 | | | Lost 09/10.37? | ? |
| 27-2 | | VB/88 | 03.37 | | | Shot down 18.04.37 | I-15 Del Rio |
| 27-3 | F | VB/88 | 03.37 | | Pablo 3 | | |
| | | A/88 | 10.37 | | | | |
| | | 8-G-27 | 08.38 | Rambaud | | Accident 10.38 | |
| 27-4 | F | VB/88 | 03.37 | | Pablo 1 | | |
| | | A/88 | 10.37 | | | | |
| | | 8-G-27 | 02.39 | | | | |
| 27-5 | E | VB/88 | 07.37 | | | Shot down 24.07.37 | |
| 27-6 | | VB/88 | 07.37 | | | | |
| | | A/88 | 08.37 | | | Lost 09/10.37? | ? |
| 27-7 | F | VB/88 | 07.37 | | | | |
| | | A/88 | | | | | |
| 27-8 | F | VB/88 | 07.37 | | | Shot down 29.12.38 | Flak |
| | | A/88 | 08.37 | | | | |
| | | 8-G-27 | 11.38 | | | | |
| 27-9 | | A/88 | 07.37 | | | | |
| | | 8-G-27 | 02.39 | | | Accident 04.04.39 | |
| 27-10 | | VB/88 | 07.37 | | | | |
| 27-11 | | VB/88 | 07.37 | | | | |
| | | A/88 | | | | Accident 15.08.37 | |
| 27-12 | | VB/88 | 07.37 | | | | |
| 27-13 | | A/88 | | Alferez Vierna | | | |
| | | 8-G-27 | 08.38 | | | | |
| 27-14 | F | A/88 | 07.38 | Hering | "Schnuckes" | | |
| 27-15 | | A/88 | 07.38 | | | | |
| 27-16 | F | A/88 | 07.38 | | "Mucki" | | |
| 27-17 | E | A/88 | 07.38 | | | Shot down 29.12.38 with 8-G-27 | Flak |

| Code | Type | Unit | Arrived | Crew | Aircraft Name | Fate | Cause |
|---|---|---|---|---|---|---|---|
| 27-18 | | A/88 | 07.38 | | | | |
| | | 8-G-27 | 02.39 | | | Accident 26.02.39 | ? |
| 27-19 | | A/88 | 07.38 | | | | |
| | | 8-G-27 | 08.38 | | | Accident 04.04.39 | ? |
| 27-20 | E | A/88 | 07.38 | | | | |
| | | 8-G-27 | 03.39 | | | Accident 04.04.39 | ? |
| 27-21 | E | A/88 | 07.38 | | | | |
| | | 8-G-27 | 08.38 | | "Comandante Rambaud" | | |
| 27-22 | | A/88 | 07.38 | | | | |
| 27-23 | E | A/88 | 07.38 | | | | |
| 27-24 | E | A/88 | 07.38 | | | | |
| 27-25 | F | A/88 | 07.38 | | "Bombenreiter" | | |
| 27-26 | | A/88 | 07.38 | | | Accident 9.38? | |
| 27-27 | F | A/88 | 07.38 | | | | |
| 27-28 | P | A/88 | 12.38 | | | | |
| 27-29 | P | A/88 | 12.38 | | | | |
| 27-30 | P | | 12.38 | | | | |
| 27-31 | P | 8-G-27 | 12.38 | | | | |
| 27-32 | P | | 12.38 | | | | |

### DORNIER DO 17 LOSSES IN CHRONOLOGICAL ORDER—14 TOTAL

| Date | A/C | Crew | Unit | Location | Fate | Cause |
|---|---|---|---|---|---|---|
| 18.04.37 | 27-2 | Sobotka | VB/88 | Bilbao | Shot down | I-15 |
| 24.07.37 | 27-5 | | VB/88 | Brunete | Shot down | |
| 15.08.37 | 27-11 | | A/88 | Santander | | Accident |
| 09.10.37 | 27-6 | | A/88 | | Lost? | |
| 07.04.38 | 27-? | Kendel | A/88 | Cubels | Shot down | Flak |
| 05.08.38 | 27-16 | Fach | | Ebro | Shot down | |
| ?? 09.38 | 27-26? | | A/88? | Llanes | | Landing accident |
| ?? 10.38 | 27-3 | Rambaud | 8-G-27 | | | Accident |
| 29.12.38 | 27-8 | | 8-G-27 | Artesa de Segre | Shot down | Flak |
| 29.12.38 | 27-17 | | 8-G-27 | Artesa de Segre | Shot down | Flak |
| 26.02.39 | 27-18 | | 8-G-27 | Medina de Røoseco | | Accident |
| 04.04.39 | 27-9 | | 8-G-27 | Alcolea del Pinar | | Accident |
| 04.04.39 | 27-19 | | 8-G-27 | Alcolea del Pinar | | Accident |
| 04.04.39 | 27-20 | | 8-G-27 | Alcolea del Pinar | | Accident |

At the end of April 1939, 27-4, 27-7, 27-13, 27-14, 27-21, 27-25, 27-27, 27-28, 27-30, 27-31, 27-32, and 27-29(?) remained at Léon.

This is most probably Dornier Do 17P 27-29 at Léon undergoing checks and maintenance. It seems to have been something of a "rogue" aircraft and may never have left the base. Here it is apparently undergoing electrical testing. Some idea of the urgency attached by the RLM to the testing of new aircraft in Spain can be gauged by the fact that the first ever flight by a Do 17P only took place on 18 June 1938, yet four had arrived in Spain by the end of the year. This hurried production may account for the problems with 27-29. 330 Do 17Ps were eventually produced.

This is Do 17F 27-3 seen in later service with A/88, location not known. When first delivered in March 1937, it had served with VB/88 as *Pablo 3* before being transferred to A/88 in August that year. In August 1938, in a very tired state, it was passed on to the Spanish unit, 8-G-27, but crashed two months later, possibly as a result of its condition. Unfortunately for modellers, the details of the personal emblem, which seem to show a someone or something wearing a top hat, are illegible.

A lineup of Dornier Do 17Fs of A/88, probably soon after they entered service in summer 1938 as number 27-4, nearest the camera, does not carry its earlier identity as *Pablo 1*, which it wore while with VB/88. By March 1939, it had been transferred to the Spanish unit 8-G-27. The other two aircraft are 27-14 and 27-22 and all are finished in the early three-tone *Luftwaffe* upper surface camouflage of the time.

This rather blurred view of Do 17E 27-5 taking off, probably from VB/88's base at Salamanca in July 1937, clearly shows how the type's slender lines gave rise to its nickname of the "Flying Pencil." The aircraft did not survive long with VB/88 as it was shot down during an action over Brunete on 24 July. Fortunately the crew survived to parachute into captivity.

Dark green SC 250 bombs await loading into the waiting Dornier 17s. This one is 27-7 and judging by its new appearance is in service with VB/88 in July 1937, either at Salamanca or Burgos.

Dornier 17s 27-9 and 27-12 appear to be in mid-term storage along with a pair of Ju-52s, the nearest of which is 22-73, sporting on its nose a badge that seems to be an ace of hearts. The nearest Dornier survived at least one crash landing which damaged its port propeller and was transferred from A/88 to 8-G-27 in February 1939 only to be lost in an accident three days after the end of the war. 27-12 was delivered to VB/88 in July 1937.

Neatly lined up with at least three He 70s and another Do 17, this is 27-14, a Do 17F. Location is not known, but the aircraft was delivered to A/88 in July 1937 and was still with the unit at Sabadell in February 1939.

Seen here in service with A/88 are Dornier 17s 27-17, 27-19, 27-8, 27-13, and 27-21. Aircraft 13, 17, 19 and 21 were all transferred to the Spanish *Grupo 8-G-27* in August 1938, although 27-17 and 27-8 were both shot down later by Republican ground fire on December 29, 1938.

Dornier Do 17E 27-21 was one of the batch delivered to A/88 in July 1938, and later transferred to 8-G-27 in August of that year. It is shown here in service with that unit, as indicated by the name, not clear here, written under the cockpit canopy, *Comandante Rambaud.*

Starboard side view of a crashlanded Do 17E, 27-24 of A/88 somewhere in a Spanish cornfield. As none of the propeller blades on this side are damaged, that engine was presumably already stopped before the impact. Date, location, crew and other details are all unknown. Note the fairing for the bombsight under the nose, which is (usually) the only means of distinguishing the "E" bomber from the "F" photo-reconnaissance variant.

Another view of Do 17E 27-24 showing only minimal damage to the airframe. The personal emblem is unfortunately illegible but may be a small child with a shock of black hair. On the other hand, the bearded devil insignia of A/88 is clearly displayed on the outer faces of both engine cowlings.

Seen from the dorsal gunner's position of an accompanying aircraft, Do 17E 27-25 drones on somewhere over Spain. The aircraft has a personal emblem of a devil riding a bomb, which is very similar to one used later in World War II by *4 Staffel* or *6 Staffel* of KG3.

Named *Bomb-rider* by its crew, this Do 17F, 27-25, remained in service with the Legion until the end of the war and then returned to Germany. The date and location of this picture are unknown.

This is Dornier 17 27-26 down in a Spanish field. The propellers were obviously turning until the moment of impact. Apart from the fact that the aircraft once flew with A/88, little is known about this incident; it is not possible to say with certainty whether it was a bomber or reconnaissance variant as the bombsight housing is not visible. This would seem something of an anomaly as A/88 was a reconnaissance outfit, but as they carried out bombing missions as well, then some of the aircraft on strength must have been E versions.

Another view of 27-26, this side from port. The emblem of A/88 is clearly visible, as is the serious damage to the wing and fuselage. It is also apparent that the machine's back is broken so it looks as this was the final landing for this Dornier.

A closer view of 27-26 reveals a small cat personal emblem below the cockpit, and severe wrinkling and tearing to the fuselage structure. Fortunately for the crew there was no fire. The date and location of this crash are not known for certain but this could be the Do 17 lost in September 1938 in a landing accident at Lanes. The presence of what looks to be barley in the field and the lack of any obvious combat damage tend to support this view. There are no crew loss records for that month so the crew presumably escaped with a shaking.

A well-detailed view of the jovial devil's head emblem of A/88, which was worn on the outer faces of the 600-horsepower BMW engine cowlings. The devil's beard could apparently bend to the front or the rear.

27-28 was presumably the first P model to be delivered to Spain; the other known Do 17P aircraft all had higher numbers. The immaculate condition of this machine suggests that it has just been delivered to A/88 at Bunuel, late in 1938.

Mechanics at work on a Dornier 17 undercarriage, a sturdy piece of equipment which gave some headaches to the maintenance crews during the early career of the aircraft.

Life was relatively comfortable at the end of the Spanish Civil War for the Legion Condor crews, and overall security allowed the aircraft to be parked within meters of the barracks.

A view of 27-29 which shows the Bramo radial engines of the Dornier Do 17P to advantage. These later models also received the devil's head emblem on their cowlings.

A clear shot of Do 17P 27-31 in immaculate condition. It has apparently just been handed over to the Spanish unit 8-G-27, as indicated by the yoke and arrows marking on the fuselage disc. Location is not known for certain but is probably Logrono.

Already found in a cruder form on a Heinkel 70, the devil's head emblem of A/88 was painted on the exterior of both engines. The inscription *Intava* that is visible below the propeller hub relates to the type of oil needed for the BMW 132N radial engines. Note the MG 15 machine gun protruding through the windscreen, probably installed as a result of earlier experience in Spain.

# The Heinkel He 45 in Spain

**Type code 15**
**Nickname** *Pavo*—"Turkey"

Records are insufficient to give a fully comprehensive listing of the fate of every one of the Heinkel 45s delivered to Spain. Indeed, there is disagreement as to how many actually arrived. Known code numbers confirmed by photographic evidence range from 15-2 to 15-38, but it is believed that up to forty-one may have been used. The Legion Condor retained at least two *Ketten* (flights of three aircraft) in A/88 between November 1936 and June 1938, when they were replaced by the Henschel Hs 126.

A very clear view of a Heinkel He 45C (15-??) somewhere on a Spanish plain (near Brunete?) wearing an interesting, and probably field-applied, camouflage pattern. This could indicate that it is one of the earliest arrivals which were delivered in the usual overall gray *Luftwaffe* finish, and has been repainted to take account of combat experience. The devil emblem on the nose may be an early version of that of A/88, while the playing card on the fin is most likely a personal marking. Note the massive wooden Heine propeller.

Many of the later He 45s delivered went straight to the Sapaniards, who quickly nicknamed them "Turkeys" and lost no time in creating appropriate emblems. This is the fin of an aircraft in service with 6-G-15, whose cartoon turkey badge it wears.

After a period of good service, the last He 45Cs of the Legion Condor were passed over to the Spaniards. Here 15-2, 15-4 and 15-7 wear another imaginative camouflage scheme. The barely discernable emblem of 6-G-15 can be made out on the fin of 15-2.

Just like the He 51, the He 45C was first used in Spain without any kind of camouflage, like numbers 15-9 and 15-3 here, but passive protection soon showed itself to be important, particularly on the northern front. Note how just the plan uppersurfaces have been given a darker color.

The He 45 15-9 survived its time of service in German hands, as it is here seen in a Spanish unit, and duly camouflaged, now in an overall dark scheme with theunit emblem on the fin. The tactical formation of two three-plane flights was more typical of the Spanish Nationalist aviation than the Legion Condor, which generally preferred to use pairs.

For the offensive against the northern provinces, the Legion Condor's He 45s received a first type of basic camouflage using large bands of green, probably over the basic grey, like here on 15-20. This aircraft would later be painted in a very World War I–like "lozenge"-type camouflage scheme. It seems fairly clear that the *Luftwaffe*'s interest in unusual camouflage schemes began in Spain.

Seen during its delivery flight (no bombs or observer) to the Spanish Grupo 6-G-15, 15-25 still sports the RLM grey livery, but has already received the *Pavo* totem on its tail fin.

Seen soon after their arrival in a Spanish unit, Heinkel He 45s 15-25 and 15-2? are being readied for still another reconnaissance/attack mission. On the tail surface is visible the *Pavo* emblem, representative of the way the Spaniards first considered the aircraft: big, and slow but dangerous. Note the pattern which has now been added to 15-25 in the background.

A skilfully drawn devil's head emblem on the nose of an unidentified Heinkel He 45. This is probably an early example of the badge of A/88. What the canvas strap might be for is unknown. The unique and enormous exhaust pipe peculiar to the He 45 is clearly visible.

Heinkel 45 15-36 awaits the next mission with the Legion during a lull in the northern campaign. Despite the fuzzy quality of this picture it can be seen that the aircraft wears a splinter camouflage, probably in the two standard *Luftwaffe* shades of green and has the devil's head insignia on the engine cowling.

He 45 15-38 was an unlucky aircraft. Here it is after being blown into the olive trees at La Cenia and wrecked during a storm on the night of 29–30 August 1938. 15-36 in the background seems to have escaped unscathed.

Another view of He 45C 15-38 at La Cenia in the morning of 30 August afer it had been wrecked in a storm the previous night. The unusual angle allows several underside details to be seen, including the observer's camera hatch and footstep, the radiator louvres in the engine cowling, and the Heine trademark on the propeller.

A more distant view of He 45 15-38 wrecked among the olive trees after the tempest that devastated the Mediterraneam coast in summer 1938. These trees were a prominent and distinctive feature of the airfield at La Cenia and can be seen in many of the photos in this book. The aircraft was subsequently scrapped.

How the Spanish conducted war. The commander of *Grupo 6-G-15*, *Capitano* Felix Bermúdez Castro, was obviously a hardy soul judging by his uniform as he climbs from his He 45. In the back seat is the senior observer of the unit, *Capitano* Juan Tornos. The date is sometime in June 1937 during the battle of Brunete when the unit was operating out of Avila and Casavieja. The ring-and-bead sight, machine gun, and striped camouflage are all worthy of note.

# The Heinkel He 46 in Spain

**Type code 11**
**Nickname** *Pava*—"Turkey Hen"

It has to be said that the Heinkel 46 was not a successful aircraft, but it did its bit in Spain like many other second-rate machines. The *Pava*, here 11-157, was probably, together with the Ju86D and a lonely He 50, the most useless aircraft brought by the Legion Condor to Spain. Big and slow, it lacked agility, stability, and offensive capacity, and worst of all, it suffered so much from vibration that it could not be used for its intended purpose, photo reconnaissance.

The limited offensive capability of the He 46C is seen here. A big aircraft for little profit, except probably for the tired crews who were happy to practice their siesta under the very generous high wing.

This Condor Legion He46C, 11-??, has received a most unusual camouflage scheme which appears to be composed of wide areas of color in two tones. It also appears to be in the shadow of the photo aircraft which adds further tones. The paint work is certainly field applied and the aircraft also wears the double black discs which are sometimes to be found in this early period of the war. These were apparently the result of a misinterpretation of orders.

A distant shot of a formation of He 46s over a typical Spanish landscape. Even at this distance, the nearest two aircraft can be seen to wear different markings and camouflage on the upper wings.

The observer in both the He 45 and He 46 had a very good MG 15 machine gun (on identical mountings) and a clear field of fire, which made them not-too-easy prey for the Republican fighters. Most losses of both types were due to ground fire.

One of the very first He 46Cs in Spain, 11-151 lived long enough to receive a mottled camouflage pattern in Spanish service.

This close-up view of 11-156 offers good detail of the crew positions. This aircraft is probably still in Legion service as it is still finished in the simple overall grey paint in which the He 46s were delivered.

This is another view of 11-156, now in flight. It carries both double black bands and double black disc markings on the upper wing. The observer's excellent field of view is obvious. What the Roman "II" marking on the fin signifies is not known.

Most of the He 46Cs were used in standard RLM light grey 63 (L40/52) livery, like here with 11-156. Noticeable is the first style of registration, with both the type number and aircraft number painted before the black fuselage disc. This was later changed by putting the cockade between them.

The pilot of the He 46C sat much higher than his observer, which probably did little for communication in the heat of combat. The observer however did have a good field of fire to the rear of the aircraft and could depress his gun to fire below the tail.

This view of 11-157 shows that it too wears the Roman "II" on the fin. As the observer appears to wear a beret, it suggests that the aircraft is in Spanish service. It is also apparent that the occupant of the rear seat had a good field of view in all directions except directly forward.

A starboard side view of He 46 11-157 in flight, still in the light grey paint finish, but now with the revised position of the code number. Not visible in other views but seen to advantage here are the black underwing stripes. Both crew members have a good view, a vital requirement in an observation aircraft. Just visible under the fuselage belly is the opening hatch for the observer's camera.

A scene of everyday life on a Nationalist airfield: a Heinkel He 51 is landing from a windless sky while two differently painted He 46Cs bake in the sun. Just visible is the tail of 11-158 which is still plain grey, while the unidentified aircraft in the foreground wears a mottle in two tones, apparently applied over the basic grey.

This formation includes at least seven aircraft, including the photo platform, but has no visible fighter cover. The big formations of He 46s were rapidly abandoned by the German crews who were quickly alert to the danger of operating such unwieldy aircraft on an active front. 11-161 is nearest to the camera.

He 46C 11-162 sports a curious camouflage scheme where the upper fuselage has a mottle over the grey background, but nothing has been applied to the generous wing. The picture is also illustrative of the distance between aircraft in a formation, as a third *Pava* can just be seen under number 162. A small village enclosed by a wall and surrounded by fields can be seen down below.

There are very few pictures of mixed combat formations in Spain, but we can see here a good example of probably two or three *Ketten* of He 46Cs with an escort of two He 51 formations; the main formation flying between 4,500 and 5,000 feet, and the top cover in echelon some 1,000 feet higher. The heavily blotched He 46 is 11-162.

Looking rather like some kind of insect, this leopard-skin mottled He 46C appears to be 11-175. As the aircraft does not appear to be armed, it may be one of the ten survivors of the type transferred to training duties. It is not known with certainty how many He 46s arrived in Spain, estimates varying between 36 and 46. Code numbers verified by photos range from 151 to 175, a total less than both estimates.

# The Heinkel He 70 in Spain

Type code 14
Nickname *Rayo*—"Lightning"

An elegantly camouflaged He 70F, probably in Spanish service in 1938. There appears to be an emblem of some sort beneath the windscreen. The fuselage number, 14-40, throws previous assumptions about the quantity of the type delivered to Spain (between 28 and 31) into some confusion as it was believed that the highest number allocated was 14-39. Location is unknown, but a Junkers 52 can be seen in the background.

The interior of the He 70 showing the pilot's seat offset to port and the entrance door open. As the type had originally been designed as a small airliner, the fuselage offered relatively generous accommodation for the rest of the crew.

This Condor Legion He 70, the number of which cannot be seen, seems to be camouflaged with wide areas of different colors on the wings over the basic grey finish (note the wing upper leading edges).

The He 70 was no newcomer to Spain, as Lufthansa had already made demonstration flights in 1935. Here the *Blitz* is seen at Madrid-Barajas in 1935. Note that the surface is still grass.

The wide track of the He 70 is quite obvious on this picture. It seems that the finish is all grey, apart from the black(?) propeller spinner, perhaps acquired after post-overhaul or post-repair delivery.

This picture of an early He 70 in Spain shows clearly the origin of some of the aircraft sent to A/88; direct from the *Luftwaffe* as all the early versions of the type were delivered in, and retained in service, the black trim and lightning flash first sported by the Lufthansa machines. Note the wide black bands under the wings.

The ellipsoid planform of the horizontal flying surfaces is perfectly apparent here. The dark blotches on the wing are not camouflage, but the shadow of the trees under which the aircraft of both sides tried to escape from the sun.

On the nose of this camouflaged He 70 can be seen an early version of what later became the official emblem of A/88 on their Do 17s: a grinning devil's head. Of interest are the projecting exhaust outlets; one from each cylinder of the BMW engine.

Spanish ground crew manhandle He 70 14-18 into position. The grey Heinkel-originated lightning flash used on aircraft in Lufthansa service was retained by most of the He 70s later delivered to the *Luftwaffe*. At the end of 1936, the He 70 was one of the fastest aircraft in Spanish skies, except for the Polikarpov I-16.

Once in Spanish service, some aircraft took on a more spectacular look, like this aircraft, 14-34, flown by the leader of Spanish *Grupo 7-G-14*. Although not certain, it is this writer's belief that the apparently bright colors were no more than white paint applied over the basic light grey and black in which the aircraft were delivered. One of the nicknames acquired by the He 70 was *Paloma Blanca* ("White Dove"), which may have some significance in this context. Behind no. 34 is an A/88 Do 17, 27-7.

Heinkel He 70 14-38 appears to have come to grief while making a belly landing with a dead engine.

He 70 14-39 awaits the next mission with A/88, well wrapped up against the Spanish weather. Note the wide variety of camouflage patterns applied to these aircraft. Compared to 14-38, this one carries a similar large blotch pattern but with harder edges to the blotches.

The paint scheme applied to He 70 14-41 was made up of wide bands of color, still with soft edges. It appears to have had some minor repair work done to the leading edge of the fin.

With time passing by and the loss rate going up, more efforts were made in passive protection methods, and the camouflage schemes got to be more sophisticated, like on 14-45 here. Here the larger areas of color (green brown and grey?) have hard edges on the uppersurface, but a soft demarcation between upper and lower, suggesting that the undersides were later resprayed. Note the introduction of white wingtips, soon to become a trademark of Nationalist aircraft.

14-47 kept its RLM 63 grey livery late in the war, together with the remnants of the glossy black engine cowling finish and *Blitz* marking. Note that this was *not* white on *Luftwaffe* examples, but the same grey as the main finish. This was one of the few *Rayos* to sport an individual emblem: a beer mug (lager of course) under the pilot's windscreen, a motif also used later by the pilot Hans Schmoller-Haldy on his Bf 109E, 6-123, while he was with 3.J/88.

The crew of 14-47 settle in prior to take-off on a mission for A/88. The aircraft looks to be in very clean condition so this is probably early in 1937.

Last-minute checks by the crew chief before He 70 14-47 begins its take-off run. The Nationalist white St. Andrew's crosses can just be made out on the wings.

A pilot poses for the family album on his He 70's wingroot. No other details known.

A *Kette* of He 70s from *Grupo 7-G-14*, all wearing a very attractive three-tone camouflage pattern. What may be an alternative version of the unit emblem, a swift on a disc, can be just made out on the fin of the neaerest aircraft, 14-5?. It is possible that these are the first three aircraft, 14-36, 14-45 and 14-56, to be transferred to the Spaniards at Seville in summer 1937.

The crew chief of a Legion Condor He 70 runs up the engine prior to a mission. The presence of three small bombs on the ground suggests that this is an He 70E version and may therefore be from the so-called *Bomberkette* of *Leutnant* Heinz Runze in late 1936–early 1937.

# The Henschel Hs 126 in Spain

**Type code 19**
**Nickname** *Superpava*—"Super Turkey Hen"

Only six Henschel Hs 16A-1s found their way to Spain as replacements for the surviving He 45s in 5.A/88. This large and heavy machine, with its resemblence to the He 46, proved quite successful in Spain, with only one being lost to enemy action. The tide of combat development was running fast, however, and the Hs 126, like other close-range reconnaissance aircraft of its type found themselves to be too slow and cumbersome in the later war. This is 19-5 in completely standard *Luftwaffe* colors of RLM 70/71 and 65 with Nationalist markings applied.

Henschel Hs 126 19-3 wears a striking camouflage scheme, possibly a *Luftwaffe* experiment, but more likely an in-the-field repaint by the Spanish unit which received all five of the survivors left in Spain by the Legion Condor.

This very dark Hs 126 carries a 100-kilogram bomb on the single portside rack and wears the devil's head of 5.A/88. Note that this is a different style from those worn by the Do 17s of A/88 and was seen on He 45s and He 70s as well. The black individual aircraft code number is not visible against the very dark green fuselage but may be 19-1.

This is Hs 126 19-6 in entirely standard *Luftwaffe* camouflage. Just visible in the background is General Franco's personal DC-2 so the location may be Léon.

As seems inevitable with the Spanish Civil War, the records turn out to differ from the photographic evidence. Only six Hs 126s were allegedly delivered, numbered 19-1 to 19-6, yet here is 19-7.

# Seefliegerstaffel AS/88

## Organization and Operations

At the end of September 1936, *Sonderstab W* took over from the *Kriegsmarine* a twin-engined He 59 biplane and a single-engined He 60. The two floatplanes and their crews were quickly shipped to Spain, where they arrived at Cadiz aboard the *Wigbert* in early October. The crews were commanded by the observers *Leutnant* Karl-Heinz Wolff and *Leutnant* Sigmund Storp.

The He 59 had been in service with the German *Seefliegergruppen* (coastal reconnaissance units) since the end of 1933. Here we are concerned with the He 59B-2 version, the first model to be produced in quantity. With two BMW 12-cylinder engines of 660 horsepower, it was usually armed with three MG 15 machine guns for defensive purposes in the nose, dorsal and ventral positions. Some of the aircraft sent to Spain, however, were up-gunned with a 20-millimeter cannon in the nose. It was capable of carrying a variety of offensive weaponry. In its internal bomb bay this could be twenty 50-kilogram bombs, while on external pylons it could take four 250-kilogram bombs or two 500-kilogram bombs. Alternatively, a 1,000-kilogram naval or "land" mine or three smoke containers could be carried. For antishipping duties, a 1,000-kilogram torpedo could be carried under the fuselage.

By virtue of the the huge floats which also served as fuel tanks, the He 59 soon acquired its Spanish nickname *Zapatones*, which translates as "big shoes" (literally "goloshes"). Martin Harlinghausen, however, preferred *Eiserne Gustav*—"Iron Gustav"—on account of the number of times it proved its robustness in combat.

In service with the Legion Condor, the primary duty of the big Heinkel was the protection of German cargo vessels in Spanish territorial waters. With the first missions came the first problems, such as that on 9 October when the *Kriegsmarine* battlecruiser *Admiral Scheer* recovered an He 59 in poor condition after a forced landing on the water. The cruiser *Königsberg* carried out a similar rescue mission on 19 December.

Like the Junkers 52s, the floatplanes were soon found more "positive" occupations, the first of these offensive missions being on 15 October when the two machines joined two Ju 52s and the first two experimental Hs 123s in an attack on the port of Cartagena, where the earliest cargos of Soviet aid were being unloaded. The results were inconclusive so the next day an alternative method was tried when Storp in the He 60 made a solo attack on a target near Malaga, with some success. As a result, *Oberst* Warlimont radioed Berlin with an urgent request for twelve more He 59s to supplement his forces.

It was the end of November, however, before reinforcements reached AS/88, by then officially part of the Legion Condor. Only two aircraft and their crews arrived: the naval observers *Oberleutnant* Werner Kluemper and *Oberleutnant* Dieter Leicht and the pilots *Oberfeldwebel* Johann Gaessler and *Unteroffizier* Bernhardt Winse, who had left Stettin aboard the cargo vessel *Strassfurt* on 19 November. The tiny unit was placed under the command of Wolff as the senior officer and left Cadiz for a new base at Melilla in North Africa at Christmas 1936. This new base had undeniable advantages over Cadiz; it was closer to the the area of operations of the floatplanes and it avoided the Straits of Gibraltar from where its movements could be monitored by the Republicans. It was also free of

A Spanish sailor poses in front of an He 59 of AS/88 at the harborside in Pollensa and offers a good view of the massive 20-millimeter gun ordered fitted to some of these aircraft in the first months of 1937. Note the enormous four-bladed wooden propellers.

bad weather as the "runway" was a small lake once used by the old Spanish air force CASA-Dornier Wals. The detachment then had two He 59s and a similar number of He 60s available. On 13 January 1937, the unit suffered its first personnel loss, when *Unteroffizier* Harald Kahl crashed into the sea off Pollensa during a night mission.

Among the tasks which fell to AS/88, experimenting with tactics was not the least. There was hardly any doubt as to which of the two aircraft types in use should be chosen as the main equipment for the He 60 had quickly proven to be really too light for offensive purposes. On the other hand, the He 59 with its primary armament of the Norwegian Horten "eel" torpedo needed trials before it could become a valuable antishipping vehicle. The first attempt proved to be less than glorious for the *Kriegsmarine*. On 30 January 1937, *Oberleutnant* Werner Klümper and his crew attacked the steamer *Delfin* off the south coast of Spain. In the first pass, the torpedo refused to drop; by the third attempt, the flight engineer had to try to open the release locks with a screwdriver. This he did and the torpedo hit the water—but then ran in circles as the steering gyros had been upset. Returning to base, Klümper and his crew immediately went back for another try in another He 59, but this time one loaded with two 250-kilogram bombs. These struck the freighter just as the Heinkel was forced to abandon the mission with the approach of three Republican fighters. The torpedo was never really a success in Spain, with only a single vessel succumbing to a torpedo strike.[16] This was the British freighter *Thorpeness*, which was sunk by *Hauptmann* Harlinghausen on 21 July 1938, one nautical mile off the port of Valencia.

Perhaps even more than their *Luftwaffe* colleagues, the naval observers of the He 59s proved to have a remarkable talent for improvisation. For example, on 31 January 1937, a transport vessel, the *Nuria*, with some 400 Republican volunteers crammed on deck, left Oran for Cartagena. It was intercepted twenty nautical miles off Cartagena by the indefatigable Klümper and his crew, among whom were a Spanish and a German radio operator. Not wishing to be responsible for a massacre, Klümper induced the captain of the ship to head for the Nationalist-held port of Melilla by means of fake messages to an imaginary submarine—and some bombs deliberately dropped wide by an accompanying He 60.

AS/88's precise role began to be more clearly defined during the campaign against Malaga. The few floatplanes available established such an effective aerial blockade that the Republican general staff more or less abandoned Andalusia. It was towards the end of this campaign that the first He 59 combat losses occured. One was shot down off Malaga—killing the pilot, *Leutnant* Dieter Leicht—on 5 February by the American mercenary pilot Charlie Koch, flying a Polikarpov I-15. In its plunge into the sea, the He 59 struck the port wing of the accompanying He 60 (numbered 512) which consequently force-landed. The crew of the He 60, who were uninjured, were rescued by the Spanish Nationalist cruiser *Canarias*, who thereafter adopted the aircraft, naming it *Fiera del Mar— The Wild Beast of the Sea*. AS/88 then transferred its base of operations to the newly captured port of Malaga, despite an almost total lack of support services.

Almost immediately afterwards *Oberleutnant* Wolff was recalled to Berlin and was replaced by *Hauptmann* Guenther Kluender. Shortly thereafter, reinforcements arrived in the form of two more He 59s and a single He 60, with their crews: *Oberfeldwebel* Herbert Schwarze, *Oberfeldwebel* Alfred Fisher, and *Feldwebel* Eugen Gries (pilots), and the observers *Leutnant* Friedrich Schallmayer, *Leutnant zur See* Albert Calmberg (*Kriegsmarine*) and *Unteroffizier* Georg Becker, *Unteroffizier* Rudolf Clauss, and *Unteroffizier* Ernst Feuchter.

The six months during which AS/88 was stationed at Malaga was a period of relative calm. The *Gruppe* took advantage of this to reorganize and increase its efficiency; the training necessary to carry out operational patrols could not be improvised. Between February and July, four more He 59s and several crews arrived, which allowed a slightly quicker rotation of the lower ranks, rather longer for the staff. In these six months, *Oberleutnant* Horst Schwilden, *Oberfeldwebel* Otto Mahl, *Oberfeldwebel* Ferdinand Schwandt, *Oberfeldwebel* Walter Gerbig, and *Unteroffizier* Rudolf Barella arrived from Germany as pilots but at the same time Gaessler, Winse, Schwarze, Fisher, and Gries returned. The arrival of *Leutnant zur See* Gerhard Bigalk, *Unteroffizier* Albin Bialek, *Unteroffizier* Arno Kleyenstuber, and *Funkmeister* Hans Beyert as observers and crew members was offset by the departure of Storp, Clauss, and Klümper. As the availability of the He 59s throughout the course of the Spanish Civil War was directly linked to the losses suffered on operations, rather than easily predictable maintenance, the personnel replacements had more effect on the intensity of operations than damage to equipment.

On 7 July 1937, AS/88 took up quarters at its final base, Puerta Pollensa on the island of Mallorca under the command of *Hauptmann* Hans Hefelel. By this date he had received a total of nine He 59s and eight He 60s. Very quickly the geographical distance engendered in the unit a character somewhat separate from the rest of the Legion. The crews were comfortably lodged in the hotel Mar i Cel, while Hefele, officially under the orders of the Spanish military commander and the commander of the air forces on Mallorca, made sure he had plenty of "elbow room."

Operations recommenced at the beginning of August, aimed this time at blockading the Republican-held Spanish coast from Port Bou to Almeria, and harassing port installations at night. For this, the crews developed an exceptional tactic. Taking advantage of the good flying qualities of the He 59, despite its size, they aimed to arrive over their objective at an altitude of 50 to 100 meters, with engines throttled back, then, after their attack making a quick escape at sea level. In order to make the He 59 more effective against coastal shipping and rail traffic, which the unit had begun to take an interest in at this time, Hefele ordered the installation of a 20-millimeter Rheinmetall cannon to be installed in the nose of some aircraft. Throughout the second month of 1937, AS/88 attacked vessels flying Greek, Danish, Norwegian, and Panamanian flags, in the knowledge that their cargos were intended for the Republicans. Out of the ten vessels attacked, three were sunk and two were forced to beach.

From the end of October 1937, the serviceable aircraft available peaked at ten He 59s and two He 60s, while personnel rotation was proceeding smoothly. New arrivals at AS/88 were the pilots *Leutnant* Volkmann Zenker, *Leutnant zur See* Erwin Brammer, and *Unteroffizier* Peter Eberhard in July; *Oberfeldwebel* Alfred Tonollo and *Unteroffizier* Otto Ossowski in November; and *Oberfeldwebel* Willi Götz and *Oberfeldwebel* Arthur Stoodt, while Mahl, Schwandt, Barello, and Gerbig left the unit. New observers to arrive were *Oberleutnant* Jürgen Janssen, *Leutnant zur See* Ernst Thomsen, *Leutnant zur See* Hans Keese, *Unteroffizier* Heinrich Schindler, *Unteroffizier* Wilhelm Siepen, *Ost. Fkg* Walter Schiller, and *Stbs. Fkg* Kurt Mommertz in July; *Unteroffizier* Heinz Logemann in August; *Oberleutnant* Heinz Golcher and *Oberleutnant* Hayo Jürgens in September; *Feldwebel* Josef Hinterberger in November; and *Leutnant zur See* Joachim Deecke and *Unteroffizier* Hans Nitzsche in December. Departees for Germany were Schallmaycr, Bigalk, Calmberg, Becker, Beyert, Schiller, Mommertz, Feuchter, and Bialek.

The arrival of a new commanding officer in January 1938 represented a turning point for AS/88. *Hauptmann* Martin Harlinghausen not only knew his business, he also enjoyed the full confidence of *Generalleutnant* Volkmann. He arrived with two He 59 as reinforcements and the pilots *Leutnant* Rudolf Meissner and *Leutnant* Karl Zunker and the observer *Leutnant zur See* Kurt Hörstke, replacing Hefele, Schwilden, Kleyenstüber, and Schindler, who left. At about this time, the unit also acquired a Junkers Ju52/3mW floatplane, which permitted heavylift transport missions.

Harlinghausen was a born leader of men. On his first mission on 19 January, he succeeded in destroying the Campsa fuel depots in Valencia, one of the priority targets of the unit. Throughout 1938, the He 59s carried out constant attacks on the Mediterranean coast of Spain and the Republican strongholds at Port-Bou, Barcelona, Palamos, San Feliu de Guixols, Villanova i Geltru, Vinaroz, Alcira, Almeria, and Cartagena. The targets were by now clearly defined: port installations where supplies and matériel were discharged were extremely important, while stations and supply trains were attacked at night with the 20-millimeter cannon. On 26 February, the He 59 flown by *Oberleutnant* Salcher was intercepted by an I-15 and damaged near San Sebastian, but the pilot managed to return to base safely despite his wounds.

Under its new commander, AS/88 little by little began to change its role, leaving daylight strikes on cargo vessels to the Ju 87s. It would be untrue, however, to pretend that attacks were successful, as on 15 March 1938 when an He 59 got too close to a train it was attacking in the Vinaroz sector. While dropping his twenty 50-kilogram bombs, the pilot, Alfred Tonollo, passed through a hail of fire from the train. Hit in the starboard engine and fuselage, Tonollo succeeded in crash-landing in an olive grove beside the Vinaroz–San Carlos road. The five crew members managed to leave their aircraft and set it on fire before being made prisoners. They were later exchanged. Again, on 30 March 1938, it took four missions by three He 59s and an He 60 and sixty 50-kilogram bombs to destroy the bridge at Amposta over the Ebro. At the same time accidents and repairs and maintenance increased in keeping with the increased tempo of operations. Fortunately for AS/88, throughout its entire time in Spain it lost only five aircraft directly due to enemy action, with twelve to other causes. The rugged quality of the *Eiserne Gustav* was demonstrated to Harlinghausen when, on an indeterminate date in 1938, during the course of a mission against Barcelona, his He 59 was hit by the blast from his own bombs and it was only by a miracle he returned to Pollensa. With half the fabric missing, the fuselage twisted and the lower wing broken in several places, the aircraft was fit only for the scrapheap.

The greatest difficulties for AS/88 revolved around maintenance. The He 59 was a very large aircraft for the period, heavy and complex, requiring constant attention in normal circumstances, even without the need to repair combat damage after a mission. The *Gruppe* was in a grotesque situation, for while the workshops in Pollensa were able to carry out normal checks, according to the manuals after every hundred hours flying time, the necessary spares were still with the *Kriegsmarine* in Kiel, yet the aircraft had been transferred to the *Luftwaffe*. The administrative complications persisted throughout the war. More difficult still, the 300-hour major services had to be undertaken back in Germany. Instead of flying back there in stages, however, the inflexible procedure was for the aircraft to fly to Cadiz, where they were dismantled and then shipped back to Germany where they were reassembled and flown to the repair depot. This whole process took three months, compared to the normal week. And again, on several occasions AS/88 found themselves with a number of aircraft immobilised with structural damage; the only qualified mechanic available was in Seville and could not be transferred.

Despite or perhaps because of the foregoing, the size of the unit became much more important in 1938 than in the previous year. Personnel rotations succeeded one another with the arrival of the following pilots: *Unteroffizier* Gerhard Franz in February; *Leutnant* Ludwig Fehling, *Oberfeldwebel* Fritz Latislau, *Feldwebel* Georg Lust, *Unteroffizier* Herbert Euen, and *Unteroffizier* Harro Prengemann in May; *Unteroffizier* Walter Ness in June; *Oberleutnant* Friedrich Verlohr and *Oberfeldwebel* Erich Furrl in July; *Leutnant* Otto Schmidt, *Unteroffizier* Ernst Hinrichs, and *Unteroffizier* Eugen Walk in September; *Oberleutnant* Egbert von Frankenberg, *Leutnant* Gerhard Werner, and *Unteroffizier* Walter Hegner in November, replacing the tour-expired Brammer, Eberhard, Tonollo (then a pris-

Basically an He 45 with floats, the Heinkel He 60E does not seem to have been as successful as its elder brother. This is probably 60-3, the lower portion of which is just visible on the fuselage, in service with the Spanish unit G-60 at Cadiz some time in 1937.

oner), Ossowski, Zenker, Götz, Stoodt, Meissner, Rathberger, Fehling, Latislaus, Prengemann, Lust, and Linge; and, finally, Harlinghausen, Franz, and Euen in December.

With regard to observers, the personnel changes were even more striking, with the arrival of *Leutnant* Franz Brey, Günther Grützmacher, *Oberfeldwebel* Hermann Strohmaier, and *Unteroffizier* Kurt Keitzel in February; *Leutnant* Karl von Bülow, *Leutnant* Peter Römisch, *Leutnant zur See* Wilhelm Fritsch, *Leutnant zur See* Ernst Poeschel, *Oberfunkmeister* Frank Westphal, *Feldwebel* Manfred Peter, *Funkmeister* Otto Wrede, *Funkmeister* Konrad Ellermann, *Unteroffizier* Ernst Langanki, *Unteroffizier* Georg Linge, and *Obergefreiter* Heinz Schinze in May; *Hauptmann* Werner Smidt and *Obergefreiter* Ottomar Gensior in August; *Oberleutnant* Klaus Havenstein, *Oberleutnant* Ludwig von Mueller, *Oberleutnant* Carl-Friedrich Printz, *Oberleutnant* Carl-Hugo Thevalt, *Leutnant zur See* Peter Lohmeyer, *Leutnant zur See* Wolf Wodtke, *Funkmeister* Gustav Schultzen, *Unteroffizier* Paul Jäck, *Unteroffizier* Rudi Schmidt, *Obergefreiter* Helmut Woch, and *Gefreiter* Erwin Sack in September; *Leutnant zur See* Hans-Jürgen Auffermann, *Unteroffizier* Hans Greve, *Unteroffizier* Bernhard Wessels, and *Unteroffizier* Josef Wirtz in November, taking over from Janssen, Siepen, Hörstke, Thomsen, Keese, Jürgens (killed), Deecke, Strohmayer, Keitzel (killed), Golcher, Ellermann, Brey, Nitzsche, von Bülow, Poeschel (killed), Peter, Wrede, Schinze, Grützmacher, Linge, and finally Fritsch, Römisch, Westphal, and Langanki.[17]

In the course of 1938, operations became longer and riskier, an indication that the war was becoming more technical. On 21 March, near Cambrills, *Oberleutnant* Jürgens and his crew, Zunker and Keitzel, were lost when their aircraft crashed in flames. According to Republican sources, Jürgens was suprised by a nightfighter and shot down by a single long burst of fire. For the record it should be noted that this would be the sole combat kill attributable to the Dewoitine D.510 anywhere. Other sources suggest that Jürgens was a victim of his own bombs which were dropped at too low a level. The victorious Republican pilot was *Teniente* José Corral, commander of the *1ª Escuadrila* of *Grupo 71*, tasked with coastal defense.

On 2 August, the He 59 of *Leutnant* Euen was on a mission in the Paitrosos sector. Hit by Republican ground fire he was obliged to make a violent forcelanding in the sea near Vinaroz. Fortunately for them, the crew were rescued by a Nationalist armed trawler and only Euen was slightly injured. On the twenty-ninth of the same month, while returning from a mission to the east coast of Spain, He 59 number 532 landed too fast and the floats were torn off by the shock, the aircraft turning over onto its nose in the bay at Pollensa. The crew were soon

A view of Pollensa's main moorings and the bay. Three He 60s can be seen on dry land, with one Cant Z.506, two Arado 95s, one Cant Z.501, and one He 59 on the water. The crane was necessary to hoist big aircraft onto the shore. Note the floats under maintenance and/or repair.

rescued, Prengemann and Bülling only slightly injured, the pilot, Römisch, more seriously.

The last commander of AS/88 was *Hauptmann* Smidt, who continued the tactics of predecessor. The last desperate struggles of the Republican death throes severely affected the *Gruppe*, which between December 1938 and March 1939 suffered its heaviest losses. Nonetheless, the cause was won and by the war's end AS/88 could claim fifty-two enemy vessels, nine of them to Franz Brey, the record holder for this type of operation.

From the end of December 1938 an unprecedented series of grim events affected AS/88. On 31 December, the He 59 of *Leutnant* Otto Schmidt was shot down by flak near Valls. The entire crew of Schmidt, Prinz, Jeck, and Bülling were killed, as well as an inspector, Ludwig Müller. The following day, 1 January, in one of a series of black days for the Legion, the *Gruppe* lost another aircraft, possibly through icing. Again the crew, Poeschel, Schöbel, Zervas, and Herold, vanished into the sea. This was not the end, for on 6 January, another He 59 returning to Pollensa was intercepted by a Republican fighter. The rugged construction of the *Zapatones* saved the crew, but the aircraft was immediately written off.

The large number of personnel transfers in this last period served to hasten the training of as many others as possible. Coming through as pilots were *Oberleutnant* Dietrich Troll and *Unteroffizier* Paul Randorf in January; *Feldwebel* Otto zum Broecke and *Unteroffizier* Heinz Schocker in February; *Leutnant* Hans-Viktor Schwencke, *Leutnant* Kurt Wacksmuth, *Unteroffizier* Heinz Cords, *Unteroffizier* Heinz Bremme, and *Unteroffizier* Priedhelm Schulz in March, which permitted the replacement of Fürrl, Schmidt (killed), and Verlohr. It was the same story with observers with the Legion trying to train as many as possible without too many risks in the last few weeks of the war.[18] These were *Oberleutnant zur See* Paul-Hugo Kettner in January; *Leutnant zur See* Herbert Schneider, *Leutnant zur See* Horst Dieterichs, *Feldwebel* Alfred Eke, *Unteroffizier* Helmuth Rudolph, *Unteroffizier* Hans Schulze in February; *Leutnant zur See* Reinhard Metzger, *Leutnant zur See* Helmuth Fiehn, *Leutnant zur See* Claus Toball, *Leutnant zur See* Wolfgang Hochbaum, *Leutnant zur See* Siegfried Jandrey, *Unteroffizier* Fritz Bätzholdt, *Unteroffizier* Hermann Einhaus, *Unteroffizier* Werner Iserloth, *Unteroffizier* Alfred Lange, and *Unteroffizier* Willi Spirka, who replaced Printz (killed), Jeck (killed), Schultzen, Gensior, and Schulze.

There still remained a bitter pill to swallow. On 22 March, one of two He 59s on reconnaisance off the east coast of Spain was forced to make an emergency landing to the north of Ibiza. It was completely destroyed when it sank, although the crew were rescued by a British destroyer, which returned them to Pollensa. On the same day, however, the Republicans announced that one of their aircraft had shot down an He 59 off the port of Cartagena, a victory attributed to a Grumman-CCF "Delfin." If correct, this would be one of very few, if not the only, claim by a Grumman biplane fighter.

New aircraft arriving were too late for AS/88, which did not have the same well-placed contacts in Berlin as the fighter Gruppe J/88, or the bomber unit K/88. Heinkel He 115s were issued but never saw combat operations. Their baptism of fire was to come some months later. Antiquated but evidently robust, the He 59 was undoubtedly the workhorse of AS/88, which had three to six machines serviceable in August–September 1938, this number subsequently reaching eleven, then back to five before the establishment was set in March as an average of seven or eight flyable aircraft. There had still been times at night during the war, however, when the one and only serviceable aircraft had taken to the air six times with different crews. A total of 17 He 59s had been lost to various causes during the course of the conflict. On 1 April 1939, ten were left. The seven best were returned to Germany, while the remainder were handed over to the Nationalist air force.

# The Heinkel He 59 in Spain

**Type code 71**
**Nickname** *Zapatones*—"Big Shoes"

Though all the He 59 aircraft had a number, it was generally painted so small that it remained unnoticed. Towards the end of the war, nevertheless, the aircraft slowly were given their full registration number, here 71-3. Note the ace of spades badge of AS/88 on the nose.

A good opportunity to have a look at one of the BMW VI engines that pulled the He 59 to a stately top speed of 220 kilometers per hour. Also remarkable is the filling of the float tanks with fuel, which gave the aircraft a more than respectable range, in spite of its weight and poor aerodynamics.

Heinkel He 59 5-12 escorted by the two He 60s, probably during the early part of 1937 while operating out of Melilla.

This He 59 is moored on a beach of Pollensa bay, ready for the next mission. The markings are typical of AS/88, though there was some liberty in their application.

Following a storm on 11 February 1938, this He 59 was left dismasted as it were, in the bay at Pollensa. It was subsequently written off as unrepairable.

This aircraft is probably undergoing overhaul, as all the armament has been taken off as well as the propellers. The scene is typical of the mess one can find in any workshop, but the sun gives a nice touch to the job. The location is not certain but may be Mellila on account of the work being done on the beach as opposed to a dockside.

This scene seems to correspond more to repairs in progress than to overhaul. Possibly this particular aircraft was damaged by flak during a night mission and the maintenance people are changing one upper wing. Note the much more sophisticated Italian CANT Z.506s in the background.

This aircraft appears to be armed with a 20-millimeter nose gun, carefully protected with a tailor-made cover. Note how light the overall grey paint appears, probably as a result of the enormous bulk of the He 59.

On some aircraft, the nose machine gun was replaced by a 20-millimeter cannon, which was far more effective against cargo freighters and locomotives. The AS/88 emblem is clearly visible on this very clean He 59. At least three more can be made out in the background, as well as an He 60. Pollensa, 1937–38.

A view from Pollensa's docks at the end of 1938 with three moored He 59s. By that date, the large and cumbersome *Zapatones* were then operating from an almost perfect base and were not under continuous threat like the land-based aircraft. The car in the foreground is a German DKW "Junior Sport" with wire wheels.

A rare formation flight by He 59Bs on reconnaissance patrol near Mallorca. Note that the farthest aircraft has an extra white cross on the wing center section.

# The Heinkel He 60 in Spain

## Type code 60

An He 60 moored in Pollensa Bay, probably while in service with the Spanish unit G-60.

AS/88 was not very lucky with its He 60s and consequently passed them over to a Spanish Nationalist unit. 60-3 has been named *Luis Cellier* by its new crew in commemoration of the first commander of the unit who was killed in He 60 60-2 on 21 August 1937. This was a custom often followed by Spanish units.

This is a port side view of He 60 60-3. It can be seen that the name and Popeye emblem were carried on both sides of the fuselage. Location is probably Puntales, Cadiz, in late 1937. Finish appears to be overall RLM grey 02 with silver-finished floats.

Originally intended for use as a torpedo bomber, the Arado Ar 95 was rejected by the *Luftwaffe* and therefore offered for export. Capable of using wheels or floats, six on floats were sent to the Legion Condor at Pollensa but were immediately handed over to the Spanish to form *Grupo 64*. Clearly, this one, 64-3, was tried out on wheels, but it seems that the Nationalists found little use for them either.

Another Ar 95, this one lacks any kind of identity marking and is therefore probably in the state in which it was first delivered in August 1938. Pollensa Bay, Mallorca.

The intended successor to the He-60, the remarkable Arado 95 was assembled and test flown by the German crews of AS/88. Here 64-2 shows off its wing-folding ability, a feature designed for use aboard ships.

# Jagdgruppe J/88

## Organization and Operations

**THE FIRST COMMANDERS**
Even though the Legion Condor still did not exist as such, a squadron of six He 51s arrived in mid-August 1936, commanded by *Leutnant* Kraft Eberhardt. At the end of September, with the arrival of the first complement of pilots, the two "squadrons" of three aircraft each had an individual commander, but Eberhardt remained the *de facto* chief of the entire operation. He was replaced after his death in combat on 13 November by *Oberleutnant* Herwig Knüppel.

Once the Legion had been officially created new aircraft arrived to create four *Staffeln*.[19] The new J/88 was placed under the command of *Major* Baier, who suddenly fell ill and had to go back to Germany. He in turn was replaced by *Hauptmann* von Mehrardt. Highly thought of by his men, who described him as a kind and gentle man, he remained in post up to 18 July 1937. It was during his mandate that the conversion to the Messerschmitt Bf 109 started.

Von Mehrardt was replaced by *Hauptmann* Gotthardt Handrick, nicknamed "Herman," a former Olympic sportsman and very characteristic of the new breed of subaltern officers of the new German army—young, athletic and as hard on themselves as on their men. Handrick remained in post until 10 September 1938, when he was replaced by *Major* Walter Grabmann. The Nationalist victory of March 1939 prevented *Major* Bustellin from succeeding him to this post.

**1.J/88**
*Hauptmann* Werner Palm led the unit into combat from the start of November 1936 to 6 April 1937, when he was succeeded by *Oberleutnant* Harro Harder, who served until 18 December of the same year; then it was the turn of *Oberleutnant* Wolfgang Schellmann up to 2 September 1938 and finally *Hauptmann* Siebel Reents. The change to the Bf 109 was carried out under the discipline of Harder.

## 2.J/88

Taken in charge in November 1936 by *Oberleutnant* Siegfried Lehmann, the unit passed to the command of *Oberleutnant* Günther Lützow on 19 March 1937; then to *Oberleutnant* Joachim-Heinrich Schlichting until 28 May 1938; to *Oberleutnant* Hubert Kroeck up to 31 October 1938 and finally to *Oberleutnant* Alfred von Lojewski. The conversion to the Bf 109 took place under Lützow, probably one of the most effective fighter pilots in Spain.

A Messerschmitt Bf 109C or D (note the wing gun openings) being readied for operations at La Cenia, the main Legion Condor base, probably in mid-1938. The man in civilian clothes is almost certainly the pilot, posing for a picture before a visit to the local town or possibly before return home to Germany. He bears some resemblance to *Oberleutnant* Kurt Müller, once of 4.J/88.

## 3.J/88

Jürgen Roth led the unit from November 1937 until 19 March 1937 before passing over command to *Oberleutnant* Douglas Pitcairn, who ceded it himself on 27 July 1937 to the celebrated Adolf Galland, at that time still an *Oberleutnant*. The conversion to the Bf 109 came about at the same time as the arrival of the new squadron chief *Oberleutnant* Werner Mölders on 24 May 1938, before the arrival on the scene, on 5 December, of the last squadron leader, *Oberleutnant* Hubertus von Bonin. All of these would gain fame in the later, greater conflict.

## 4.J/88

This was without doubt the *Staffel* with the most troubled career. It was taken over in November 1936 by *Oberleutnant* Kraft Eberhardt, who was already a veteran; it was in fact only the continuation of the first unit which had arrived during the course of the summer. Eberhardt, killed on 13 November, was replaced by *Oberleutnant* Herwig Knüppel, another veteran, who remained until 1 March 1937. Next came *Oberleutnant* Walter Kienzle, who commanded from the end of the same month to the disbanding of the unit for reasons which we shall examine later.

*4 Staffel* was reformed on 2 November following under the command of *Oberleutnant* Eberhardt d'Elsa until 17 June 1938, when it was definitively dissolved. It was not converted to the Bf 109 due to lack of aircraft.

## 5.J/88

On 15 February 1938, the Ju 87 *Kette* was temporarily reattached to J/88, under the command of *Leutnant* Hermann Haas. This new squadron only remained a few weeks before changing its Ju 87s for the Arado Ar 68, with which it carried out the first experiments with night fighting by the Legion Condor, experiments quickly abandoned in view of the small chances of success.

It is curious to note from the scoreboard (although now and then fanciful in its claims) that, besides such "stars" as Harder, Lützow, and Mölders, a good number of unit leaders did not obtain a single official victory in Spain: von Mehrardt, Palm, Lehmann, Kroeck, Roth, Pitcairn, Galland, d'Elsa, and Kienzle were not credited with any combat successes, whereas Reents only marked up a single victory and Lojewski two.

One of the last aircraft flown by 4.J/88 (the aircraft number is obviously over 100) this Heinkel He 51 carries a typical three-tone camouflage scheme. It has just left the workshops of the park at Logrono, where it had an armor plate fitted behind the pilots seat in order to protect his back and head. The plate can be seen protruding above the fuselage spine.

Probably the most dangerous enemy to be met in the air by the Legion was the Polikarpov I-16. This Type 5 may be the very first example to be captured by the Nationalists, shown after rebuilding and in service with *Grupo 1-W*, but it shows all the main features of the airframe. Location is probably Cuatro Vientos, 1939.

This is the mount of Walter Oesau, as it wears seven victory bars on the fin, and a small shield on the spinner although the the number of this Bf 109B (no wing guns) is not known.

## SQUADRON LIFE

### 1 Staffel

The three new He 51s were not really operational until the end of November and were installed at Burgos for several days before taking up duty at Vitoria from 4 December. To be found under the discipline of

Palm at that time were *Oberleutnant* Harro Harder, *Oberfeldwebel* Karl Wilfert, *Leutnant* Hans-Jürgen Hepe, *Oberfeldwebel* Heinz Braunschweiger, *Leutnant* Wilhelm Blankenagel, *Oberleutnant* Günther Schulze-Blank, *Oberleutnant* Joachim Wandel, *Leutnant* Ernst Reutter, *Unteroffizier* Ernst Terry, and *Unteroffizier* Hans Kolbow.

At the end of the month, the entire *Gruppe* was based at Avila and Escalona and carried out their first missions over the Madrid front. The inexperience of the new group was amply demonstrated on 20 December when *1 Staffel* downed a friendly Italian Romeo Ro 37 in error. The incident did nothing to bring the two expeditionary corps together, who already viewed one another with some suspicion.

In February, several new pilots arrived, among them Adolf Galland, who then, of course, had no idea that he would become famous, nor that he would stay very much longer in Spain than planned; he was just a pilot like the others, charged equally with the technical maintenance of the *Staffel*.

At the start of February, the *Staffel* was at Escalona, but come the twelfth, Hepe and Palm himself were surprised on their patrol and forced to parachute out. Then the big northern campaign erupted and the entire J/88 *Gruppe* moved to a base at Vitoria, with *1 Staffel* reduced to ten aircraft. The offensive that started on 31 March saw the He 51s effect their first *Cadenas*-style[20] ground-support attacks. The perfecting of the *Cadenas* techniques did not happen without problems, the most evident being that, often, the infantry did not follow up the assault, as for instance on 1 and 2 April, when *1 Staffel* intervened at Corbea and Chiqui. After its combat blooding, *2 Staffel* could use its brand-new Messerschmitts and the He 51s to concentrate with increasing success on ground attacks. This type of operation, which the British in World War II later called "Rhubarbs," was a sweep by four aircraft in loose formation looking for targets of opportunity on vehicles, troop formations, installations, and so on. This quickly became the speciality of *1 Staffel* and *3 Staffel*. For example, on 31 April, about forty lorries were destroyed in six missions, missions which became known as "louse hunting" to some pilots of the Legion. This was not always without danger, and on 13 May, *1 Staffel* lost the aircraft flown by *Leutnant* Wandel and *Unteroffizier* Kolbow, who were downed by the dangerous light flak. Wandel was imprisoned, condemned to death, then finally exchanged.

The ten available machines of *1 Staffel* participated in the bombing of Guernica—more precisely, by strafing the roads and streets after the passing of units of K/88. For a long time, the pilots were reluctant to tell the story of this event.

A mechanic seated on the lower wing root of an Heinkel He 51C, 2-60, flown by *Leutnant* Kurt Müller of 4.J/88, whose ace of spades insignia can be seen on the fuselage. This aircraft and pilot were with the unit at Calamocha in January 1938 during the Teruel campaign when it was commanded by *Oberleutnant* Eberhardt d'Elsa. At this time, the He 51s were finding more and more difficulty in coping with the enemy fighters and the unit was disbanded for the second time in June 1938 and the aircraft passed on to the Spaniards. The pilots were then dispersed through the other fighter *Staffeln* of the Legion.

In June, the He 112V-4 piloted by *Unteroffizier* Max Schulz (nicknamed *Dosen Max*—"Dozy Max") was attached to *1 Staffel* and employed principally against tanks for which the 20-millimeter cannon firing through the propeller spinner was eminently suited. At least three tanks were confirmed to Schulz before he totally obliterated the aircraft when landing on 19 July. In fact, according to certain witnesses, it would rather seem that the He 112 came back with serious combat damage and was not able to reach the runway. The intensity of the air defenses was confirmed by Harro Harder who, on 18 July, warned that numerous aircraft were returning riddled, including his own 2-64. Thus poor Schulz had to return to He 51s.

For the battle of Brunete, the General Staff of J/88 had to leave for Valdemorillo, and *1 Staffel* returned to Escalona on 8 July. Although now well understood, the *Cadenas* tactics were not at all easy for the units of He 51s; the barren territory of Brunete did not lend itself to the game of "hide and seek" possible in the Basque country. The *Staffel* had a bad day on 24 July when in the course of the last mission, carried out jointly with

*3 Staffel, Leutnant* Reutter was hit squarely by ground fire and killed; according to Harder, he was the most experienced pilot of the unit. For his part, *Unteroffizier* Beurer took several very near hits and, because of his seniority, was able to leave Spain after having seen the impressive damage inflicted upon his biplane. He proceeded to test the Hs 123 as part of the experimental *Gruppe VJ/88*. All the other aircraft had been hit. Notable participants were Handrick and *Leutnant* Galland, as well as Wilfert, Kolbow, and Terry. The doctor of *1 Staffel* ordered three weeks of enforced leave for the five longest-serving pilots of the unit, but the campaign was reaching its conclusion, and the last missions were on 27 July.

All the He 51s were more or less worn out by this campaign, and so, on 30 July, the *Gruppe* went to lick its wounds in the area of Alar and Calahorra. By then, *1 Staffel* had only nine machines left. The rest was not long because the offensive against Santander began on 7 August. The two units of He 51s were charged with "doing the housework" on the left flank of the operation. On the eighteenth, *1 Staffel* occupied the ground around Orzales. At the beginning of the month, the unit lost Terry, who, to his great relief, was transferred to *2 Staffel*. For his part, Adolf Galland, who had participated in the terrible mission of 24 July, left to command *3 Staffel* with his new *Oberleutnant* bars. The campaign against Santander did not cut into the combat capability of the unit; on the contrary, during the transition to Bf 109Bs, the unit at one time had available seven Bf 109s and fourteen He 51s.

On 2 September, the entire *Gruppe* of J/88 was at Pontejos, west of Santander, with *1 Staffel* and *3 Staffel* giving themselves up to the delights of *Freijagd* patrols chasing targets of opportunity. By mid-September, however, there remained only fourteen He 51s available between the two squadrons. As the *Freijagd* fighter sweeps started to become more systematic, they were frequently followed by a hunt for vehicles called colloquially *Kochenjagd*—akin to "pigsticking" in English. The great specialist in this was *Feldwebel* Ignaz Prestele, nicknamed *Igel*—"Hedgehog."

Then, on the ground, the race for the sea began. On 8 March 1938, Awe announced a new victory against an I-15 above Puebla de Hijar. Finishing with the *Kochenjagd* patrols, *1 Staffel* then began exclusively to escort the He 111s of K/88. On 10 March, Prestele claimed an I-15 but the Republican Air Force was not as yet bled dry, and despite the technical superiority of the Bf 109, many encounters ended in a draw, such as the one on 15 March, during an escort for a Do 17. The first part of this campaign, the first real strategic movement of the Nationalist forces, ended on 17 March. J/88 then regrouped in the area of Sanjurjo-Saragossa.

This is the young *Oberleutnant* Hannes Trautloft, later to become one of the greatest fighter leaders in the *Luftwaffe* seated in his He 51, 2-23, in summer 1936. The aircraft survived to be transferred to the Spanish unit 1-G-2. When it first reached Spain, the Heinkel 51, though the pride of the new *Luftwaffe*, was already inferior to the Fiat C.R.32, but still vastly superior to the assorted Republican Nieuport fighters. The problems came when the German (or Spanish) pilots went into a fight against a Fury, Dewoitine, or Loire, as Trautloft was able to testify.

Republican aviation reacted again with some vigor, but in the overall picture, the Nationalist air force, and in particular the Legion Condor, became the masters of the sky. *1 Staffel* intervened on 24 March in a combat between Nationalist-flown Fiat CR.32s engaged against a unit of "Chatos."[21] In the ensuing dogfight, *Leutnant* Awe and *Unteroffizier* Stark each bagged an I-15. Another was claimed by *Oberleutnant* Schellman in controversial fashion in Bf 109 6-51 when he shot down the Republican Sergeant Domingo Hueso, who had been wounded by the Nationalist Captain Angel Salas Larrazabal and was being escorted in his I-15 back to Nationalist territory so that he could surrender. On the twenty-ninth, Hans-Karl Mayer (*Mayer-Ast*) claimed an I-15 above Lerida.

On 4 April, the two units of Bf 109s moved to Larraja to the south of Huesca, where *General* Volkmann was to pay them a visit. On landing at about 12.00 hours, the 109s of Awe and Borchers were in collision. The propeller of Borchers's machine sliced through the cockpit part of Awe's aircraft, decapitating the pilot at the same time. Borchers survived despite overturning on landing.

In the same period, Otto Bertram was transferred from *4 Staffel* to *1 Staffel* and allocated Bf 109 6-82. On his first day in the unit he "enjoyed" no fewer than four missions at 08.00, 11.00, 14.00, and 17.00. By month's end, the race towards the "orchard" of Valencia was well underway.

On 18 May, Gotthardt Handrick (*Gruppen Kommandeur* of J/88, flying an aircraft from the Stab/88) brought down an I-16 over Castellón, the unidentified pilot of which was announced as being an American. It was June before *1 Staffel* could add to its victory list when an SB-2 was credited to *Leutnant* Mayer on the tenth, which made him an ace. The thirteenth was both a good and a bad day; having arrived too late for the planned escort duty for K/88, *1 Staffel* redeemed itself by virtue of a incredible mêlée with Republican fighters. *Leutnant* Keller and *Unteroffizier* Erich Kuhlmann were each credited with an I-15 and *Oberleutnant*

The most ferocious enemy of the He 51 in Spain ceased to be the Polikarpov I-15 (in itself serious competition for the German biplane) when the Heinkel was assigned to ground attack. This one has been shot down by the Thaelmann flak battery manned by international volunteers. One of these men, either the one in overalls or the one on the right, is Laco Holdos, a Czech member of the unit and political commissar. Note the man wearing the standard-issue Spanish army steel helmet, which never looked as though it fit the owner.

Schellmann with an I-16, with *Leutnant* Walter Maurer, *Oberleutnant* Kurt Müller, and *Oberleutnant* Meyer being awarded three "probables." The next day, *1 Staffel* came across yet more "Chatos" and "Moscas"[22] when escorting a group of Stukas. In the dogfight, the newly promoted *Feldwebel* Kuhlmann downed an I-15, but Priebe was shot down by an I-15 while trying to dislodge a particularly tenacious aircraft off the tail of *Leutnant* Rudolf Rech of *2 Staffel*. Wounded in the lungs and the shoulder blade, he managed with difficulty to land in a field at Villafames, insisting, by his own account, he had been saved by the several seconds it took for his Bf 109 to break up, and on his difficulties in landing with a throttle lever, so to say, almost shot off. The same day, the group lost *Leutnant* Helmut Henz, hit south of Castellón by Republican fighters, who was obliged to land on a bank of the River Mijares and give himself up. Very soon, however, before the government forces were able to get hold of this juicy prize, his companions burned the aircraft on the ground.

At this time, the situation with regard to available aircraft was extremely grave, with *1 Staffel* being in the worst condition with only four fighters in flying condition with which to carry out the essential ten sorties per day. Back in Germany, Spain was of lesser importance than the *Anschluss*[23]; there was no question at that moment of waiting for reinforcements. From 17 to 24 June, the Legion Condor remained on the ground. On the twenty-fifth, *Oberleutnant* Schellmann celebrated the renewal of operations by downing an I-16.

On 15 July, another great aerial combat permitted *Oberleutnant* Muller, *Leutnant* Keller, *Feldwebel* Kuhlmann, and *Unteroffizier* Quasinowski to each gain a victory against as many Republican I-15s. Against the same type of aeroplane, Quasinowski scored again on 17 July and downed another the following day. That same day, Schellmann and Kuhlmann shared a claim for yet another. On the twentieth, Schellmann downed two "Moscas" and *Unteroffizier* Helmut Brucks another. Next, it was the turn of *Feldwebel* Robert Menge, who, on the twenty-third, gained his first official victory against an I-16. At the end of the month of July, *1 Staffel* was reinforced by *Leutnant* Otto "Otsch" Bertram, who transferred from *3 Staffel* to his great satisfaction. He was allocated Bf 109 2-67. On 1 August, *Leutnant* Karl Ebbighausen, *Unteroffizier* Franz Jaenisch, and *Unteroffizier* Josef Bauer were each able to claim a score against a formation of I-15s estimated at thirty, but *Leutnant* Horst Tietzen had to make a forced landing in no-man's-land twelve kilometers northeast of Gandesa.

The big thrust towards the sea again cut the Republican territory in two. The Nationalist forces prepared to follow up, but it was the Government forces that took the initiative; this was to become the battle of the

Ebro. It was therefore not until 12 August that the unit gained more laurels when Brucks and Schellmann downed an SB-2 and Bertram an I-16, the leader of the squadron being equally credited with a probable second Katiuska, which was later confirmed.[24]

The new intake of pilots acquitted themselves well when, after Menge and Bertram, it was *Unteroffizier* Willy Szuggar who opened his prize list on 14 August with an I-16, and Bertram and Schellmann each took one on the same occasion. Otsch was in good form when he downed a third I-16 the following day. On 19 August, *Oberleutnant* Keller added a new Mosca to his claims, imitated the following day by Schellmann, who thereby gained his second victory and his last in Spain. On the twenty-third, Bertram and *Oberleutnant* Muller each brought down an I-16. On 2 September, *Oberleutnant* Reents arrived for one week in joint command of the Staffel.

Otto Bertram revealed his talent when he gained a double on 7 September in the face of opposition from other I-16s. On the tenth, Schellmann ceded for good the command of the *Staffel* to Siebel Reents. At this time, *1 Staffel*, as other squadrons of the Legion Condor, suffered a large drain of experienced personnel. Many key men were sent back to their homes as the Sudetenland crisis menaced. In spite of everything this hardly changed the fact of the superiority of the German fighter squadrons, and on the twentieth, *Leutnant* Tietzen brought down two I-16s. This was repeated by Bertram on the twenty-third, this being already the seventh score of the month. On the twenty-seventh, *1 Staffel* particularly distinguished itself when Tietzen accounted for two more I-16s, Bertram another and *Oberleutnant* Rudolf Unger opened his account with the same type. Tietzen finished nonetheless with a forced landing in a field one kilometer northeast of Gandesa.

The month of October confirmed the growing weakness of the Republican Air Force, and on the fourth, Bertram and Szuggar each took out an I-15. This eighth kill for Bertram, previously a reconnaissance pilot, was his last in Spain as he was shot down in his faithful 6-67 and made prisoner. He was finally exchanged on 8 February 1939, along with *Leutnant* Fritz Losigkeit and *Leutnant* Helmut Henz. The loss of Bertram was compounded by an attack on La Cenia by some SB-2s that destroyed a Bf 109 on the ground and damaged four others. A black day for J./88.

On the seventh, things started off again with two I-16s going to *Feldwebel* Menge and *Leutnant* Ehring for his first kill. After this, Menge had to wait until 1 November for another victory. On the fifth, *Unteroffizier* Hans Nirminger was wounded in combat. On the twelfth, *Unteroffizier* Szuggar and *Unteroffizier* Fisher came back from the front, each of them with an I-16 in the bag; for Fisher, it was the first kill. The Ebro campaign finished in mid-November and was the last opportunity for Republicans to redress the situation. From now on, the Nationalist air force feared nothing more than sudden moves, and there would be some, but victory was in view.

It was now a question of the liquidation of Catalonia. Other than Reents, the *Staffel* had *Leutnant* Albrecht von Minnigerode, *Leutnant* Hermann Hollweg, *Leutnant* Horst Tietzen, *Leutnant* Wolf-Dietrich Wilcke, *Leutnant* Karl-Heinz Sandmann, *Leutnant* Gustav Roedel, and *Leutnant* August-Wilhelm Schumann, plus *Unteroffizier* Hans Nirminger, *Unteroffizier* Gerhard Herzog, *Unteroffizier* Halupczek, *Unteroffizier* Willy Szuggar, and *Unteroffizier* Heinrich Windemuth. The number of aerial victories claimed by *1 Staffel* now began to decline, first because the major part of the pilots were inexperienced but, above all, because there was by now a lack of opposition and hence nothing to shoot down. On the twenty-first, *Leutnant* Tietzen got an I-16, repeating the feat on the twenty-ninth. 16 December saw SB-2s again destroy two German fighters at La Cenia. Szuggar "made ace" on 3 January 1939 after he downed an I-15, after which it was necessary to await the mopping-up of the plains of Catalonia before the young pilots of *1 Staffel* had the opportunity to open their accounts. This was not to prove easy as the last Republican pilots were combat-hardened survivors, as when *1 Staffel* arrived over the aerodrome of Vilajuiga on 6 February (where the last Government combat aircraft were regrouping before leaving for France) just as the Republican machines were about to take-off. *Leutnant* Hauptmann and *Leutnant* Reents and *Unteroffizier* Halupczek and *Unteroffizier* Herzog each got an I-15, while *Unteroffizier* Nirminger destroyed a Grumman Delfin on take-off before being shot down by another one of the veterans who was able to get off. Immediately afterwards, *Unteroffizier* Windemuth made the mistake of engaging the same I-15 (flown by José Falco, commanding officer of the night-fighter squadron) in a frontal pass and was shot down in 6-98. Crashing in flames and trapped in the wreck, he was mercifully finished off on the ground by a Spanish pilot. On the tenth, the General Staff of the Legion came to the place to see the results for themselves.

**2 Staffel**

At the time of its formation at the end of November 1936, *2 Staffel*, other than its commander, *Hauptmann* Siegfried Lehmann, was comprised of *Leutnant* Franzl Lützow, *Leutnant* Rolf Pingel, *Leutnant* Urban Schlaffer, *Leutnant* Karl-Heinz Greisert, *Feldwebel* Peter Boddem, *Feldwebel* Franz Heilmayer, *Unteroffizier* Guido Höness, *Unteroffizier* Edgar Rempel, *Unterof-*

*fizier* Norbert Flegel, *Unteroffizier* Jansen, and *Unteroffizier* Hillmann. After a period of acclimatization and training and after several careful missions (for they were not yet the experienced "Old Hares"[25] of *4 Staffel*) on 22 December, *2 Staffel* was installed at Villa del Prado, forty kilometers southwest of Madrid. Pingel, Schlaffer, Boddem, Heilmayer, and Flegel were quickly lost, being sent to Seville to rejoin Knüppel for tests on the first Bf 109s. The first real combat of the *Staffel* took place on 4 January 1937 above Brunete, when the *Staffel*, then based at Avila, took off on alert at 11.10 hours and formed up at Torrijos with two units of Ju 52s. So far as the *Staffel* was concerned, this encounter served no purpose.

At the beginning of February, after a short detour via Saragossa and Huesca, the unit returned to Madrid, or more precisely, Villa del Prado. The arrival was in unusual circumstances since Lehmann was very ill from nephritis and unable to continue in command. This was passed temporarily to *Oberleutnant* Otto-Hans Winterer who, on the fourth of the month, had obtained from von Richthoffen agreement to leave Stab/88 and to fly with *1 Staffel* for two weeks. Based at Almorox on the eleventh, the unit did not participate in the first mission of the twelfth but did in those following. Events do not always take place as planned, such as for instance the fifteenth, which was spent in fruitless take-offs after a series of alarms.

Spain seen from the air could also be attractive, particularly when it appears to be undamaged by war, as seen by the pilot of this Bf 109 who has dropped his wing to see better. No doubt the stories brought back home in 1939 helped to launch German tourism to Spain in the fifties.

The He 51s began to have more and more problems in taking the load against the Republican fighters, and evidently going by the book no longer applied. It was about this time that *Ritter* von Greim, a former fighter ace, and *Oberst* Seidemann arrived from Berlin on a fact-finding mission. The latter took part in a single operation and only got back to Escalona with difficulty, crash-landing at base, thereafter returning to Germany to report.

On 20 February, Lehmann returned, although as a result Winterer did not do any less flying with the *Staffel* but continued to do so for several more days. These turned out to be several days too many as he was hit on the twenty-fifth and had to land at Navalmorales in Republican territory and was made a prisoner of war.

The sixth of March saw the *Staffel* rejoined by the flight detached to Talavera the previous month, and on the tenth, everybody was installed at Almorox, a welcome change as, at last, there were proper barracks. After the first trials with VJ/88, the squadron had the honor of being the first squadron of J/88 to convert to Messerschmitt Bf 109Bs. The first operational patrol was made up of Knüppel, Schlaffer, and Gödecke. This conversion was by no means painless as the Jumo engines of 680 horsepower frequently went unserviceable.

Lehmann having gone back to Germany, *2 Staffel* was then commanded by Franzl Lützow. Very quickly, they had adopted the insignia of the *4 Staffel*, the *Zylinder Hut*—"Top Hat," which gave birth to a celebrated saying: "We go faster. This is normal as we have one more 'cylinder' than you." Effectively, however, *2 Staffel* functioned as an operational conversion unit where pilots did two flights under instruction before being sent to the front on a rollover basis during a nine-month period.

During the course of the month of March, the He 51s of the unit were passed to the Spanish but the Northern Campaign started, and *2 Staffel* soon found itself at Vitoria, on a concrete runway with seven Bf 109s available. The first victory of the squadron, and thus of the Bf 109, was when *Leutnant* Lützow shot down an I-15 northwest of Ochandiano at 17.15 hours on 6 April. On the twenty-second, while protecting some Do 17s from VB/88, *Leutnant* Radusch and *Feldwebel* Heilmayer shot down two I-15s, one of them probably being that of the Republican ace from the Northern Zone, Felipe del rio Crespo. Another victory against an I-15 is attributed in Legion archives to a *Hauptmann* von Janson, probably a "guest" on an inspection tour from Germany.

The few Bf 109s present took part in the operation against Guernica, but it certainly seems that the strafing of the streets was the work of the He 51s of *1 Staffel* under Harro Harder.

# Jagdgruppe J/88

With the passing of time, the superiority of the 109s became evident and so the escort missions developed into a routine: two squadrons of Ju 52s along the Basque line of retreat Bermeo-Menaca on 3 May; some He 70s and some Do17s to Santander on 7 and 8 May. On the twenty-second, Lützow shot down another I-15 above Bilbao and again on the twenty-eighth near Santander, with *Feldwebel* Braunschweiger taking another. On 5 June, Pingel opened his score also with a Chato at San Julián de Musques.

On 2 July, the friction between the Germans and the Italians grew when Lützow and *Unteroffizier* Hillmann, escorting some Ju 52s to Villaverde, were jumped by some Fiat CR.32s who obliged them to flee in haste. On the seventh, the squadron was installed at Avila. The next day, two of the twelve Bf 109s in service were damaged on the ground by an attack of Republican Tupolev SB-2s; *Leutnant* Pingel and *Unteroffizier* Höness saved the honor of the squadron by each claiming a bomber. The ten remaining aircraft passed the rest of the day at *Kochenjagd*. By then, the pilots had the Bf 109 well in hand, and results were not slow to come.

A well-known and probably faked picture supposedly showing a Bf 109 strafing Republican trenches. It does, however, show what an enemy view of a Bf 109E would look like and gives an idea of the confused situation in the front lines of a civil war.

On the twelfth, Pingel claimed two kills (an SB-2 and an I-16), and *Unteroffizier* Adolf Bühl and *Unteroffizier* Boddem each claimed an I-16, whereas Höness got to his credit two "Praga [*sic*]" (Aero A-101, in fact most probably the very similar Polikarpov R-5 or R-Z) types not easy to differentiate under fire. Sometimes, however, things are not so simple, and Gotthard Handrick, during one of his first missions in a Bf 109, almost did not get back to Santander, having had the enterprise to engage an I-15 in a dogfight. The chase having led over enemy territory, in an ill-judged maneuver he almost brought disaster upon himself when he collided with the Polikarpov, but survived to bring back a piece of the Chato stuck in his aircraft's undercarriage mounting. Even so, it only needed two days' work to fly again.

On 8 July, the biggest of the escorts was confided to the Bf 109s of *2 Staffel*. Very quickly, however, the unit was to suffer its first serious setback. First, on the tenth, during an interception exercise with Italian Savoia SM.79 bombers, Lützow was wounded in the leg and the right hand by an overly nervous Italian machine gunner; next, on the eleventh, Flegel mowed off the undercarriage of his machine when landing, officially due to an engine failure, resulting in the machine being scrapped. The following day *2 Staffel* lost its first pilot in a Bf 109 when *Unteroffizier* Guido Höness was shot down above Brunete by Republican fighters. The unit closed ranks, and on the thirteenth, following a heroic fight for mastery of the sky, *Feldwebel* Boddem got an I-15, which was without a doubt that of the American Harold Dahl, while *Feldwebel* Braunschweiger claimed an I-16.

On 16 July, *Leutnant* Pingel shot down a Mosca which crashed near to Fuenlabrada. Despite Republicans claims of having downed, on the same day, two Messerschmitts, it appears that all the Bf 109s returned to base. Later, the base became the preferred target of the Tupolev SB-2 Katiuska bombers, which gave it a first visit at dawn, in vain, after being in the air since 05.30, and then a second visit in the evening with no more success. On the seventeenth, the flight was on escort duty for He 111s from VB/88 to Alcalá, and then for K/88 and A/88, who attempted to create a bridgehead. The Messerschmitts threw themselves at a small formation of I-16s, and Handrick had to make an emergency landing at Escalona due to an engine failure. The following day everyone was in the air early, and even though *Oberfeldwebel* Hillmann announced a victory over an I-16, a Mosca shot down the Bf 109 of *Unteroffizier* Haarbach, who succeeded nonetheless in parachuting to safety behind his own lines. The twenty-first and twenty-fifth saw *Feldwebel* Boddem shoot down two I-16s. Also on the twenty-first, Lützow, much against his wishes, had to let slip four SB-2s which were flying on a heading for Madrid. First the bulb of the gunsight burned out, then all three guns jammed after a single burst of fire from afar. The Republican machine gunners having equally missed, the two pilots of the alert patrol had their chance, of whom one was Boddem, who announced upon his return that he had downed a Tupolev which was in the process of landing, but his wing man was in between times lost in the clouds.

This was a very trying period for *2 Staffel*, which carried out three missions each day as high cover at 6,000 to 7,000 meters for about an hour and a half each, all without oxygen. The system of alert patrols noted above was heavily criticised as it wore the pilots out, often for nothing. In addition the availability of Bf 109s was not exactly ideal. Other than the two aircraft shot down, 6-9 was at Burgos being overhauled, 6-10 was under repair on the base, 6-13 was clearly already too worn out to return to combat (it did, however, come back again after overhaul) and 6-15's generator was broken. All this means that on 21 July, there were only three machines available for the 16.00 duty. Happily some new ones were delivered in mid-July just as the battle of Brunete finished. *2 Staffel* was soon transferred north where the climate is more temperate than that of Castille in summer.

With its refurbished Bf 109s, *2 Staffel* set itself up on 30 July at Calahorra near Herrera de Pisuerga. Very quickly, however, the structural fatigue of the first 109Bs started to show and 6-8 and 6-9 were withdrawn from duty, while 6-5 was not far from the same fate. Operations only started on the eighth, and Boddem announced the first kill for the unit in the northern campaign on the thirteenth, an I-16 downed near Santander. On the sixteenth, it was *Leutnant* Edgar Rempel's turn, while *Feldwebel* Flegel claimed an unidentified enemy aircraft. On the seventeenth, Boddem again claimed an I-15 and an I-16; he also awarded himself a Chato the following day, the same as Lützow.

With hindsight, the claims against the weak Republican fighter forces on the northern front continued rather too quickly if one considers the number of actual aeroplanes available to sustain the "Red" resistance. On the twenty-second, three I-15s were credited to *2 Staffel*—Lützow, Pingel, and Flegel. The unit moved to West Santander on 2 September. On 4 September, *Feldwebel* Reinhard "Sepp" Seiler, a new pilot, claimed the destruction of an I-16 followed by Boddem on the sixth and by Brücker on the seventh, who claimed a kill against a Mosca.

By 15 September, there were only seven Bf 109s available when the squadron met its new chief, *Oberleutnant* Joachim Schlichting, who obtained his first confirmed kill against an I-16 on 23 September. On the

An unidentified pilot poses in front of a Bf 109D, 6-52 of 2.J/88. The aircraft is probably finished in RLM 02 and 65 and has a single white victory bar on the fin. Note that it is not fitted with a radio mast.

last day of the month, the Bf 109s of *1 Staffel* and *2 Staffel* came upon a formation of four Chatos and two Moscas in one of the last engagements in this zone. The German pilots admitted to being very impressed by the aggressiveness and effectiveness of these last Republican fighters and, even though Flegel gained a kill against a Chato, the Bf 109s, at the end of their ammunition, finally had to break off the fiercely fought dogfight after twenty minutes and return to base behind Handrick.

From the point of view of aerial operations, the rest of the campaign was almost without incident; the Republican forces had been neutralized, and *2 Staffel* had hardly more to do than escort duties without any real opposition. Gijón finally fell on 21 October. Afterwards, as for every campaign, the units of the Legion returned to the aircraft park at León to rest and recuperate before transferring to Burgo de Osma for the future battle of Teruel.

The first combats of that murderous campaign took place on 29 November as far as *2 Staffel* was concerned, showing a net claim of three I-16s claimed by Schlichting, *Unteroffizier* Kurt Rochel, and Seiler. The following day, *Leutnant* Greisert, *Unteroffizier* Wilhelm Staege, and *Unteroffizier* Hermann Stange announced exactly the same score, but a new pilot, *Unteroffizier* Otto Polenz, landed in Republican territory with one of the first Bf 109Bs to arrive in Spain and was taken prisoner.

Teruel clearly promised not to be a picnic as, when for example, on 5 November, a formation of 15 Bf 109s of *1 Staffel* and *2 Staffel* were set upon by a squadron of I-16s coming from the east. While Harder could claim a Mosca shot down in the proximity of Bujaraloz, the aircraft of the other recently arrived pilot, *Feldwebel* Leo Sigmund, did not come back. It was learned later that he was a prisoner.

This was a period of doubt for the Legion—above all, in view of the ambivalent attitude of their Mediterranean allies. In honestly determining the effectiveness of the organization of the Republican camp (areas well camouflaged, instructions strictly observed), the future *General* Galland wondered if Germany was on the right side in this conflict. Was aerial superiority necessary to lead to a hoax on the ground?

Then, in mid-December, the Republicans attacked on the north and west of the corridor to Teruel, which was thirty kilometers wide. After inital uncertainty, the Nationalist command decided that the military situation now rendered it out of the question to envisage an offensive toward Madrid. In addition, the weather forecast was anything but favorable,

This is the Messerschmitt Bf 109B, 6-15, which was force-landed by newly arrived *Oberfeldwebel* Otto Polenz in Republican-held territory on 30 November 1937. He was taken prisoner and the aircraft then passed through the hands of a special French evaluation unit at Sabadell before being handed over to the Soviet Union, where it was extensively examined at the various technical centers.

with temperatures of -18°C with heavy falls of snow; the mechanics of the three *Staffeln* of J./88 had to regularly turn the engines of their aircraft each night to prevent them from freezing solid.

On 12 January, *Oberfeldwebel* Seiler and *Unteroffizier* Staege on "alert" patrol at Calamocha claimed victories over two Tupolev SB-2s. The event was particularly fêted as it was the hundredth victory of the *Gruppe*. On the twentieth, *Unteroffizier* Rochel notched up a victory against an I-15. Two days later, it was the turn of Seiler to announce his fifth victory, against an I-16. On 5 February, at the beginning of the Nationalist counteroffensive, another new pilot, *Unteroffizier* Lohrer, obtained confirmation of his first success against an I-15. The following day, *Unteroffizier* Strange destroyed a Mosca piloted by Luis de Frutos, one of the survivors of the terrible Northern Campaign.

J./88 particularly distinguished itself on 7 February at the time of the breakthrough to Alfambra. 2 *Staffel* was in advance covering for K/88, and as it was passing over the front lines, the German formation encountered a large number of twin-engined aircraft coming from Valencia, SB-2s. There were twenty-two of them, without any close escort, following their flight path without divergence. A furious mêlée started during which the Bf 109s had even more of an advantage than usual since the bombers were still loaded with their bombs, and the finish was quick. Before the escort of two squadrons of I-16s could get close enough to intervene, eight SB-2s were on fire or had been shot down, to be followed by two of their fighter companions. *Oberfeldwebel* Seiler was awarded two Katiuskas, an I-16 going to the credit of *Oberleutnant* Schlichting, the leader of the unit. But it was *Leutnant* Wilhelm Balthasar, the refugee from the reconnaissance *Gruppe*, A/88, which won the cup with four confirmed successes against SB-2s, which exploded rapidly from his point-blank bursts of gunfire, the first target being hit from only thirty meters. He was to crown the day by bagging one of the I-16 support fighters, piloted by Francisco Chumillas. On the other hand, his 109C was hit all over, the oil cooler was pierced, and he had to get away from the combat area by diving towards the ground and making his return at ten meters altitude. Even so, he did not arrive back at base, having to land in a field. Afterwards, he admitted to having been very scared: control surfaces riddled, oil and petrol tanks holed, wings transformed into sieves, the cockpit gutted. In his words, "Theoretically I am dead." The machine was only good for the scrap heap; it never flew again.

*Unteroffizier* Strange had to wait until the nineteenth to add another I-15 to his prize list. Then, on the twenty-first, it was Schlichting, *Leutnant* Rempel, *Unteroffizier* Rochel, and *Unteroffizier* Herbert Ihlefeld, who got themselves four victories against some I-16s. The following day, *Leutnant* Seiler played his part in the Teruel campaign by claiming two I-16s. The operational lessons learnt at Teruel served many others besides *2 Staffel*, especially when the *Luftwaffe* was confronted by the Russian winter. On 23 February, *2 Staffel* moved to take up residence at Gallur, on the Ebro, northwest of Saragossa. Like those of *1 Staffel*, their aircraft were worn out, but the unit was soon to benefit from some new Bf 109Cs and Ds, which arrived in March.

Operations recommenced for the Legion Condor on 7 March with an escorted bombing raid on Puebla de Hijar. On the tenth, J./88 was operating on the Belchite/Jatiel sector, and Rochel and Schlichting each came back with another I-16 added to their list of kills. The next day, *Leutnant* Alexander Graf zu Dohna, Schlichting's new wingman, was shot down above Caspe by an I-16. The escort duties were soon going to multiply for the two *Staffeln* of Bf 109s. Caspe, Albalate, and Hijar on the eleventh; Semper de Calanda, Puebla de Hijar, and Castellote on the twelfth; Caspe again on the thirteenth. On his last mission, *Unteroffizier* Ihlefeld and *Leutnant* Armin Ettling each claimed an I-15. Caspe fell on the fourteenth, but that did not mean the end of the combats. On the fifteenth, for example,

Aircraft 6-15 was captured intact by the Republicans after *Oberfeldwebel* Otto Polenz of 2.J/88 landed it near Bujaraloz. It was intensively tested and eventually sent to the USSR, from which the *Wehrmacht* recovered it during Barbarossa. It is seen here repainted with Republican red stripes, and flown by Konstantin Rozanof, who was to be a famous French test pilot after World War II.

the escort for Do 17s over the front line was no less evident, as elsewhere with the following day's escort of K/88 to Maella. On the seventeenth, however, the party was forgotten and the whole of J./88 was reunited at Saragossa on the aerodrome of Sanjurjo.

In effect, activity was about to shift to the northern sector of the Ebro. After having started operating from Sanjurjo, the two units of Bf 109s were going to be isolated at Larraja to the south of Huesca, where *General* Volkmann visited them. The race to Valencia was soon about to begin.

The Republican Air Force was already very tired and clearly numerically inferior, whereas the effectiveness of the German fighter units continued to grow. On 11 May, *Unteroffizier* Ihlefeld claimed a victory against an I-16. On the eighteenth, a violent combat awaited the 109s at Castellón from which they officially emerged with four kills against I-16s, of which three were for *2 Staffel* (*Unteroffizier* Rochel, *Unteroffizier* Bernard Seufert, and *Unteroffizier* Ihlefeld). After this, aerial combats were rarer up to 2 June, when the SB-2s of Republican *Grupo 24* attacked La Cenia. Officially, five of the nine aircraft fell to the "alert patrol" of *2 Staffel*, credited to *Unteroffizier* Willi Meyer and *Unteroffizier* Ihlefeld (one each) and to *Leutnant* Kurt Heinrich, who opened his prize list with a hat trick. Whatever the true results were, the technique of harassing the fast Republican twin-engined aircraft was starting to wear out the machines and equipment, and soon the "alert patrols" had to be dispersed to Cabi and Alcalá de Chivert.

A skirmish on the ninth finished with no result on either side but, on the tenth, a fresh takeoff on alert allowed *Unteroffizier* Seufert and *Unteroffizier* Rochel to add another I-16 to their lists of kills (Utrilla and Antonio Días Perez of 3 Mosca squadron), plus another probable for *Leutnant* Heinrich. On the thirteenth, there was a new and unwelcome scenario when J./88 limped back to the fold with six aircraft badly hit after a brush above Castellón with a formation of only six I-15s and two I-16s. For *2 Staffel*, *Unteroffizier* Staege and *Unteroffizier* Seufert and *Leutnant* Wolfgang Ewald obtained respectively two I-15s and an I-16. On the twenty-fifth, Ihlefeld claimed to have shot down an I-16, which was, however, downgraded to a "probable." Over two weeks later, on 12 July, Ihlefeld and *Leutnant* Wilhelm Keidel each wrote another I-15 on their list of kills, and on the fifteenth, Ihlefeld added yet another two of the same. This gained him rapid promotion to *Leutnant*. *Leutnant* Resch gained his first victory, against an I-15, on 17 July. It was then necessary to wait until the twenty-third before *Unteroffizier* Georg Braunschirn obtained a "probable" against an I-16 above Viver. In the meantime, on 30 June, *Feldwebel* Alfred Held, who was to later distinguish himself by getting the first aircraft of the RAF in the Second World War, destroyed an aircraft in a forced landing and was seriously wounded.

The start of the battle of the Ebro on the twenty-fifth rather caught the Nationalists offguard. Risking the Nationalist superiority in the air, the government air force decided to throw its last squadrons into the battle. For the pilots of the three squadrons of Bf 109s, this soon signified more targets and more opportunities to add to their victory lists. On 2 August, *Oberleutnant* Hubert Kroeck obtained his first success in combat against an I-16; there were no more claims until the fifteenth, when *Unteroffizier* Kuell downed an I-15. He repeated this feat on the nineteenth against an I-16. August was decidedly the month of baptisms when, on the twenty-third, *Leutnant* Wilhelm Ensslen opened his personal score with an I-15, an exploit repeated on 5 September and again on the twentieth, this time with an I-16, whereas Keidel was only able to be credited with a single probable victory. On the twenty-third, Braunschirn downed an SB-2, and on the twenty-fourth, *Unteroffizier* Herbert Schob was also credited with his first success in combat, against an I-16. He repeated this on 13 October against the same type of aircraft. On the last day of October, another new pilot, *Leutnant* Martin Lutz, was credited with his first I-16 while Braunschirn got an I-15, imitated in this by *Leutnant* Heinz Schumann, who also opened his score.

From 1 November, *Oberleutnant* Alfred von Lojewski took over command, Kroeck returning to Germany. On 3 November, *Obergefreiter* Freund

A Legion Condor officer examining all that is left of a Bf 109 that was probably destroyed by a direct bomb hit and burnt out on 16 December 1938 at La Cenia. In the background, a second fighter still shows one relatively intact wing.

downed his first adversary, an I-15, Braunschirn adding another to his list with Schob claiming the destruction of an I-16. The roll of pilots starting their victory lists lengthened on the fifth, with *Leutnant* Heinz Bretnütz knocking down an I-15. Braunschirn, meanwhile, became an ace with a victory over a Chato.

After a lean time, Schob added a Katiuska on the sixteenth. There was then a relatively long period of calm following the end of the battle of Ebro, which took *2 Staffel* to the end of December until, in a clash on the twenty-eighth, the unit notched six victories, among them the first (an I-16) for *Feldwebel* Schott. Ensslen claimed an I-16 and an SB-2, one each of the latter type also being awarded to Bretnütz and Redlich. Combat recommenced on the thirtieth, with the first victory for *Oberleutnant* von Lojewski (I-15) and successes for Schott (I-15), Schob, and Ensslen (I-16). The year ended for *2 Staffel* with Schott's third victory, an I-16.

At that time, the *Staffel* pilots were, apart from their chief, Lojewski, *Oberleutnant* Karl-Wolfgang Redlich, *Oberleutnant* Ernst Boenigk, *Leutnant* Werner Ursinus, *Leutnant* Ernst-Peter Karpenkiel, *Leutnant* Heinz Gresens, *Leutnant* Heinz Bretnütz, *Leutnant* Hans Hasselmann, *Feldwebel* Schott, and *Unteroffizier* Herbert Schob.

The year 1939 began as 1938 finished, with Ensslen putting another I-16 onto his score sheet. Then on the fourth, Redlich obtained a "probable" against an SB-2, and on the ninth, Ensslen obtained his eighth victory against an I-16. On 21 January, *2 Staffel* moved with the rest of the *Gruppe* to set themselves up at Valls, one of the biggest Republican areas. The following day, Schob claimed an I-15. The enemy proved that they could still inflict damage, however, when, on 29 January, *Leutnant* Karl-August Bötticher was shot down and killed by Republican ground fire over Mollet.

There were no longer many targets to pursue, and the last three victories were claimed at the beginning of February. On the third, Schumann claimed a probable against an I-15, followed the next day by Ensslen and Redlich and *Hauptmann* Walter Rubensdörfer, of the Stab, who laid claim to three I-15s shot down at Puerto de la Selva (a probable only for Redlich). There was very little more active service before the end of the war, which was by then generally devoid of encounters. One of the last events of note was on 4 March, when *Oberleutnant* Lutz was posted to the Stab.

## 3 Staffel

*Leutnant* Douglas Pitcairn, *Leutnant* Walter Kienitz, *Leutnant* Gerhard Rutsch, *Leutnant* Hans-Peter von Gallera, *Unteroffizier* Kurt Kneiding,

*Unteroffizier* Walter Leyerer, *Feldwebel* Erwin Kley, *Feldwebel* Reidinger, and *Feldwebel* Walter Fenske, among others, were under the leadership of *Oberleutnant* Jürgen Roth at the end of November 1936. From the beginning, *3 Staffel* was dedicated to ground attack, leaving the "glory" of aerial combat to *1 Staffel* and *2 Staffel*. It is not surprising, therefore, that there is little detail of their exploits. Nonetheless, on 6 January 1937, the *Staffel* suffered a serious setback when an aerial combat over Madrid saw Gallera and his wingman go down while Leyerer had to crash-land in the countryside with a dozen hits to his aircraft.

At the beginning of February, the unit was based at Villar del Prado. At the start of April, *4 Staffel* was disbanded, and *2 Staffel* was re-equipped with Bf 109s. The idea seems to have been to give the fighter *Gruppe* two functions: aerial combat, which was to be confined to the modern aircraft (Bf 109), and ground attack, which was to be carried out by the aged biplanes (He 51). From the last days of March and under the leadership of Douglas Pitcairn, the three *Staffeln* of the *Gruppe* were based at Vitoria for the northern campaign. Roth carried out the duties of commandant of the airfield. *3 Staffel* had ten aircraft and was based on the more humid northwestern side of the runway. It was at this time, particularly during the attacks against Ochandiano, Elgueta, and Elorrio, that the pilots perfected the technique of *Cadena* ("chain") attacks, which derived from a variation of a *Noria* ("water wheel") attack with a change of axis.

On 1 April, the Nationalist attack commenced with the whole of J./88 in the air from 10.00 hours. The personnel of the squadrons were rarely fully engaged; thus, at 13.36 hours on the front at Santa Agueda, *3 Staffel* lined up only five of its aircraft. The task of the He 51s was as already described with *1 Staffel*, and the poor follow-up by the ground troops was quite demoralizing for the professional Germans. This was also the period of the attacks against urban centers such as Durango and Guernica, which left a bitter taste for most of the fighter pilots.

From 8 July, during the battle for Brunete, *3 Staffel* was based at Villa del Prado. It was from here on the seventeenth that it participated in the first great push to create a bridgehead. On the twenty-seventh, a pilot from *1 Staffel* took over command. He was to become celebrated somewhat later; this was *Oberleutnant* Adolf Galland. Another notable individual rejoining the ranks of J./88 at this time was Wilhelm Balthasar, who abandoned for some time his beloved He 112.

Once the battle of Brunete reached its conclusion, *3 Staffel* went up north with nine aircraft and was based at Calahorra near to Herrera de Pisuerga. On 18 August, in the company of *1 Staffel*, *3 Staffel* left for Orzales.

In September, this was the only unit remaining with He 51s. Staying on the northern front, it profited from fine-tuning the ground-attack techniques under the imaginative direction of Galland. Then an early type of napalm bomb was knocked up, initially using containers filled with oil and petrol and sporting a fragmentation bomb. After consideration, the under-fuselage auxiliary fuel tanks on the aircraft, never really used on that fairly narrow front, were transformed into napalm bombs thanks to the addition on each side of a small incendiary bomb of one kilogram. The General Staff was somewhat intrigued by the petrol consumption figures of *3 Staffel*.

On 2 September, the whole of J./88 moved off towards Pontejos and Santander-West. It was here that the technique of *Kochenjagd* was perfected. This consisted of making a detour of seventy to eighty kilometers out to sea at a very low altitude (according to Galland himself, one meter), returning behind the defender's backs, each pilot then choosing his own target in a free-for-all. On 4 September, *3 Staffel* was surprised and jumped by a dozen mixed I-15s and I-16s skimming along the ground. An He 51, holed in its tanks, quickly made a dash for home by tacking between the trees, and the defensive circle quickly collapsed, leaving every man for himself, as in the Great War. Once back in the fold, only the aircraft of *Leutnant* Eduard Neumann was missing. He, however, eventually made a jubilant return, having shot down an I-15 above the area of Los Llanos. For the others this was no picnic, and most of the aircraft were out of service, with the record for one machine being thirty-seven hits at the rear and four in the wings.

*3 Staffel* was close to the front on 21 September and stayed there until the fall of Gijón a month later. It was this unit that marked up the most conspicuous consumption for the whole of this campaign, not only of fuel but also of munitions, drawing 25,000 cartridges per day. The "Mickeys"[26] of Galland, as for everyone else, were sent for rest and recuperation at the aircraft park at León.

Teruel and its dreadful freezing weather followed, as did the doubts that sprang up among the oldest members of the Legion. On 7 January 1938, *3 Staffel* and *4 Staffel* were surprised on the ground at Calamocha by two squadrons of SB-2s, which damaged five aircraft, two of them beyond repair. Teruel was taken on 21 February, but it had become clear that the He 51s would be incapable of continuing combat at such a pace for much longer. The steady buildup of Republican machine guns and light antiaircraft guns had become too much for the *Cadena* tactic, which required an approach in "Indian file"; in the two squadrons equipped with He 51s, there were disputes about who was to be the last in the line.

A move to Gallur, along with the rest of the *Gruppe*, took place on 23 February. The offensive towards the east then began. From the beginning of March, *3 Staffel* and *4 Staffel* plunged back into the struggle to support the troops on the ground, notably on the ninth in the sector Fuendetodos/Herrera de los Navarros, then on the tenth between Fuendetodos and Belchite, then again the same day between Azuara and Almonacid de la Cuba. On 11 March, the unit was engaged in combat for fifteen minutes of the seventy-minute flight, this being a ratio of more than 20 percent, a very high figure. On the following day, the *Staffel* strafed the Escatrón road and destroyed five enemy lorries. The strongpoints held by the XIth, XIIIth, and XIVth International Brigades were attacked on the fifteenth, while, on the seventeenth, *3 Staffel* returned to the "Rhubarb" technique against the roads neighboring the front.

As the movement towards the north of the Ebro began on 22 March, *Hauptmann* Hubertus Hering arrived to relieve Galland, but even before the transfer of command, *3 Staffel* was surprised in the air by a squadron of I-15s, and Galland's wingman had to put down in the middle of the countryside with wounds to his lungs and shoulder and more than thirty hits to his aircraft. Afterwards, *3 Staffel* and *4 Staffel* were transferred to Aragon, at Sariñena, a former Republican base. Then, on the twenty-seventh, they set up a shared base at Bujaraloz. The thirtieth saw a drama without combat when the machines of Hering and *Leutnant* Manfred Michaelis collided in midair to the west of Cinca, killing the two pilots, consequently obliging Galland to stay in command for a while longer. He had already had problems finding a replacement, one candidate having been rapidly repatriated because of obvious inability. The bad luck story was not yet finished, for on 10 April, *3 Staffel* was again badly shaken by the Republican antiaircraft fire, coming back with one aircraft in flames and another 40 percent damaged, clearly condemned to being cannibalized. Happily, the pilots were uninjured. On the twelfth, *Unteroffizier* Waldemar Gerstmann, wounded in combat, brought his damaged machine back to friendly lines. In the emergency landing that followed, to the west of Balaguer, he suffered a broken collarbone.

The race to Valencia gained maximum momentum, and on 26 April, the He 51s attacked four heavy antiaircraft batteries. Events continued in this pattern until 31 May, the date at which, during operations in support of the Aranda Corps progressing towards Valencia, *3 Staffel* lost the machine of *Leutnant* Fritz Losigkeit, shot down by efficient enemy 20-millimeter ground fire. Losigkeit was saved thanks to his parachute but was made a prisoner of war. On 2 June, *Leutnant* Martin Haupt was also shot down and made prisoner. Finally, on the eighth, after an objective report by Harro Harder to the General Staff of the Legion, *3 Staffel* and *4 Staffel* were stood down.

*3 Staffel* had better luck than 4./88 as it was not be disbanded. While Galland finally returned to Germany, the unit came under the command of newly arrived Werner Mölders, who was to be one of the most brilliant pilots of the Spanish Civil War. The Bf 109s allotted to *3 Staffel* had only started arriving from 2 June, which enabled everybody to enjoy some welcome holidays. Other new pilots arrived with Mölders, such as *Leutnant* Walter Oesau (transferred from *4 Staffel*), *Unteroffizier* Kiening, and the Austrian *Leutnant* Josef Fözö.

Mölders proceeded to open his score very quickly in his faithful 6-79, which had been baptized *Luchs* ("Lynx"), a name that corresponded well with the agility and extraordinary precision of the pilot. On 15 July, he shot down his first I-15. On the twenty-third, *Unteroffizier* Boer damaged one of the squadron's aircraft during a not very successful landing. The unit lost one of its oldest machines, 6-6, on 25 July when it was destroyed upon landing by Franz Jaenisch, Mölders's faithful wingman. He redeemed himself by claiming an I-15 on 1 August, but on the third, *Leutnant* Siegfried Lehrmann was shot down over Flix. By 23 August, the SB-2 that Mölders claimed already constituted his fifth victory. On 5 September, following a sustained combat to the northwest of La Cenia, *Leutnant* Lutz had to make an emergency landing, causing 85 to 90 percent damage to his Bf 109 according to Legion Condor reports. Little could have been left of it. The sixth victory for the chief came on 9 September (an I-16), but it was a bad day for the squadron as *Leutnant* Kiening was shot down by some I-15s; he succeeded, however, in making a forced landing to the north of Gandesa, his aircraft 50 percent destroyed. On 13 September, yet another I-15 was added to Mölders's account. Five days later, Fözö got his first I-16. While Mölders added an I-16 to his prizes on the twenty-third, *Unteroffizier* März opened his score, and *Leutnant* Rudolf Goy added a second and third victory, all against I-16s.

There was no lack of combats at this time, and Mölders claimed yet another I-16 on 10 October, the day when *Leutnant* Johann Gamringer claimed his first victory against an SB-2, in exchange for a forced landing in open country and a wound to his arm. On 30 October, Mölders claimed two I-16s shot down, as did *Feldwebel* Fleischmann, with *Leutnant* Kiening contenting himself with one. *Unteroffizier* Fözö and *Unteroffizier* Theodor Rossiwall were only able to bag "probables." The fourteenth and last victory for Mölders came on 3 November, just as Oesau marked up his ninth personal success. The work and the luck of *3 Staffel* had changed considerably since the days of the He 51s, and in the course of the battle of the Ebro alone, the squadron had recorded forty-two victories. On 12 December, the charismatic Mölders returned to Germany, handing over command to *Oberleutnant* Hubertus von Bonin. Overall, J./88 then had thirty-seven Bf 109s of types B, C, and D on strength.

The Republican Air Force, however, still remained dangerous, and on 16 December, a formation of SB-2s destroyed two Messerschmitts on the ground at the base of La Cenia. The German "alert patrol" claimed two of the Russian twin-engined aircraft in exchange.

One of the last major aerial combats of the Spanish Civil War took place on 12 January 1939, involving the whole of J/88. In the fight against what remained of the Republican fighter force above the Vallas/Vendrell/Villafranca del Panadés sector, the action resulted in net victory for the Nationalists, with thirteen claimed kills, shared with the Fiat CR32s.[27]

The "game" became rare, and von Bonin had to wait until 3 February to get his first I-15, claiming a second two days later above Alicante. On 5 March, aircraft 6-101 of *Leutnant* Jung had to make an emergency landing at Calamocha, without any major problems, due to an engine failure. By 11 March, the Messerschmitts had no more opposition and had free rein in the sector of Madrid. *Kochenjagd* operations returned,

*Leutnant* Ursinus poses with the unit mascot in front of his Bf 109E-1, number 6-111, christened *Bärchen* in white under the windscreen. The name was a pun, as it is the German translation of his Latin name (*ursus* means "bear"). The aircraft was still flying in 1943 within the Spanish air force.

but even on the ground, there was nothing much to chase. The last days in Spain for J/88 were, however, darkened by the collision in flight on 16 March of two Bf 109s, fortunately without the loss of either pilot, *Leutnant* Rolf Strössner being only lightly wounded.

## 4 Staffel

The official formation date of the first *4 Staffel* is fairly unclear as, even as the elements of the three other units were disembarking on 18 November 1936, not yet operational, the "old sweats" of the first weeks were already "on the job" with or without an official title. It therefore seems logical not to take this theoretical date as the starting point but the start of the first campaign against Madrid, in the course of which *4 Staffel* was to be severely tested. During these first days, from 4 to 8 November, it was the Italian Fiat fighters that took the brunt of the work of supporting the Ju 52s, and that rather well. Nonetheless, on the sixth, the squadron was hit on the ground with several aircraft damaged when Republican bombers attacked the area of Avila.

It will be recalled that *Oberleutnant* Herwig Knüppel was in command, and serving under him were *Leutnant* Kraft Eberhardt, *Leutnant* Hannes Trautloft, *Leutnant* Gerhard Klein, *Leutnant* Ekkehard Hefter, *Leutnant* Hennig Strümpell, *Leutnant* Ottheinrich von Houwald, *Leutnant* Dietrich von Bothmer, *Leutnant* Oskar Henrici, *Leutnant* Paul Rehahn, *Leutnant* Kurt von Gilsa, *Unteroffizier* Erwin Sawallisch, *Unteroffizier* Willi Gödecke, and *Unteroffizier* Ernst Mratzek. This plethora of pilots was to be quickly put to the test in the face of I-15s piloted by the finest of the Soviet fighter pilots. On 13 November, nine He 51s took off as cover for five Ju 52s and three He 46s heading for the west bank of the River Manzanares. In the course of the furious mêlée that followed their interception of a group of I-15s and I-16s, the Germans credited an I-15 each to Mratzek, Strumpell, Knüppel, von Bothmer, Henrici, and Eberhardt. The Republicans admitted to the loss of two aircraft. The price was high; Henrici landed mortally wounded in his lungs, Eberhardt was shot down and killed and the aircraft flown by Sawallisch got back by a miracle, its tail unit destroyed. Knüppel took leave. It was a Friday. The damage was such that, on the fifteenth, the squadron had only three aircraft in flying condition.

On 19 November, the *Staffel* was part of a mixed formation of He 51s and Fiat CR.32s that participated in the last aerial combat of 1936 of any importance and claimed the destruction of four enemy fighters, the Republicans admitting the loss of two. On the twenty-fifth, because of very bad weather conditions, the He 51s regrouped at Burgos, moving to

Vitoria on 4 December for the first campaign of the north against Bilbao. When twelve new He 51s arrived in Spain it was the "Old Hares" of *4 Staffel* who got them first, leaving the earlier worn out Heinkels to the Spaniards.

The first official victory of the unit during the northern campaign went to Rehahn, who shot down a Breguet XIX on 8 December. Trautloft and von Bothmer each claimed an I-15 after taking off on the "alert patrol" at Avila the same day. The third man of the patrol, Mratzek, had been shot down in flames at 150 meters altitude but, all the same, was able to parachute to safety. On the following day, the unit lost the services of Trautloft, who was sent to Seville to test the first Messerschmitt Bf 109 in Spain, of which more later. On 12 December, the unit was credited with five victories against some SB-2s, these going to Knüppel, von Gilsa, Rehahn, Sawallisch, and Godecke. Rehahn, von Gilsa, and Godecke were also later recompensed by joining the Bf 109 test team at Seville.

By 3 January 1937, *4 Staffel* was in top form and stationed at Vitoria. Sawallisch added an I-15 to his score at Bilbao. At the beginning of February, the unit was at León, still under the command of Knüppel. On 2 March, the first volunteers went back to Germany, among them Klein, Trautloft, Knüppel, von Houwald, and Sawallisch. Theoretically, they were to be replaced by at least five new pilots, including *Unteroffizier* Kühl and *Oberleutnant* Walter Kienzle, but the Legion Condor, having more and more difficulty in maintaining four fighter squadrons, disbanded *4 Staffel* in April 1937, even though *Oberleutnant* Kienzle took charge on 1 March. The disbandment was perhaps brought on by the capture of Kienzle at the front on 4 April while accompanied by *Leutnant* Schultze-Blanke. According to the official history, he was also accompanied by *Oberleutnant* Karsten von Harling, the interpreter Paul Freese and three new pilots playing at tourists at the front, made prisoner in their car; this was without doubt a bad omen. There is, however, a strong doubt as to the exact truth of this matter, in so far as the Franco-era state archives hold returns of German aircraft shot down showing that a Harling of J./88 was brought down on 5 April near to the hill of Urquiola, on the road to Vitoria and of a Freese likewise brought down in almost the same place, but on 18 April! It should be noted that if this information was false, it would constitute a rare exception as the Nationalist military security was very precise.

The unit was only reformed on 2 November with the following pilots: *Leutnant* Helmut Henz, *Leutnant* Wilhelm Keidel, *Leutnant* Eckehardt Priebe, *Oberfeldwebel* Hans Ries, *Unteroffizier* Heinrich Torner, *Unteroffizier* Cuhlmann, *Unteroffizier* Friedrich von Cramon, *Unteroffizier* Anton Kurz,

*Unteroffizier* Willy Meier, and *Unteroffizier* Fritz Rabeneck. The unit commander, *Oberleutnant* Eberhardt d'Elsa, did not arrive until 9 November. All the personnel and matériel disembarked from the *Karla 2*, renamed *Golfo de Panama* for the occasion, the aircraft being brought to León under the orders of "Eckie" Priebe. If the origins of the pilots was very diverse (they came from Jever, Cologne, Döberitz, Wiesbaden, Jesau, Aiblingen, and Bernburg), the ground personnel were very much the opposite, being entirely detached from *Stammtruppenteil I (I)/JG.136* at Jever.

Somewhat more than an operational squadron, the new No. 4 was at its debut rather a sort of OTU[28] in which the turnover was rapid. Thus, by the end of the month of November, Keidel and Reis had already left (sent to *3 Staffel* on the eleventh) to be replaced by *Leutnant* Fritz Awe and *Oberfeldwebel* Ignaz Prestele, who themselves appeared only briefly in the unit before being allocated to *1 Staffel* during the month of December (the movement of Prestele, coming already from *1 Staffel*, was without a doubt due to the necessity of finding former experienced pilots to train the novices during the course of their first missions). On the twenty-fourth, *Leutnant* Kurt Mueller arrived to take their place. On 4 January 1938, *4 Staffel* was at the front at Teruel, with all the difficulties that that implies. *Leutnant* Gerhardt Klein was lost on 18 January, shot down in flames over enemy territory on board 2-59. The unit personnel roster then stabilized for a time.

*Unteroffizier* Heinrich Torner was killed by ground fire at the front in 2-105 on 19 February. The Republicans had installed more and more "aircraft traps" in the form of 20-millimeter Oerlikon cannons to counter the *Kochenjagd* and *Cadenas* maneuvers, and the earlier fear of these aerial attacks disappeared. Torner was in some way avenged the following day by Priebe when he skilfully scored a direct hit against a T-26 tank in the streets of Teruel, destroying it with a salvo of his six ten-kilogram bombs. As recompense, he was immediately transferred to Gallur at the heart of *1 Staffel* in the company of Borchers. It was becoming abundantly clear that the He 51s constituted a sort of "Purgatory" for fighter pilots, with those of the Bf 109 being "Paradise." *4 Staffel*, as well as *3 Staffel*, remained in the breach for several more months and was generally engaged at the same time as its sister squadron, but independent from the Spanish units flying He 51s.

Since *4 Staffel* had only seven pilots, it was necessary to recruit, and during February, *Unteroffizier* Kurt Schaeffer was transferred from *1 Staffel*. On the thirteenth and twenty-first of the month, respectively, it was the turn of *Unteroffizier* Heinrich Vielhaber and *Gefreiter* Rudolf Horn from *2 Staffel*. With the arrival of *Leutnant* Lothar Keller, *Leutnant* Horst Rech, and *Unteroffizier* Karl van Kueck, who had all left Germany in November, and of *Unteroffizier* Andreas Hester, who arrived on 1 March, and finally *Leutnant* Otto Bertram on the nineteenth, the squadron had become overmanned, even considering that Vielhaber had been sent back to Germany on the twenty-first of the month. The *Staffel* then had *Unteroffizier* Franz Albert arrive on 22 March, followed by *Leutnant* Wilhelm Ensslen on 1 April and *Leutnant* Walter Oesau on the twentieth.

Life became unbearable for the He 51s, as noted by Otto Bertram, who was astonished to have to cover four sorties on 4 April at 08.00, 11.00, 14.00, and 17.00 hours above the trenches of the River Segre—according to him, "a hard nut to crack." By now, there were only eight aircraft in the unit. At the end of the month, the race towards Valencia started, and the He 51s were given the job of neutralizing the 76.2-millimeter flak batteries put in place by the Republicans. Once again, new pilots were called up and *Feldwebel* Hubert Menge arrived on 23 April, followed by *Unteroffizier* Georg Braunschirm on the twenty-eighth and *Unteroffizier* Helmut Brucks on the thirtieth.

On 4 May, the squadron lost another aircraft, that of Hester, who had to land in flames near Albocacer as he was too low to be able to jump. He died in the accident. On 7 May, *4 Staffel* also included *Leutnant* Horst Tietzen. This was a bad period for the whole of the Legion Condor, the German authorities then being too occupied with international politics nearer home, to think of properly provisioning the expeditionary corps, which was starting to cost dearly. The final blow arrived on 8 June with the loss of *Leutnant* Erick Beyer, called "the Fakir," shot down and made prisoner at the front. As already noted, *3 Staffel* and *4 Staffel* were forbidden to fly after the intervention of Harder. Their aircraft were soon passed on to Spanish units. *4 Staffel* was never reformed as there were not enough Bf 109s to sacrifice to the Spanish adventure.

## 5 Staffel

For the first part of the history of this very secretive unit, see the section called "Stuka 88." When the Ju 87s were under the direct control of K/88, the fighter group received three Arado Ar 68s. It was obvious that the machine had no part to play in Spain for diurnal fighter missions, the I-15s and I-16s being so much better. In order to find them something useful to do, it was thought to make them into night fighters; the aeroplane was stable, had a wider undercarriage and was infinitely more reliable than the Bf 109, which justly permitted it to land with less risk in poor visibility.

It was necessary nonetheless to wait until the nights of 5–6 September 1938 to carry out the first operational flight of the aircraft in the Castellón sector, without encountering any enemy activity. The rest of the short career of the Ar 68 in Spain is unknown—it is quite possible that it ended there.

At first sight, this would seem to be probably the most famous tailfin in Spain, that of Messerchmitt Bf 109D-1, 6-79, flown by Werner Mölders of 3.J/88. It had fifteen victories marked on it, although only fourteen were officially granted. However, not previously known is the Bf 109B-1, 6-10, which also carried fifteen such kill markings. Did Mölders fly another aircraft? Did he fly both aircraft? Did another pilot claim fifteen kills? The Spanish conundrums continue.

With the Kleinbahn aircraft waiting in the background, Werner Mölders gets ready to climb aboard for his trip back to Germany. The bottle he is being offered is probably *aniseta*, one of the favorite alcoholic beverages of the German soldiers in Spain.

Like aircraft 2-19 shown here, most of the He 51s were used until March 1937, with their original factory light grey color.

# The Heinkel He 51 in Spain

## Type code 2

| Code | Unit | Pilot | Fate |
|---|---|---|---|
| 2-1 | | | |
| 2-2 | | | |
| 2-3 | | | |
| 2-4 | 2E2 | Oblt Herwig Knüppel | Shot down 02.04.36, D.371 |
| 2-5 | | | |
| 2-6 | | | |
| 2-7 | | | |
| 2-8 | 1G2 | Rey-Stolle | |
| 2-9 | | | |
| 2-10 | | | |
| 2-11 | | | |
| 2-12 | 1G2 | | |
| 2-13 | | | |
| 2-14 | | | |
| 2-15 | | | |
| 2-16 | 2E2 | | |
| 2-17 | | | |
| 2-18 | | | |
| 2-19 | | | |
| 2-20 | | | |
| 2-21 | | Oblt Hannes Trautloft | |
| 2-22 | 1G2 | Ozores | |
| 2-23 | 2.J/88 | Oblt Hannes Trautloft? | |
| 2-24 | 1G2 | Ozores | |
| | 2.J/88 | | |
| 2-25 | 4.J/88 | Herwig Knüppel | |
| | | Branning | |
| | | Ernst Mratzek | |
| | | Günther Radusch | |
| 2-26 | 2E2 | | |
| 2-27 | 1G2 | Rey-Stolle | |
| | | J.Mir Astrie | Shot down 12.37, Seros |
| 2-28 | | | |

| Code | Unit | Pilot | Fate |
|---|---|---|---|
| 2-29 | 1G2 | Jiménez Arenas | Shot down 30.07.38, Mequin |
| 2-30 | | | |
| 2-31 | 1G2 | Medrano | |
| | | Jiménez Arenas | |
| 2-32 | | | |
| 2-33 | | | |
| 2-34 | | | |
| 2-35 | | | |
| 2-36 | | | |
| 2-37 | | | |
| 2-38 | | | |
| 2-39 | | | |
| 2-40 | | | |
| 2-41 | | Lt Paul Rehahn | |
| 2-42 | | Willi Gödecke | |
| 2-43 | | | |
| 2-44 | | Uffz Kowalski | |
| 2-45 | | | |
| 2-46 | | | |
| 2-47 | | Lt Alfons Klein | |
| 2-48 | | | |
| 2-49 | | | |
| 2-50 | | Kraft Eberhardt | |
| 2-51 | | | |
| 2-52 | | | |
| 2-53 "Z" | | | |
| 2-54 "T" | 1G2 | Guervos | |
| 2-55 "H" | | | |
| 2-56 | | | |
| 2-57 | | | |
| 2-58 | | | |
| 2-59 | 1.J/88 | | |
| | 4.J/88 | | Lost |
| 2-60 | 4.J/88 | Lt Kurt Müller | |
| 2-61 | 1G2 | Muñoz | |
| 2-62 | 3.J/88 | | |
| | 4.J/88 | | |
| 2-63 | | | |
| 2-64 | 1.J/88 | Oblt Harro Harder | |
| | 4.J/88 | Oblt Eberhard d'Elsa | |
| 2-65 | | | |
| 2-66 | | | |
| 2-67 | | | |
| 2-68 | | | |
| 2-69 | | | |

# The Heinkel He 51 in Spain

| Code | Unit | Pilot | Fate |
|---|---|---|---|
| 2-70 | 4.J/88 | Lt Henz | |
| 2-71 | 4.J/88 | | |
| 2-72 | | | |
| 2-73 | | | |
| 2-74 | | | |
| 2-75 | | | |
| 2-76 | 4.J/88 | Meyer | |
| 2-77 | | | |
| 2-78 | 3.J/88 | Oblt Adolf Galland | |
| 2-79 | 4.J/88 | Uffz Fritz Rabeneck | |
| 2-80 | | | |
| 2-81 | | | |
| 2-82 | 4.J/88 | Lt Otto Bertram | |
| | | Uffz Adolf Borchers | |
| 2-83 | | | |
| 2-84 | | | |
| 2-85 | | Oblt Eduard Neumann | |
| 2-86 | 4.J/88 | Fw Erich Kuhlmann | "Heidi" |
| 2-87 | 1G2 | Oliveira | Shot down 28.8.38 |
| 2-88 | | | |
| 2-89 | 2.J/88 | | |
| | 3.J/88 | | |
| 2-90 | | | |
| 2-91 | | | |
| 2-92 | | | |
| 2-93 | 4.J/88 | | |
| 2-94 | | | |
| 2-95 | 4.J/88 | | |
| 2-96 | | | |
| 2-97 | | | |
| 2-98 | 3.J/88 | Strümpell | |
| 2-99 | | | |
| 2-100 | | | |
| 2-101 | | | |
| 2-102 | 4.J/88 | Oblt Heinrich Neumann | "Annalis" |
| 2-103 | | | |
| 2-104 | 4.J/88 | | |
| 2-105 | 4.J/88 | Uffz H.Torner | Shot down 19.02.38 |
| 2-106 | 4.J/88 | | |
| 2-107 | | | |
| 2-108 | 1G2 | Llobet | |
| 2-109 | | | |
| 2-110 | 4.J/88 | Lt Klein | |
| 2-111 | 4.J/88 | Oblt Eberhard d'Elsa | |
| 2-112 | 4.J/88 | Fw Friedrich von Cramon | |

| Code | Unit | Pilot | Fate |
|---|---|---|---|
| 2-113 | 4.J/88 | Oblt Eckehardt Priebe | |
| 2-114 | 4.J/88 | | |
| 2-115 | 4.J/88 | | |
| 2-116 | | | |
| 2-117 | | | |
| 2-118 | | | |
| 2-119 | | | |
| 2-120 | | | |
| 2-121 | | | |
| 2-122 | | | |
| 2-123 | 4.J/88 | | |
| 2-124 | 4.J/88 | | |
| 2-125 | 4.J/88 | | |
| 2-126 | 4.J/88 | | |
| 2-127 | | | |
| 2-128 | | | |
| 2-129 | | | |
| 2-130 | | | |
| 2-131 | | | |

## HEINKEL HE 51 LOSSES IN CHRONOLOGICAL ORDER—79 TOTAL

| Date | A/C | Pilot | Unit | Location | Fate | Cause |
|---|---|---|---|---|---|---|
| 30.08.36 | | Hannes Trautloft | | D.371 | Shot down | |
| ??.10.36 | | | | Avila | Accident | Ground collision |
| ??.10.36 | | | | Avila | Accident | Ground collision |
| 13.11.36 | | Oblt Kraft Eberhardt | | Madrid | Shot down | |
| 13.11.36 | | Lt Oskar Henrici | | Madrid | Shot down | |
| 08.12.36 | | Uffz Mratzek | 4.J/88 | Vitoria | Shot down I-15 | |
| 26.12.36 | | Senra | | Concud | Accident | |
| 27.12.36 | | Cne Arija | | Teruel | Shot down I-15 | |
| 27.12.36 | | | | Concud | Bombed on ground | I-15/Potez |
| 27.12.36 | | | | Concud | Bombed on ground | I-15/Potez |
| 27.12.36 | | | | Concud | Bombed on ground | I-15/Potez |
| 27.12.36 | | | | Concud | Bombed on ground | I-15/Potez |
| 04.01.37 | | | | Bilbao | Shot down | I-15 (Maranchov) |
| 06.01.37 | | Lt H.P. von Gallera | | Madrid | Shot down | I-16 |
| 06.01.37 | | Uffz K.Kneiding | | Madrid | Shot down | I-16 |
| 06.01.37 | | Uffz Walter Leyerer | | Vitoria | Accident | Crash-landed |
| 12.02.37 | | Hptm Walter Palm | 1.J/88 | Jarama | Shot down | I-16 |
| 12.02.37 | | Lt Hans-Jurgen Hepe | 1.J/88 | Jarama | Shot down | I-16 |
| 14.02.37 | | | | Jarama | Shot down | I-16 |
| 14.02.37 | | | | Jarama | Shot down | I-16 |
| 16.02.37 | | Francisco Bofill | | Saragossa | Accident | Mid-air collision with He 51 16.02.37 |
| | | Krug | | Saragossa | Accident | Mid-air collision with He 51 25.02.37 |
| | | Lt Otto-Hans Winterer | 2.J/88 | Navalmoral | Shot down | Flak |

## HEINKEL HE 51 LOSSES IN CHRONOLOGICAL ORDER—79 TOTAL (continued)

| Date | A/C | Pilot | Unit | Location | Fate | Cause |
|---|---|---|---|---|---|---|
| 01.04.37 | | Blankenagel | | Vitoria | Shot down | |
| 01.04.37 | | | 3.J/88 | Santa Aguada | Shot down | |
| 01.04.37 | | | 3.J/88 | Santa Aguada | Shot down | |
| 01.04.37 | | | 3.J/88 | Santa Aguada | Shot down | |
| 01.04.37 | | | 3.J/88 | Santa Aguada | Shot down | |
| 01.04.37 | | | 3.J/88 | Santa Aguada | Shot down | |
| C5.04.37 | | Oblt Christian von Harling | | Vitoria | Shot down | |
| 18.04.37 | | Freese | | Vitoria | Shot down | |
| 12.04.37 | | | | | Shot down | |
| 17.04.37 | | Palmero | 2-E-2 | | Mid-air collision | I-15 |
| 17.04.37 | | Allende | 2-E-2 | | Shot down | I-15 (Comas) |
| 13.05.37 | | Lt Joachim Wandel | 1.J/88 | Durango | Shot down | |
| 13.05.37 | | Uffz Hans Kolbow | 1.J/88 | Durango | Shot down | |
| 24.06.37 | | F.Cándido | 1-G-2 | Gandesa | Forcelanded | |
| 06.07.37 | | | | Illescas | Shot down | |
| 06.07.37 | | | | Illescas | Shot down | |
| 06.07.37 | | | | Illescas | Shot down | |
| 19.07.37 | | | | | Shot down | Flak |
| | | C.Fernández Pérez | | Aragon | | |
| | | Adj. P.Ruiz Vazquez | | León | Accident | |
| 24.07.37 | | Lt Ernst Reutter | 1.J/88 | | Shot down | |
| 24.37.37 | | Uffz Hermann Beurer | 1.J/88 | | Rebuilt | |
| 20.08.37 | | Martin Campos | 2-E-2 | | Accident | Mid-air collision with He 51 |
| 20.08.37 | | Ferreras | 2-E-2 | | Accident | Mid-air collision with He 51 |
| 26.08.37 | | S.Blasco | 2-E-2 | Osera | Shot down | |
| 11.09.37 | | Leske | J/88 | | Shot down | |

## HEINKEL HE 51 LOSSES IN CHRONOLOGICAL ORDER—79 TOTAL (continued)

| Date | A/C | Pilot | Unit | Location | Fate | Cause |
|---|---|---|---|---|---|---|
| 22.09.37 | | M.Ruiz de Alda | 1-E-2 | Santander 0 | Accident | Mid-air collision with He70 |
| 02.09.37 | | | | | | |
| 10.12.37 | | Lt Klein (Alfons?) | J/88 | Candasnos | Shot down | |
| 03.01.38 | | Hunze | J/88 | | Shot down | |
| 07.01.38 | | | 3.J/88 | Calamocha | Bombed on ground | SB-2 |
| 07.01.38 | | | 4.J/88 | Calamocha | Bombed on ground | SB-2 |
| 15.01.38 | | L.Palacios Vega | 1-G-2 | Teruel | Shot down | |
| 18.01.38 | | Lt Gerhard Klein | 4.J/88 | Teruel | Shot down | |
| ??.01.38 | | Amoedo | 1-G-2 | Alfambra | Shot down | |
| 19.02.38 | | Uffz Heinrich Torner | 4.J/88 | | Shot down | |
| 22.02.38 | | A.Carreras García | 1-G-2 | Teruel | Shot down | |
| 11.03.38 | | Graf | J/88 | Sastago | Shot down | |
| 20.03.38 | | Jiménez Guerra | 1-G-2 | Caspe | Shot down | |
| 23.03.38 | | (ailier Galland) | 3.J/88 | | | |
| 18.06.38 | | Alegria | | Crementela | Shot down | Flak |
| 26.03.38 | | Lt Aragón Muñoz | 1-G-2 | Teruel | Shot down | |
| 30.03.38 | | Lt Hubert Hering | 3.J/88 | Bujaraloz | Accident | Mid-air collision |
| 30.03.38 | | Lt Manfred Michaelis | 3.J/88 | Bujaraloz | Accident | Mid-air collision |
| 10.04.38 | | | 3.J/88 | | Shot down and burned | |
| 10.04.38 | | | 3.J/88 | | Shot down 40% damaged | |
| 12.04.38 | | Uffz Waldemar Gerstmann | 3.J/88 | | Shot down | |
| 26.04.38 | | Lt Fritz Losigkeit | 3.J/88 | | Shot down | |
| 04.05.38 | | Lt Hester | 4.J/88 | Albocacer | Shot down | |
| 12.05.38 | | Cuadra | 1-G-2 | Teruel | Shot down | |
| 02.06.38 | | Lt Martin Haupt | 3.J/88 | | Shot down | |
| 08.06.38 | | Lt Erich Beyer | 4.J/88 | | Shot down | |

## HEINKEL HE 51 LOSSES IN CHRONOLOGICAL ORDER—79 TOTAL (continued)

| Date | A/C | Pilot | Unit | Location | Fate | Cause |
|---|---|---|---|---|---|---|
| 09.06.38 | | Medrano | J/88 | | Shot down | |
| 06.38 | | R.Serra Hamilton | | | Shot down | |
| 13.07.38 | | R.Serra Hamilton | | Tortosa | Shot down | Flak |
| 14.07.38 | | Ruy Ozores | | Corbalán | Shot down | Flak |
| 14.07.38 | | Adj F.Encinas | | Corbalán | Shot down | Flak |
| 17.07.38 | | Jimènez Arenas | 1-G-2 | Teruel | Shot down | |
| 30.07.38 | | González del Valle | | Mequinenza | Shot down | Flak |
| 05.08.38 | | Oliveira | | Cote 471 | Shot down | |
| 28.08.38 | | Macias | | | Shot down | |
| 27.09.38 | | Melían | 1-G-2 | Recapo | Accident | |
| ??.10.38 | | Mir | 1-G-2 | | Shot down | |
| 23.12.38 | | F.Segovia | | | | |
| ??.12.38 | | ? | | | Lost | |

A close view of the fuselage of He 51 2-102 flown by Dr. Heinrich Neumann, the medical officer of the Legion from February 1938. Although not a fully qualified pilot, he used this aircraft to travel to visit his patients. The motto translates as "Don't bother me and I won't bother you."

Three mechanics are using the shade projected by He 51 2-22. The aircraft still seems quite new, to judge by the condition of the propeller and the presence of the Schwarz factory transfer on the visible blade. Though the aircraft had arrived with their FuGe 7 or 7a radio equipment, the use of radio in the first months of the war was considered a heavy luxury and the sets were not installed until 1938.

He 51 2-23, with the pilot neatly enclosed in his cockpit with the access flap closed up. The wing root panel appears to be natural metal, which may indicate a repair.

The He 51 in flight was an elegant aircraft and sturdy enough to withstand ill treatment from foe and friends alike. This aircraft of a Spanish unit sports on the black cockade the two six-point stars that correspond to the Spanish rank of *Teniente (Oberleutnant)*.

As a demonstration of the He 51B's solidity, this somersault at landing seems to have had little technical consequence apart from a broken propeller, bent struts, and a slightly bruised tail fin: perhaps two days of work. This aircraft, 2-64, is already in service with the Spanish *Cadenas del Aire* ground-attack unit.

A line-up of 3.J/88's He 51s including aircraft 2-105, 2-101 and 2-78. All are now fully camouflaged. Location not known.

The pilot of this Condor Legion aircraft has been deceived by the waterlogged ground and has made a *caballito*, but the propeller seems to be intact, and the aircraft should be back on the flight line after cleaning of the brakes and wheel spats.

A typical sight in the early months of fighting, although the unusual-for-the-He 51 "splinter" camouflage suggests a later period. This *4 Staffel* aircraft sits in front of two He 45Cs.

Four He 51s, probably of J/88, in the skies over Brunete. 2-63 in the foreground has a white cross on the front of its engine cowling. The white spinnner tip may indicate it is from *1 Staffel*.

The last aircraft of the 4.J/88 have been called in in order to be picked up by Spanish pilots who will form a new *Cadenas* unit with them. Visible are aircraft 2-73 and 2-70. All seem very tired, but notice the differences in the spinner coloring, including a rare example of striping on that belonging to 2-70. Aircraft 73 sports a name under the pilot's access flap that is unfortunately unreadable.

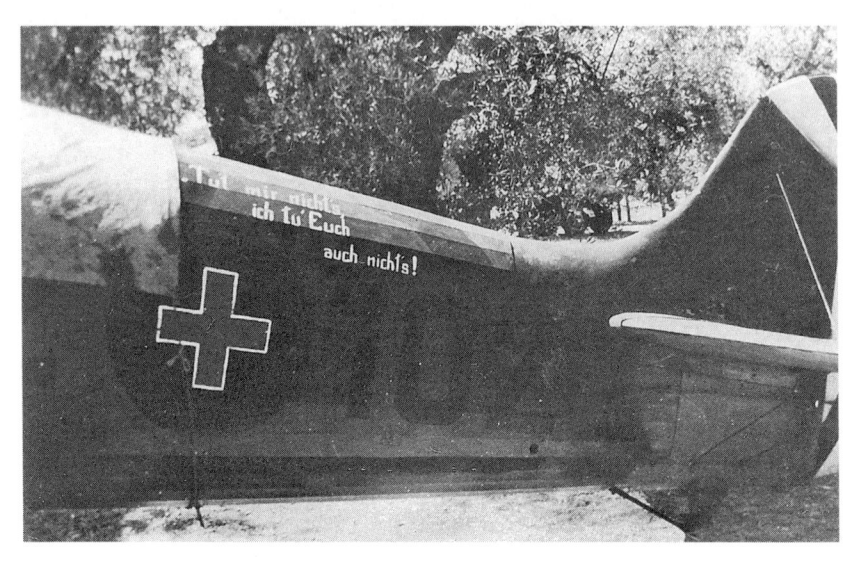

Aircraft 2-102 was flown by *Stabsarzt* Dr. Heinrich Neumann, who showed his profession, if not his vows, by the red cross decorating the black disc. The advert in German, apart from being hardly legible at some distance, was probably more a fervent wish than a serious hope: *Tut mir nicht's, ich tu Euch auch nicht's* ("If you don't mess with me, I won't mess with you"). It was probably the most decorated He 51 in the Legion as it also carried a Mickey Mouse and the name *Annelis*.

A good example of the painting scheme used by most aircraft in 3.J/88 (although actually in later service with the *Cadenas*) with a very vague mottle over the whole fuselage. Though clearly obsolete as an intercepter, the He 51 could still hold its own as a ground-attack machine and did not need fighter cover. In over 280 combat missions logged by Adolf Galland in Spain with 3.J/88, the unit only met enemy fighters ten times, always acquitting themselves well. Just behind 2-108 can be seen the fuel bowser.

Contrary to the aircraft of 3.J/88 shown in the previous photo, this camouflage scheme (here on aircraft 2-111) was in general use among *4 Staffel*'s aircraft, with irregular broad areas of grey, brown and green.

Sometimes the V-12 BMW engine needed some help to be cranked up.

Mickey Mouse (here on a He-51B, probably 2-102) started a second career in Spain as a *Luftwaffe* totem for fighter aircraft. Introduced by Douglas Pitcairn, it spread among 3.J/88 to become one of the classics in combat aircraft artwork.

Front view of the He51B, a classic plane of the thirties. Date, unit, and location are all unknown.

It is apparent that this He 51 has had camouflage applied over the uppersurfaces with the underside remaining in the original grey. The white spinner may indicate it is in service with 1.J/88.

This He 51 has not been camouflaged for winter duties with washable paint; it is just snow gathering on exposed areas, during the bitter 1937–38 winter on the Teruel front, where the He 51 pilots suffered more from adverse climatic conditions than the enemy. The location may be León and the unit 3.J/88, although the cloak worn by the pilot (?) was a popular item of clothing with Spanish officers.

This close-up of the nose of an He 51 offers many details: the separate exhausts pipes for each cylinder, the oil filler access flap, and the neat detailing of the engine cowling panels. Note the footsteps on the front edge of the undercarriage legs and the starting crank. The propeller also has brass sheathing to its leading edge.

A line-up of He 51s, all apparently wearing the ace of spades emblem adopted by 4.J/88 the second time it was formed. The location is probably Calamocha in 1938 during Teruel shortly before the aircraft were handed over to the Spanish Nationalists. Aircraft visible are, from the front, 2-104, 2-123, and 2-88.

Another view of the wreckage of a J/88 He 51 which has been shot down, allegedly in spring 1937, by an International Brigade antiaircraft gun, manned by at least one Czech volunteer and commanded by a German. The most likely candidate for this misfortune is *Leutnant* Otto-Hans Winterer of 2.J/88, who was brought down on 25 February near Navalmoral.

A closeup of one of the crew of the Republican Thaelmann flak battery manned by international volunteers, standing in front of the tail of an He 51 they have shot down.

# The Messerschmitt Bf 109 in Spain

## Type code 6

| Code | Type | Unit | Arrived | Pilot | A/C Name | Fate |
|---|---|---|---|---|---|---|
| s/n | V3 | VJ/88 | 12.36 | Uffz Erwin Kley | | Crashed on takeoff, 10.12.36 |
| 6-1 | V4 | VJ/88 | 12.36 | Lt Hannes Trautloft | | |
| | | 2.J/88 | | Oblt Herwig Knüppel | | |
| 6-2 | V3 | VJ/88 | 12.36 | Lt Paul Rehahn | | Destroyed in accident 11.2.37? |
| 6-3 | V5 | VJ/88 | 12.36 | Oblt Hennig Strümpell | | |
| | | 2.J/88 | | | | |
| 6-4 | B-1 | VJ/88 | 03.37 | Lt Kurt von Gilsa | | |
| | | 2.J/88 | | Uffz Guido Höness | | Withdrawn from service end 37 |
| 6-5 | B | VJ/88 | 03.37 | Lt Dietrich von Bothmer | | Withdrawn from service end 37 |
| | | 2.J/88 | | | | |
| 6-6 | B | VJ/88 | 03.37 | Lt Urban Schlaffer | | |
| | | 2.J/88 | | Fw Herbert Ihlefeld | | |
| | | 3.J/88 | | Lt Franz Jaenisch | | Crashed on takeoff, 25.07.38 |
| 6-7 | B | VJ/88 | 03.37 | Lt Rolf Pingel | | |
| | | 2.J/88 | | Fw Norbert Flegel | | |
| | | 3.J/88 | | Oblt Werner Mölders | | |
| 6-8 | B | VJ/88 | 03.37 | Fw Franz Heilmayer | | |
| | | 2.J/88 | | | | Withdrawn from service, 08.37 Takeoff accident |
| 6-9 | B | VJ/88 | 03.37 | Uffz Willi Gödecke | | |
| | | 2.J/88 | | | | Withdrawn from service, 08.37 |
| 6-10 | B | VJ/88 | 03.37 | Uffz Ernst Mratzek | | |
| | | 2.J/88 | | Hptmn Günther Lützow | "Altertum" | To Spanish AF |
| 6-11 | B | VJ/88 | 03.37 | Uffz Adolf Buhl | | |
| | | 2.J/88 | | | | |

| Code | Type | Unit | Arrived | Pilot | A/C Name | Fate |
|---|---|---|---|---|---|---|
| 6-12 | B | VJ/88 | 03.37 | Uffz Boddem | | |
| | | 2.J/88 | | Uffz Hermann Stange | | Crashed on takeoff |
| 6-13 | B | VJ/88 | 03.37 | Uffz Harbach | | |
| | | 2.J/88 | | Fw Heinz Braunschweiger | | |
| 6-14 | B | VJ/88 | 03.37 | Oblt Otto-Hans Winterer | | |
| | | 2.J/88 | | Uffz Harbach | | Shot down |
| 6-15 | B | VJ/88 | 03.37 | | | |
| | | 2.J/88 | | | | |
| | | 1.J/88 | | Uffz Otto Polenz | | Captured 4.12.37 |
| 6-16 | B | VJ/88 | 03.37 | | | |
| | | 2.J/88 | | | | |
| | | 3.J/88 | | Lt Josef Fözö | | |
| 6-17 | B | | 07.37 | | | |
| 6-18 | B | | 07.37 | | | |
| 6-19 | B-1 | | 07.37 | | | |
| 6-20 | B | 1.J/88 | 07.37 | Lt Fritz Awe | | Lost 4/4/38 Mid-air collision |
| 6-21 | B | 2.J/88 | 07.37 | Lt Rolf Pingel | | |
| 6-22 | B | | 07.37 | | | |
| 6-23 | B | | 07.37 | | | |
| 6-24 | B | | 07.37 | | | |
| 6-25 | B | | 07.37 | | | |
| 6-26 | B | | 07.37 | | | |
| 6-27 | B | | 07.37 | | | |
| 6-28 | B | | 07.37 | | | |
| 6-29 | B | 2.J/88 | 07.37 | | | |
| 6-30 | B | 2.J/88 | 07.37 | Fw Reinhard Seiler | | Crashed on landing Alar del Rey |
| 6-31 | B | 1.J/88 | 07.37 | | | |
| 6-32 | B | 2.J/88 | 07.37 | Obfw Reinhard Seiler | | |
| 6-33 | B | 1.J/88 | 07.37 | Lt Eckehardt Priebe | | Shot down 14.06.38 Villafames ? |
| 6-34 | B | 1.J/88 | 07.37 | Oblt Erich Woitke | | |
| 6-35 | B | | 07.37 | | | |
| 6-36 | B | 1.J/88 | 07.37 | Oblt Harro Harder | | |
| 6-37 | B | | 07.37 | | | |
| 6-38 | B | 1.J/88 | 07.37 | Uffz Ernst Terry | | |
| 6-39 | B | | | | | |
| 6-40 | B-2 | 1.J/88 | | Uffz Willy Szuggar | | |
| 6-41 | B | | | | | |
| 6-42 | B | 1.J/88 | | | | |
| 6-43 | B | | | | | |
| 6-44 | B | | | | | |
| 6-45 | B | | | | | |
| 6-46 | C | | | | | |

# The Messerschmitt Bf 109 in Spain

| Code | Type | Unit | Arrived | Pilot | A/C Name | Fate |
|---|---|---|---|---|---|---|
| 6-47 | C | | | | | |
| 6-48 | C | | | | | |
| 6-49 | C | | | | | |
| 6-50 | C | | | | | |
| 6-51 | D | 1.J/88 | | Hpt Wolfgang Schellmann | | To Spanish AF |
| 6-52 | D | 2.J/88 | | | | To Spanish AF |
| 6-53 | D | 2.J/88 | | | | To Spanish AF |
| 6-54 | D | | | | | |
| 6-55 | D | | | | | |
| 6-56 | D | Stab 88 | | Hpt Gotthard Handrick | | |
| | | | | Hpt Walter Grabmann | | To Spanish AF |
| 6-57 | D | | | | | |
| 6-58 | D | 2.J/88 | | | | |
| 6-59 | D | | | | | |
| 6-60 | D | 2.J/88 | | Uffz Herbert Schob | "NNWW" | |
| 6-61 | D | | | | | |
| 6-62 | D | | | | | |
| 6-63 | D | | | | | |
| 6-64 | D | | | | | |
| 6-65 | D | | | | | |
| 6-66 | D | | | | | |
| 6-67 | D | 1.J/88 | | Otto Bertram | | Shot down, 4.10.38 |
| 6-67 | D | | | | | |
| 6-68 | D | | | | | |
| 6-69 | D | | | | | |
| 6-70 | D | | | | | |
| 6-71 | D | | | | | |
| 6-72 | D | | | | | |
| 6-73 | D | | | | | |
| 6-74 | D | | | | | |
| 6-75 | D | | | | | |
| 6-76 | D | | | | | |
| 6-77 | D | | | | | |
| 6-78 | D | | | | | |
| 6-79 | D1 | 3.J/88 | | Oblt Werner Mölders | "Luchs" | |
| 6-80 | D | | | | | |
| 6-81 | D | | | | | |
| 6-82 | D | 1.J/88 | | Lt Otto Bertram | | |
| | | 3.J/88 | | | | |
| 6-83 | D | 3.J/88 | | | | |
| 6-84 | D | 3.J/88 | | | | |
| 6-85 | D | | | | | |
| 6-86 | D | 1.J/88 | | Oblt Siebert Reents | | |
| 6-87 | E | | | | | |
| 6-88 | E | | | | | |

| Code | Type | Unit | Arrived | Pilot | A/C Name | Fate |
|---|---|---|---|---|---|---|
| 6-89 | E | | | | | |
| 6-90 | E | | | | | |
| 6-91 | E | 3.J/88 | | Uff Herbert Schob | | |
| 6-92 | E | | | | | |
| 6-93 | E | 1.J/88 | | Uffz Hans Nirminger | | Shot down 6.2.39, Vilajuiga, by Lt José Falco |
| 6-94 | E | | | | | |
| 6-95 | E | 2.J/88 | | | | |
| 6-96 | E | | | | | |
| 6-97 | E | 1.J/88 | | | | |
| 6-98 | E | 1.J/88 | | Uffz Heinrich Windemuth | | Shot down 6.2.39, Vilajuiga, by Lt José Falco |
| 6-99 | E-3 | 3.J/88 | | | | |
| 6-100 | E | | | | | |
| 6-101 | E | 3.J/88 | | Oblt Jung | | |
| 6-102 | E | | | | | |
| 6-103 | E | | | | | |
| 6-104 | E | 1.J/88 | | Rey-Stolle | | |
| 6-105 | E | | | | | |
| 6-106 | E | 3.J/88 | | | | |
| 6-107 | E-4 | 2.J/88 | | | "Mors-Mors!" | |
| 6-108 | E | | | | | |
| 6-109 | E | 3.J/88 | | Kurt Sochatzki | | |
| 6-110 | E | | | | | |
| 6-111 | E-3 | 2.J/88 | | Lt Werner Ursinus | "Bärchen" | |
| 6-112 | E | 2.J/88 | | | | |
| 6-113 | E | 2.J/88 | | | | |
| 6-114 | E | | | | | |
| 6-115 | E | | | | | |
| 6-116 | E | | | | | |
| 6-117 | E | 3.J/88 | | | | |
| 6-118 | E | | | | | |
| 6-119 | E | 1.J/88 | | Oblt Siebert Reents | | |
| 6-120 | E | | | | | |
| 6-121 | E | 2.J/88 | | Lt Karl-Wolfgang Redlich | | |
| 6-122 | E | | | | | |
| 6-123 | E-1 | 3.J/88 | | Oblt Hans Schmoller-Haldy | | |
| 6-124 | E | | | | | |
| 6-125 | E | 1.J/88 | | | | |
| 6-126 | E-3 | 2.J/88 | | | | To Spanish AF |
| 6-127 | E | | | | | |
| 6-128 | E | | | | | To Spanish AF |
| 6-129 | E | 3.J/88 | | Lt Josef Fözö | | |
| 6-130 | E | Stab.J/88 | | Major Walter Grabmann | | |
| 6-131 | E | | | | | |

## MESSERSCHMITT BF 109 LOSSES IN CHRONOLOGICAL ORDER—40 TOTAL

| Date | A/C | Pilot | Unit | Location | Fate | Cause |
|---|---|---|---|---|---|---|
| 10.12.36 | V-3/6-3 | Uffz Erich Kley | | Tablada | Accident | Crashed on takeoff |
| 11.02.37 | 6-2 | Lt Paul Rehahn | | Cáceres | Accident | |
| 12.07.37 | 6-4 | Lt Guido Höness | | Brunete | Shot down | Air combat |
| 17.07.37 | ? | Lt Gotthard Handrick | | Escalona | Shot down | I-16 (Tinker) |
| 18.07.37 | 6-14 | Uffz Haarbach | | | Shot down | I-16 |
| ??.07.37 | 6-13 | | | | Written off | |
| 11.07.37 | ? | Uffz Norbert Flegel | | | Accident | Crash-landed |
| ??.08.37 | 6-8 | | | | Accident | Crash-landed |
| ??.08.37 | 6-9 | | | | Written off | |
| ??.08.37 | 6-30 | Ofw Reinhard Seiler | | Alar del Rey | Accident | Crash-landed |
| ??.09.37 | 6-7 | Fw Norbert Flegel | | Santander-0 | Accident | Crash-landed |
| ??.09.37 | 6-12 | Uffz Hermann Stange | | Santander-0 | Accident | Crash-landed |
| 05?.09.37 | ? | Lt Walter Adolph | | Llanes | Accident | Crash-landed |
| 05.11.37 | ? | Fw Leo Sigmund | | Teruel | Shot down | |
| 30.11.37 | 6-15 | Fw Otto Polenz | | | Shot down, POW | |
| 23.12.37 | ? | Uffz Anton Kurz | | Teruel | Shot down | |
| 07.02.38 | | Oblt Wilhelm Balthasar | | Teruel | Shot down | SB-2 |
| 11.03.38 | | Fw Alexander Graf zu Dohna | | Caspe/Sastago | Shot down | I-16 (J.Bosch, 21/4) |
| 04.04.38 | 6-20 | Lt Fritz Awe | | Lanaja | Mid-air collision | Bf 109 |
| 04.04.38 | 6-21 | Uffz Adolf Borchers | | Lanaja | Mid-air collision | Bf 109 |
| 20.04.38 | | | | Sagunto | Shot down | I-16 (21/3) |
| 11.05.38 | | | | Sra Espadán | Shot down | I-16 (21/3) Tarazona |
| 14.06.38 | | Lt Helmut Henz | | Mijares | Shot down | I-16 (21/4) |

## MESSERSCHMITT BF 109 LOSSES IN CHRONOLOGICAL ORDER—40 TOTAL (continued)

| Date | A/C | Pilot | Unit | Location | Fate | Cause |
|---|---|---|---|---|---|---|
| 14.06.38 | 6-33 | Lt Eckehardt Priebe | | Villafames | Shot down | I-15 ? |
| 14.07.38 | | | | Teruel | Mid-air collision | I-15 (Redondo) |
| 23.07.38 | | Uffz Boer | (3.J) | La Cenia | Accident | |
| 25.07.38 | 6-6 | Lt Franz Jaenisch | | | Accident | Crashlanded |
| 03.08.38 | | Lt Horst Lehmann | | Flix | Shot down | Flak |
| 05.09.38 | | Lt Martin Lutz | (3.J) | | Shot down | |
| 09.09.38 | | | | Gandesa | Accident (50%) | Engine failure? |
| 04.10.38 | 6-67 | Lt Otto Bertram | | Venta de C. | Shot down | I-16 (Cortizo, 21/4) |
| 11.38 | 6-74 | | | La Cenia | Accident | Crashlanded |
| 13.12.38 | | | | | Shot down | |
| 16.12.38 | | | | La Cenia | Bombed on ground | SB-2 |
| 16.12.38 | | | | La Cenia | Bombed on ground | SB-2 |
| 29.01.39 | | Lt K.Bötticher | | Mollet | Shot down | Flak |
| 06.22.39 | | Uffz Hans Nirminger | | Vilajuiga | Shot down | G-23 'I-15' |
| 06.02.39 | 6-98 | Uffz Heinrich Windemuth | | Vilajuiga | Shot down | G-23 'I-15' |
| 16.03.38 | | Lt Rolf Strössner | | | Collision | Bf 109 |
| 16.03.38 | | | | | Collision | Bf 109 |

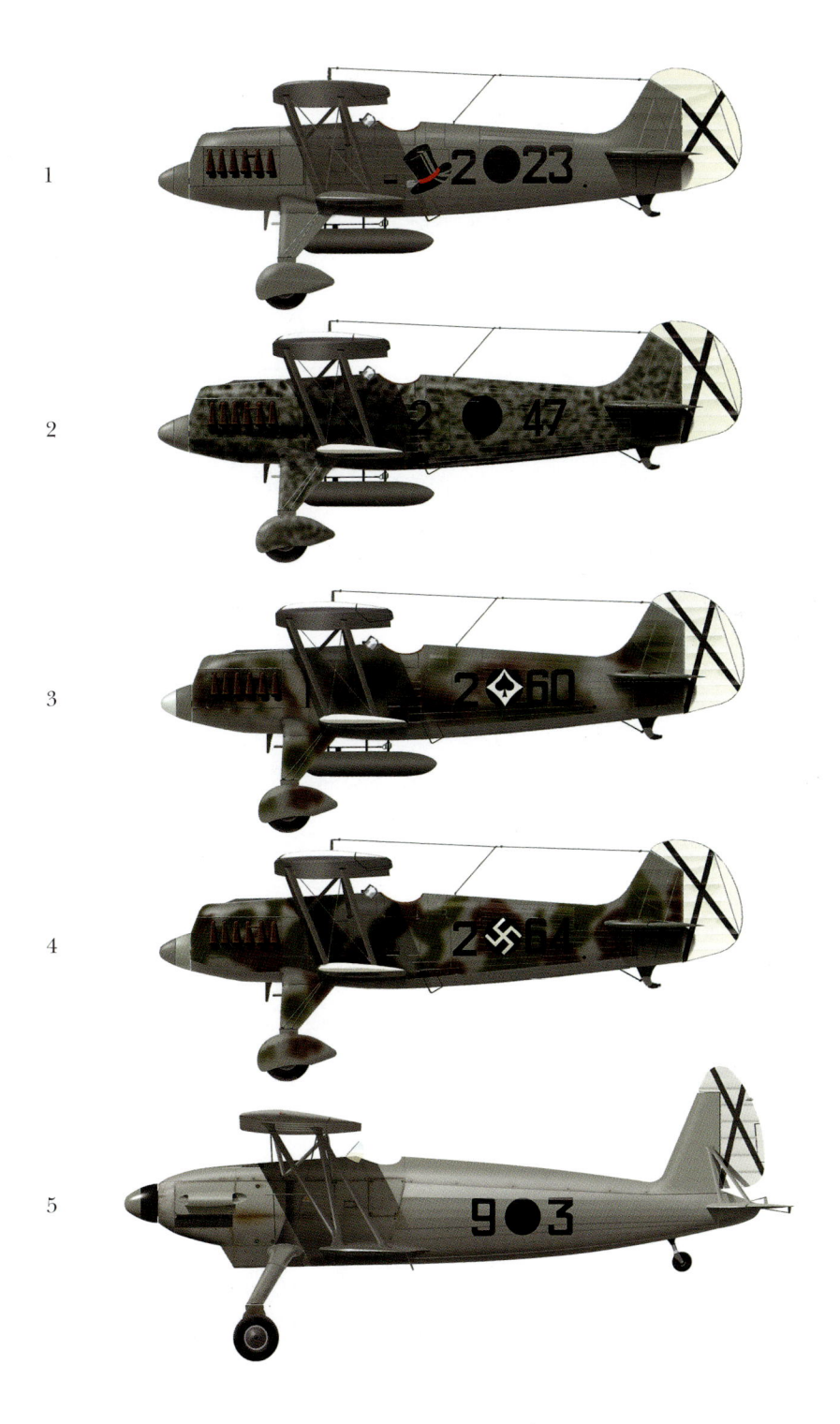

For captions, see page 375.

6

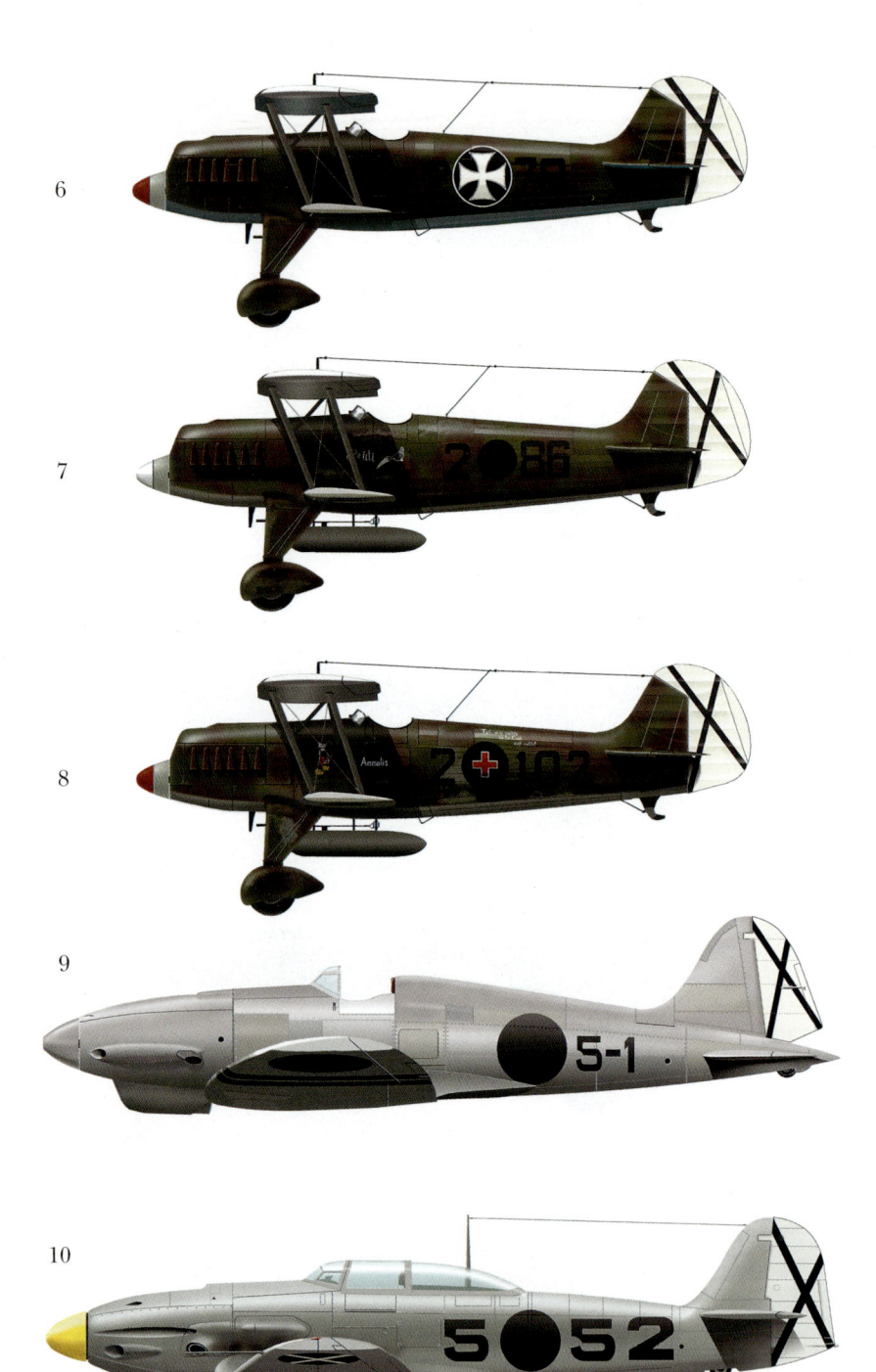

7

8

9

10

11

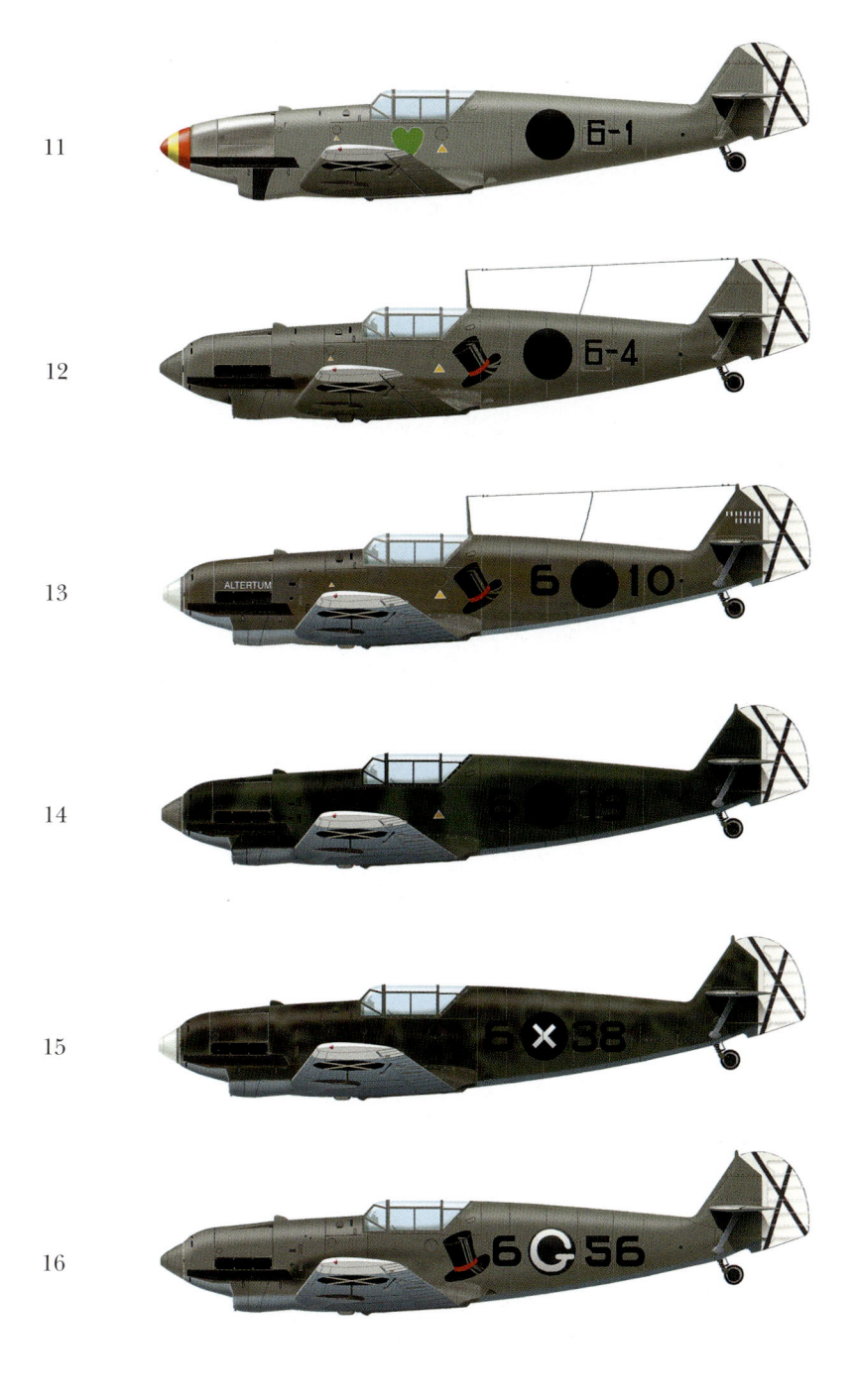

12

13

14

15

16

17

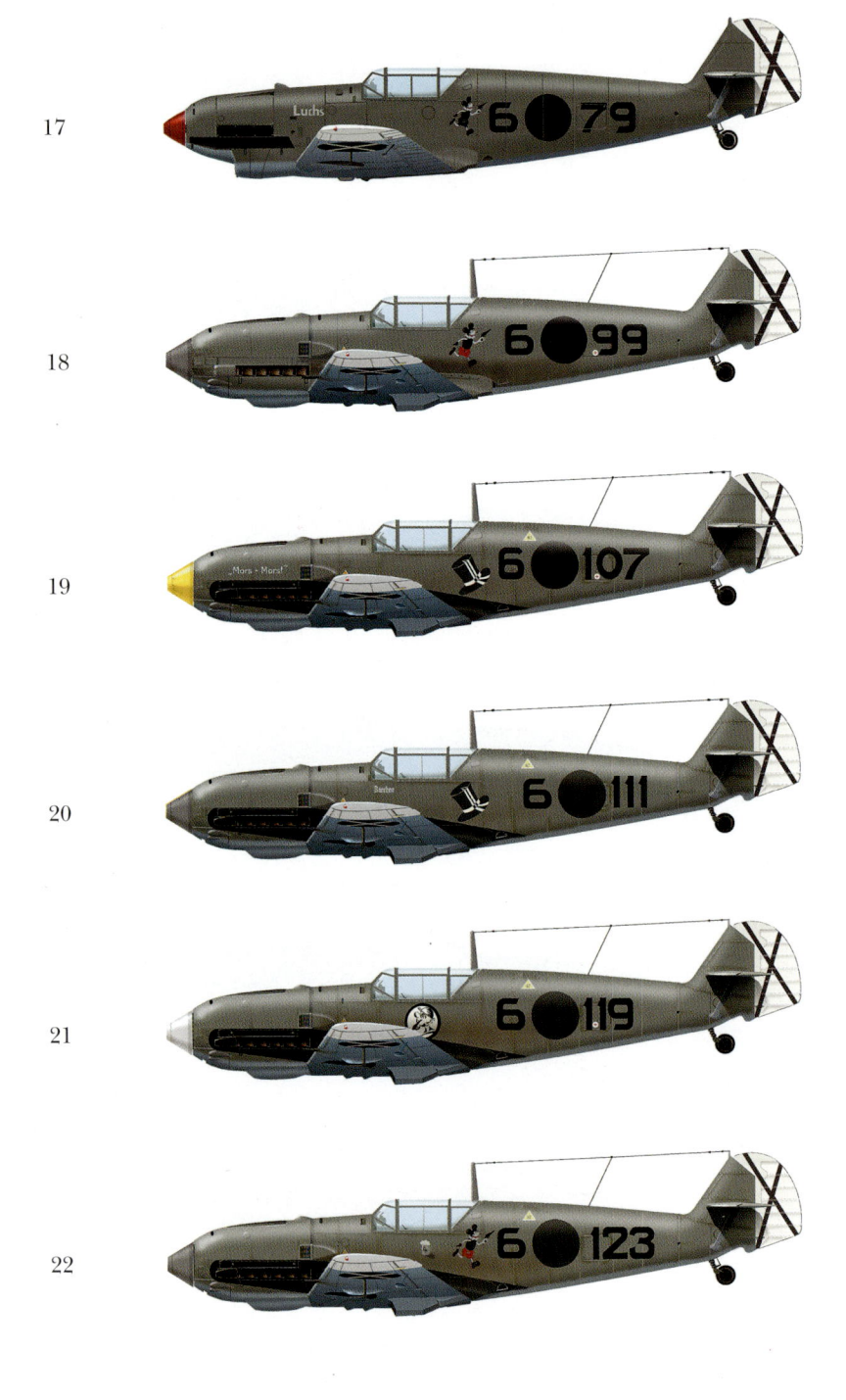

18

19

20

21

22

23

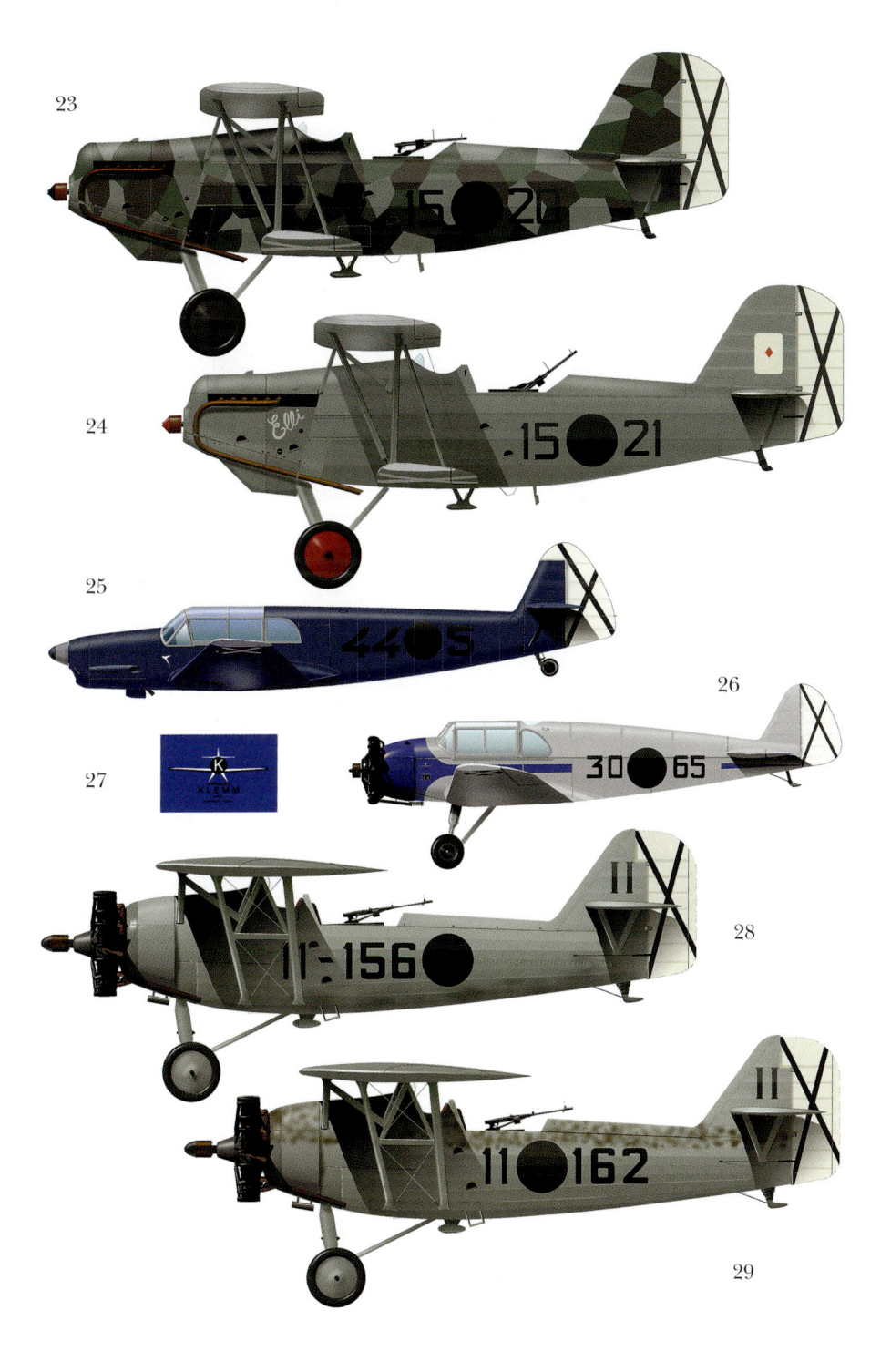

24

25

27

26

28

29

30

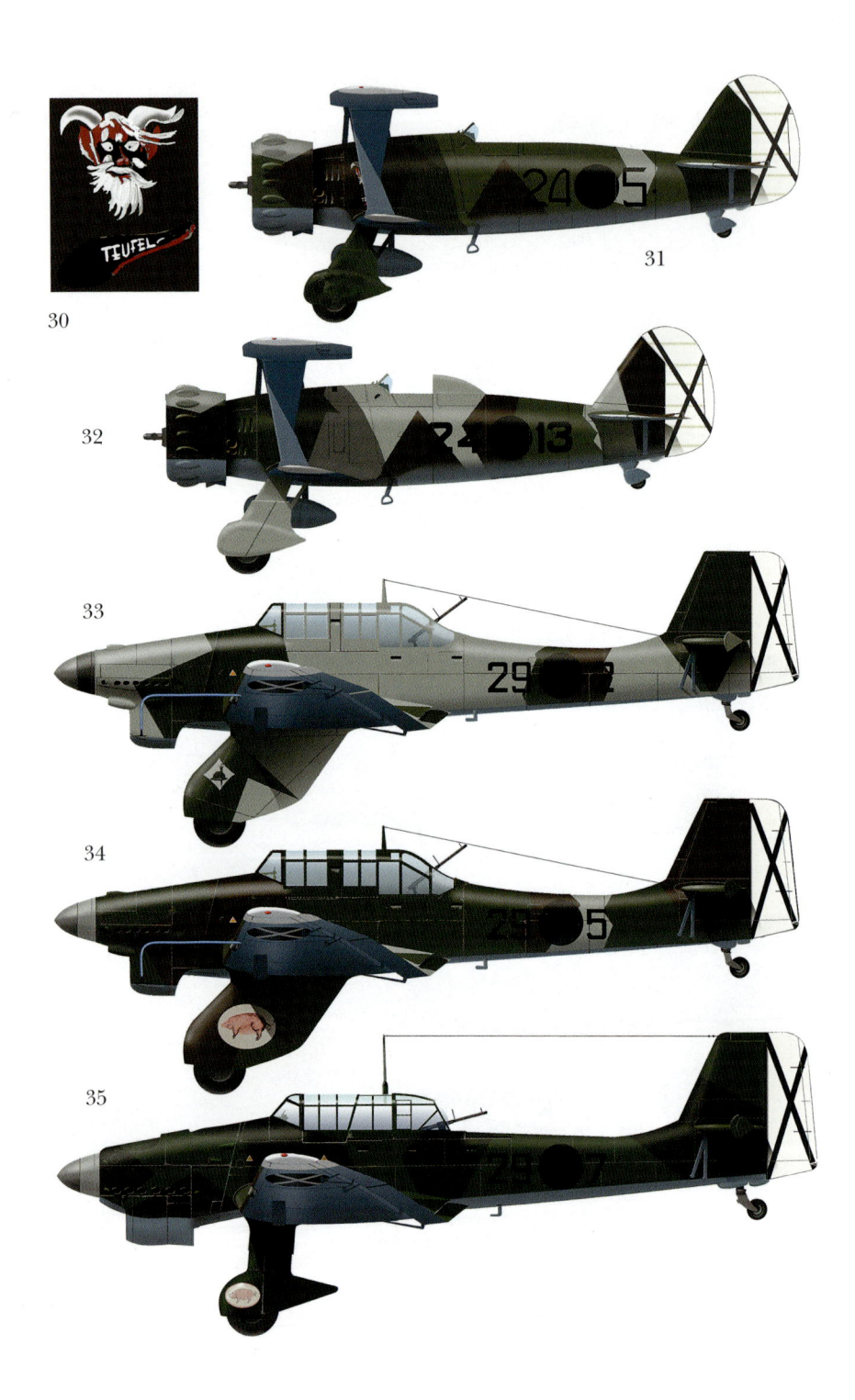

31

32

33

34

35

36

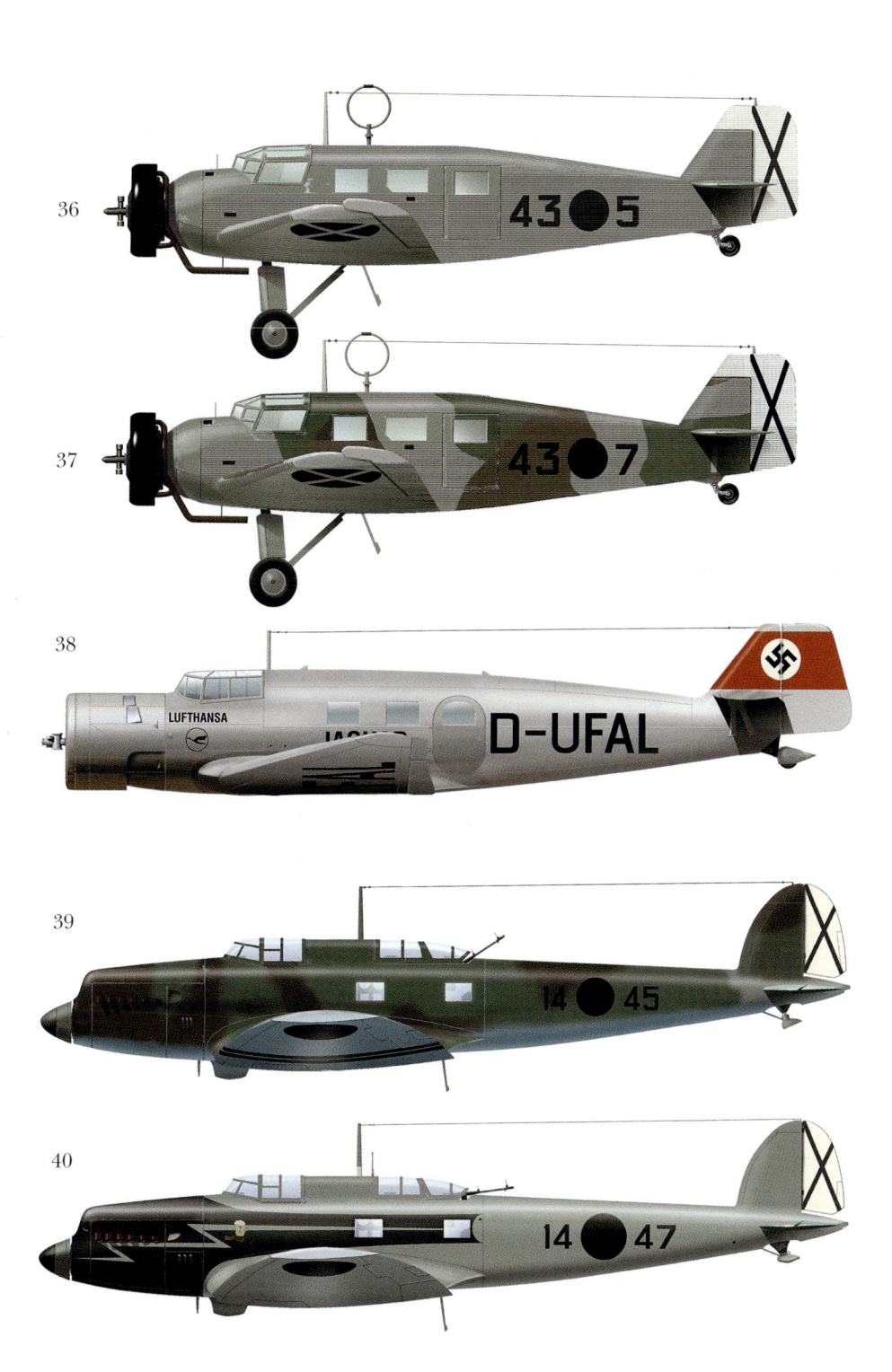

37

38 LUFTHANSA D-UFAL

39 14●45

40 14●47

41

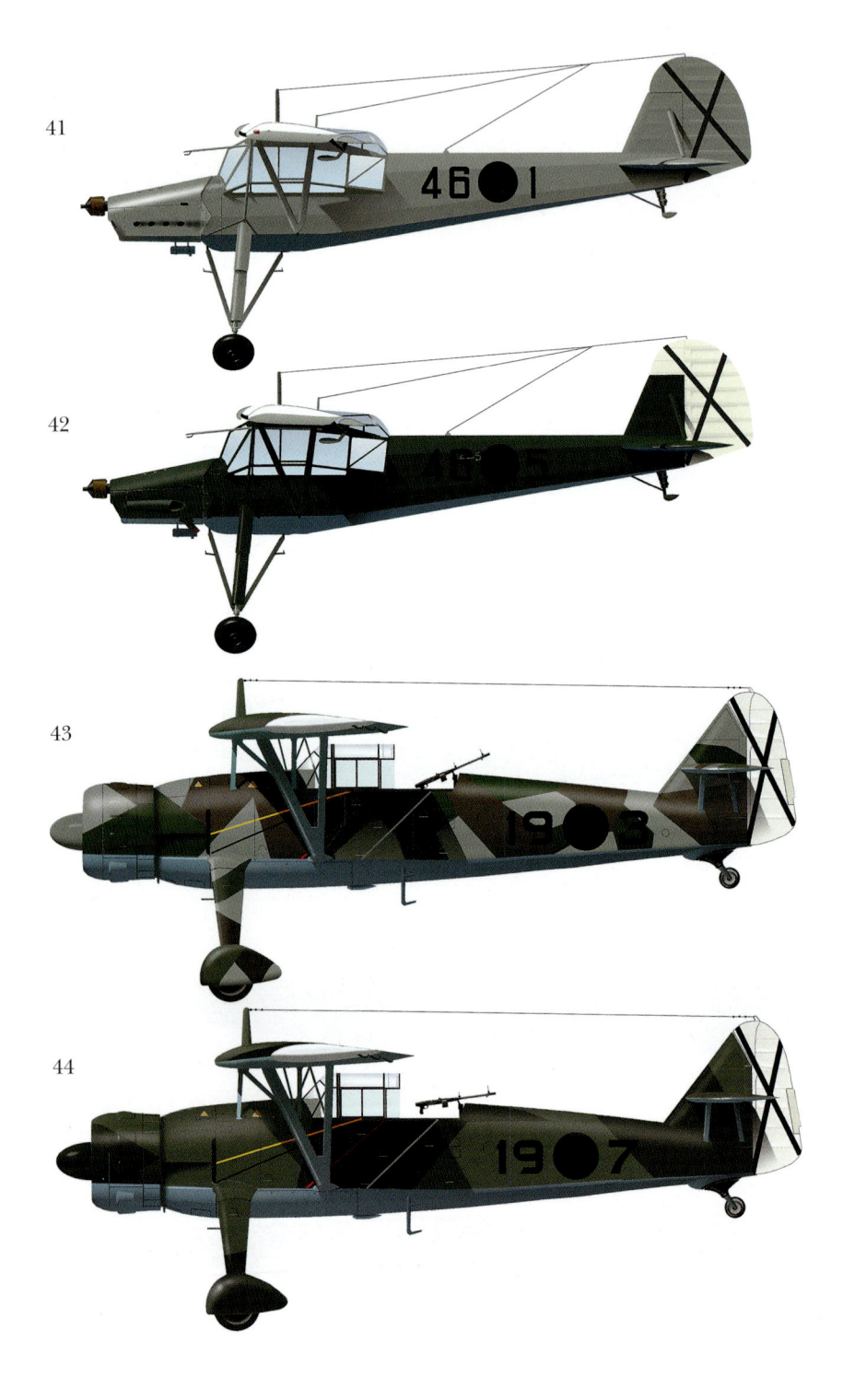

42

43

44

45

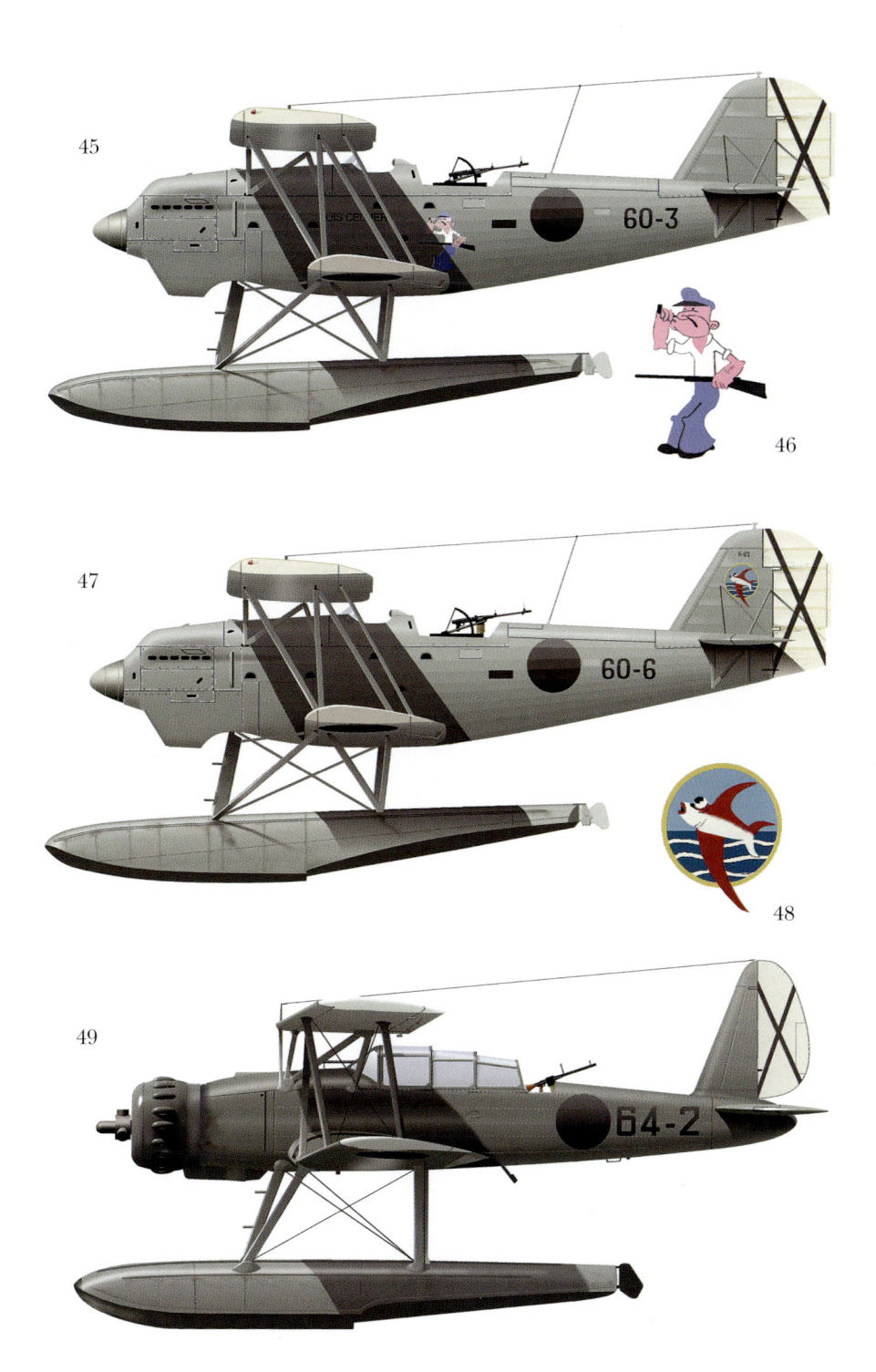

46

47

48

49

50

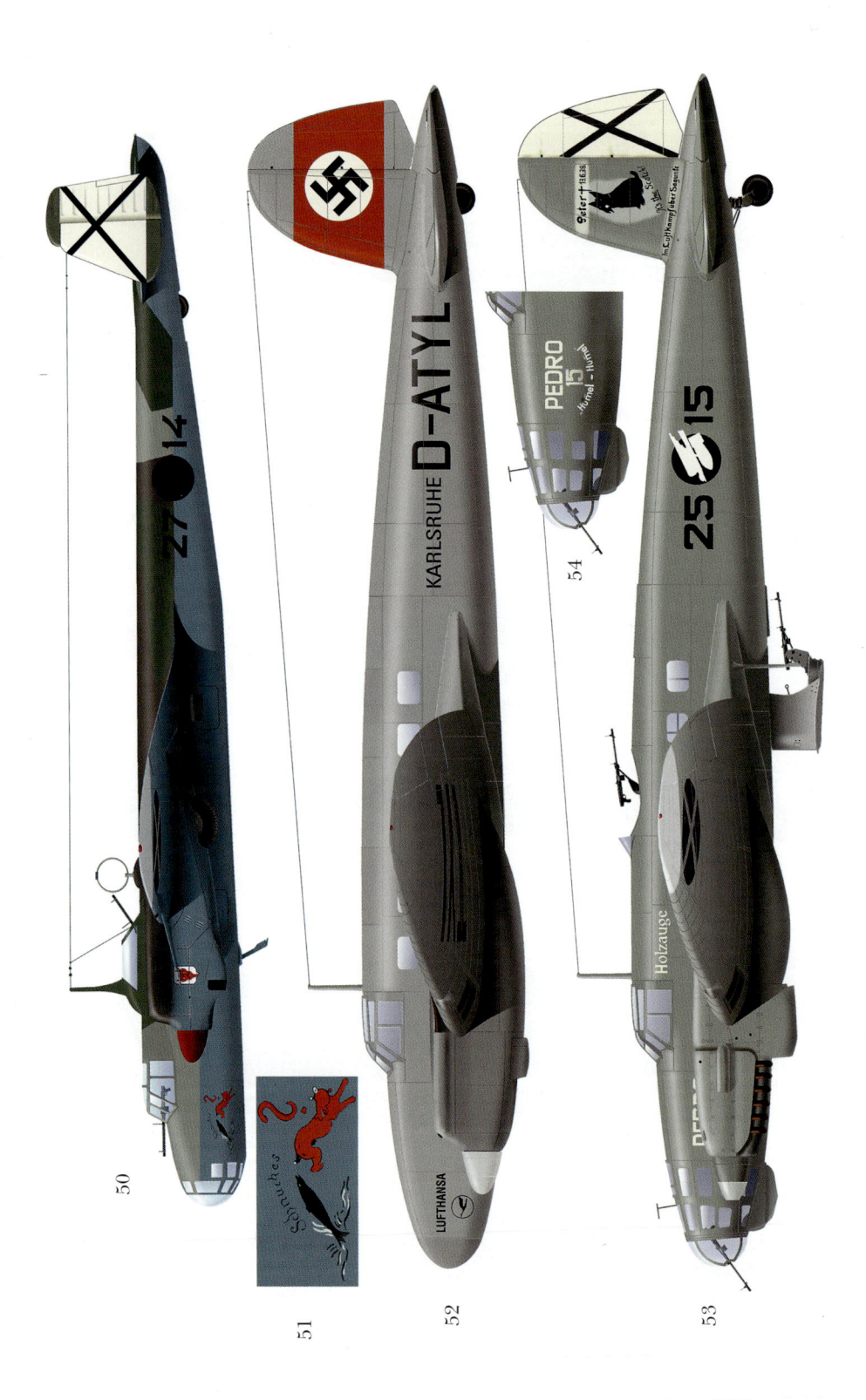

51

52

53

54

55

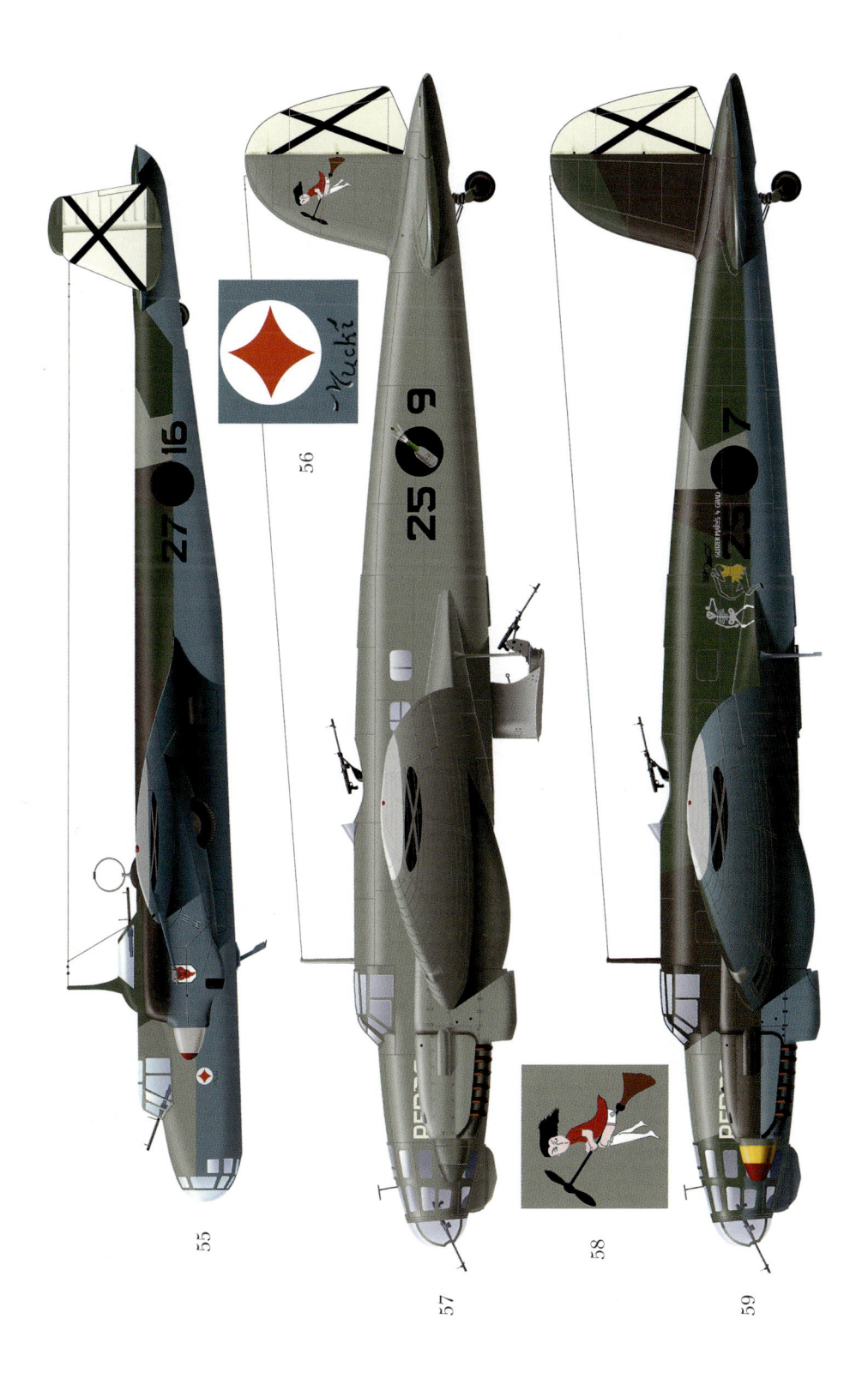

56

Mucki

57

25 9

58

59

27 16

23 7

60

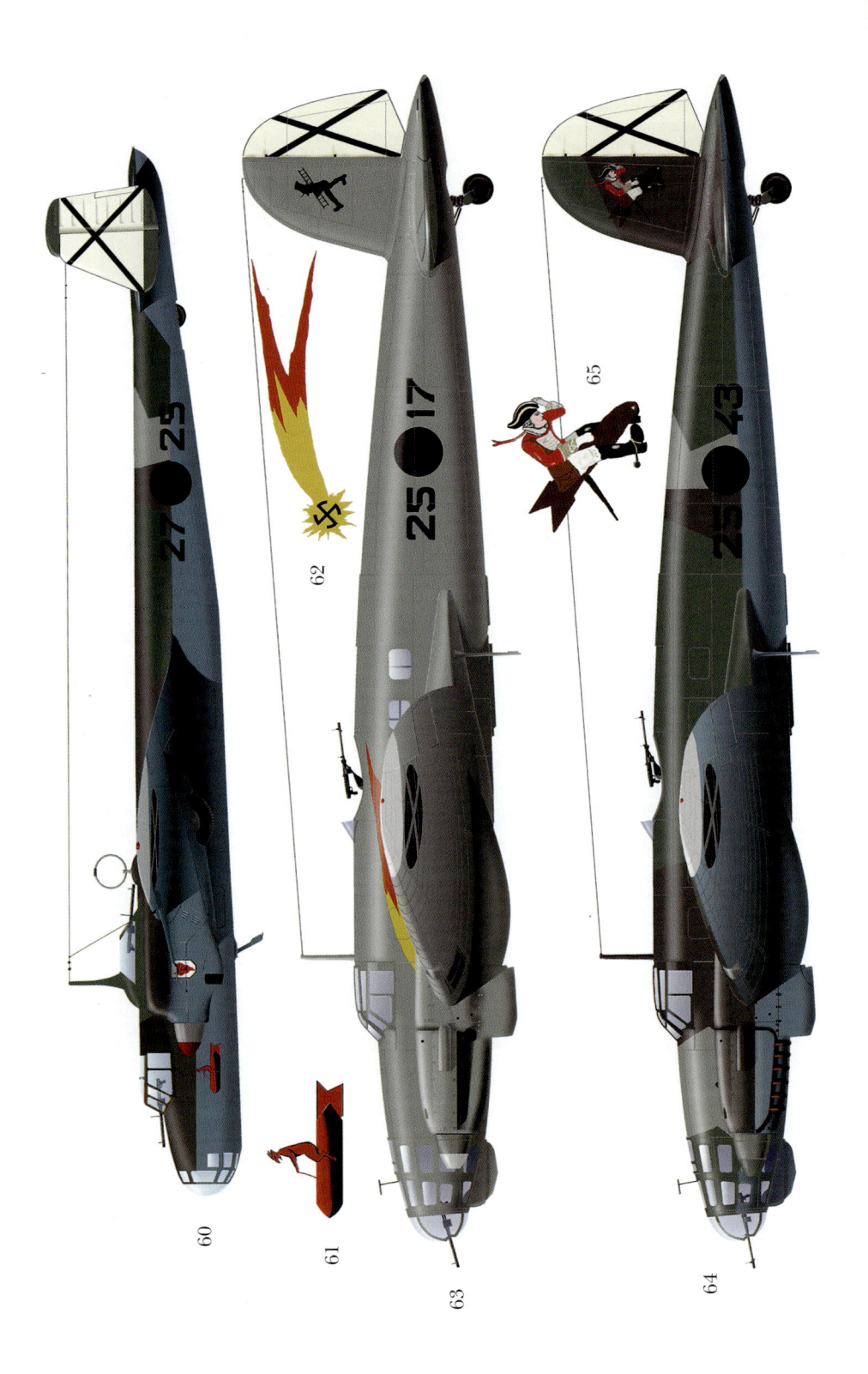

61

62

63

64

65

66

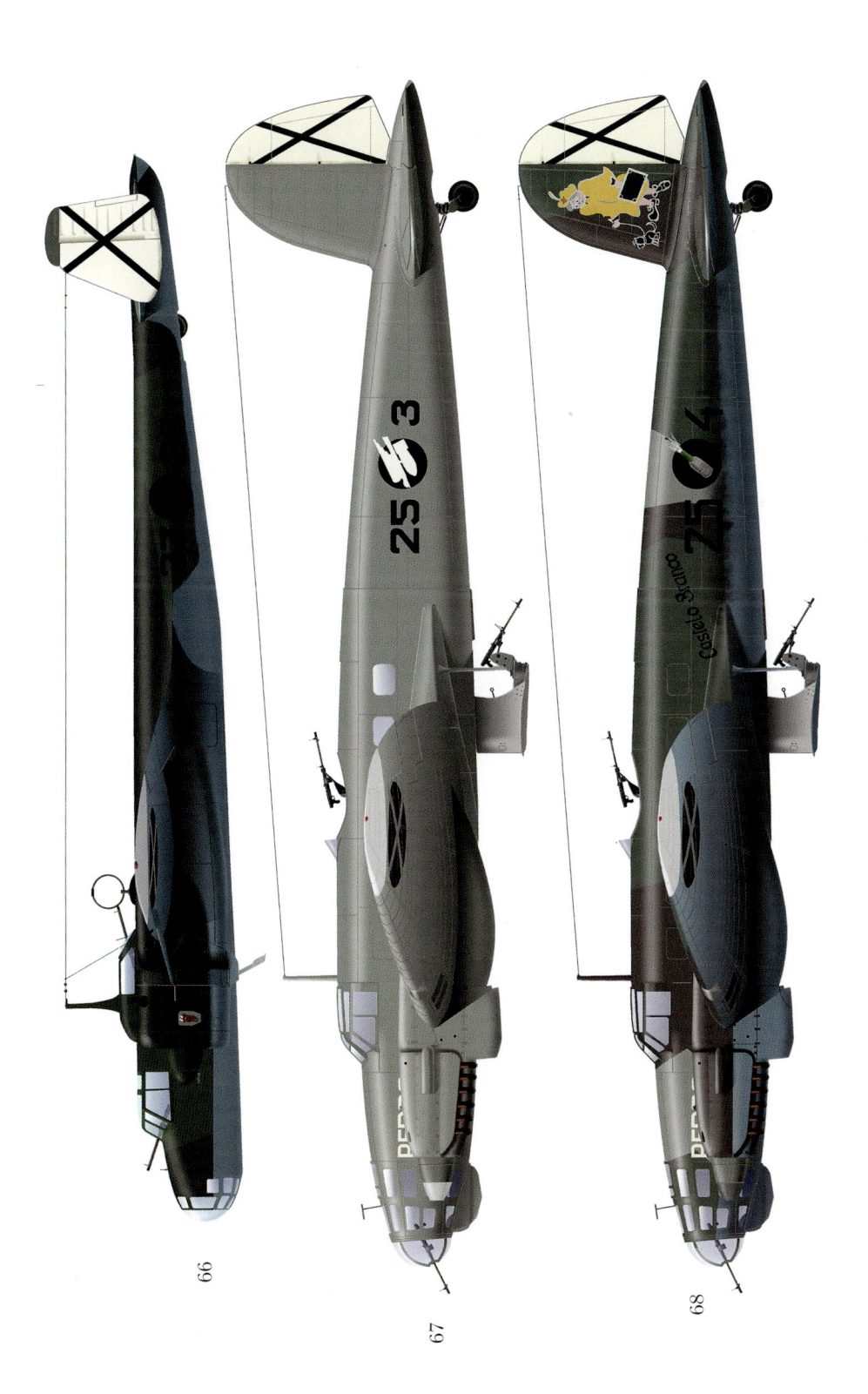

67

68

69
70
71
72

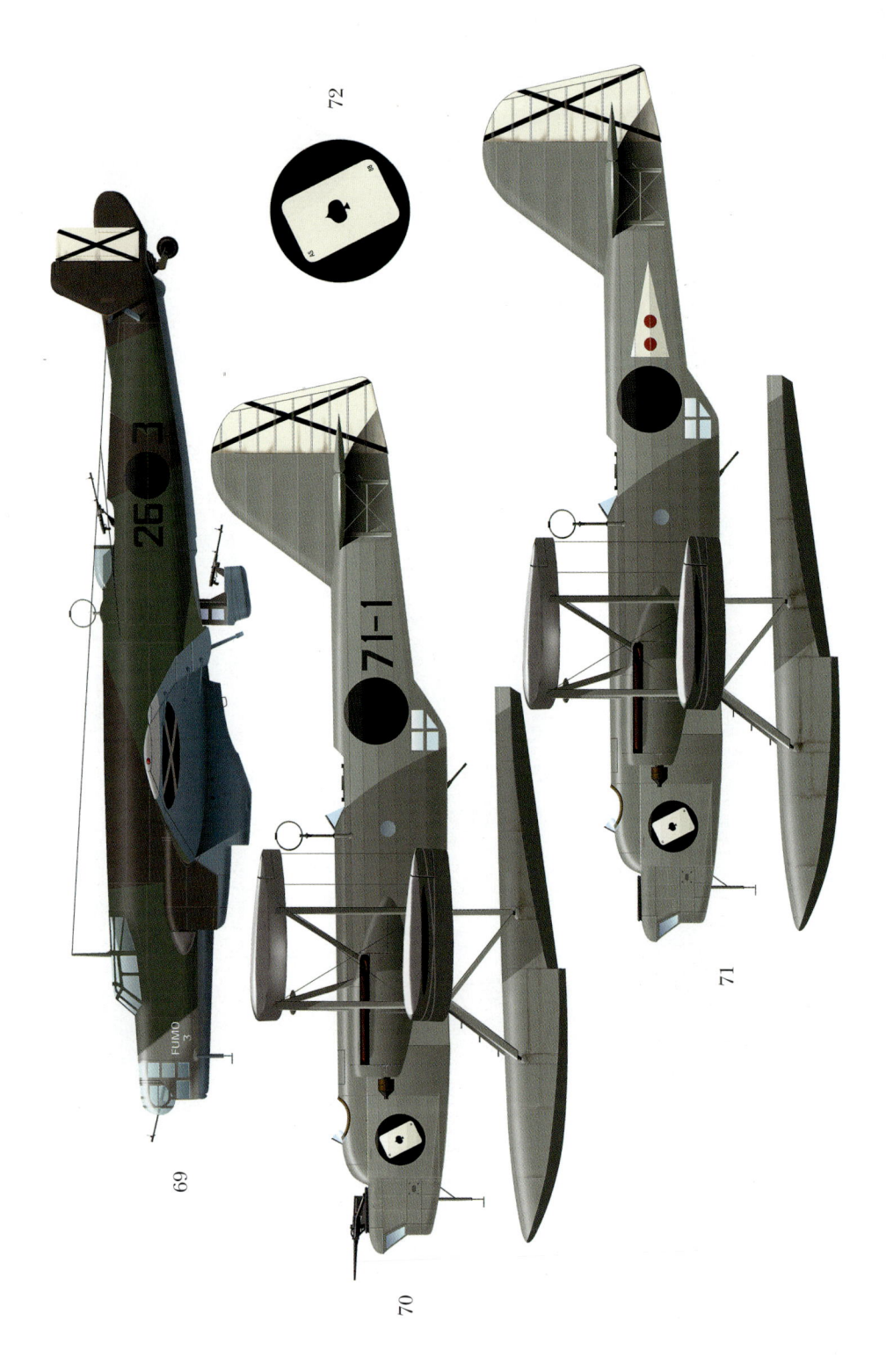

73

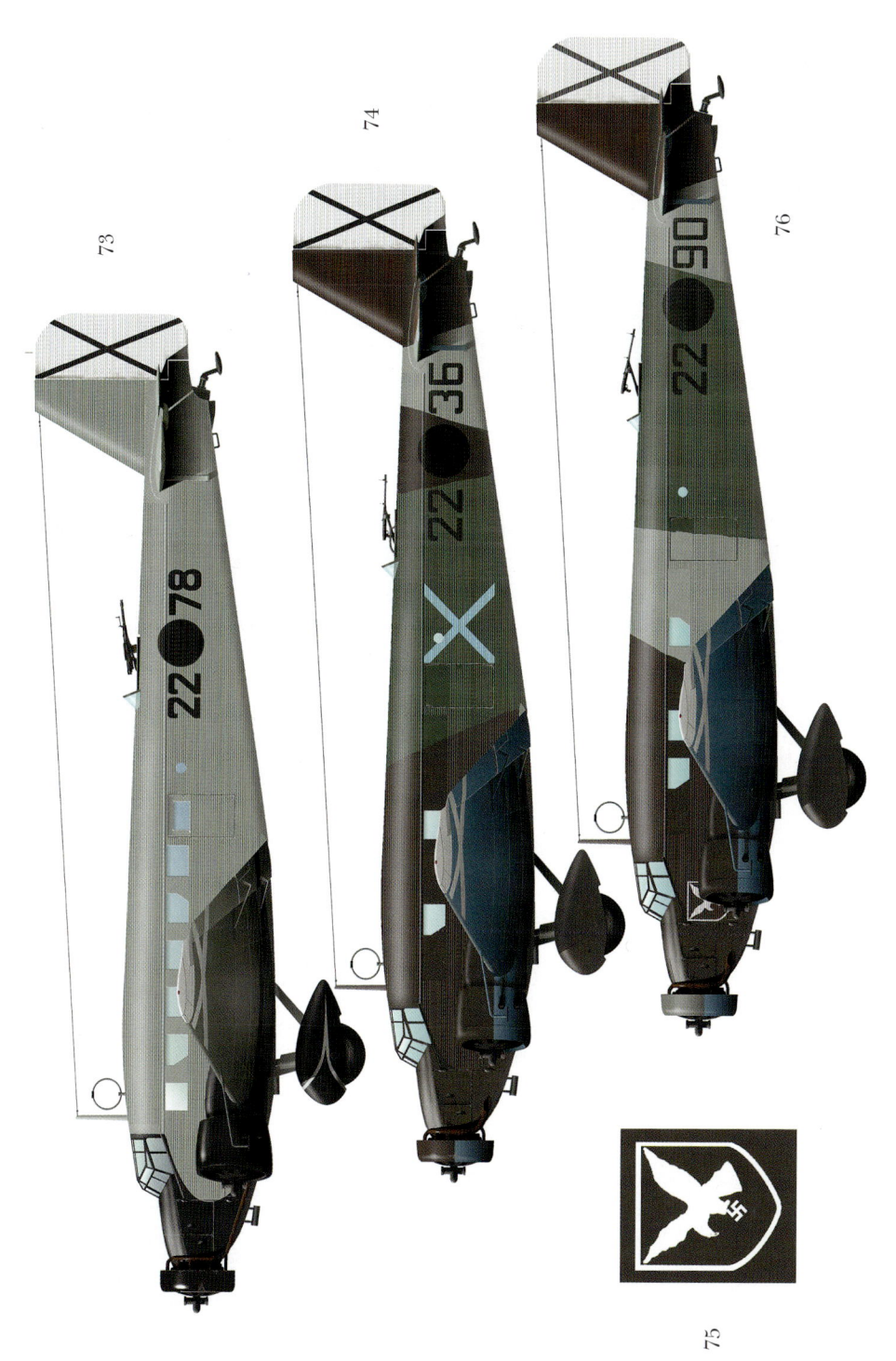

74

75

76

77

78

79

80

81

82 Tut mir nichts, ich tu' Euch auch nichts!

83 Annalis

84

85

86

87

88

89

90

91

92

93

94

95

96

97

98

99 GLITZER MARY'S 4 GRAD

100 Peter † 13.6.38. It's the Scotch! Im Luftkampf über Sagunto

101

102

Recovery operations in progress after Bf 109E-4, 6-107, named *Mors-Mors*, had suffered a typical Bf 109 landing accident and collapsed the starboard undercarriage leg. The identity of the pilot is not known, but either he or the ground crew probably came from Hamburg, the shout "Mors-mors!" being Hamburg slang and the riposte to the cry "Hümel-hümel!" This verbal exchange originated hundreds of years ago and relates to a water seller in that city.

One of two Bf 109s destroyed on the ground at La Cenia by Republican SB bombers on 16 December 1938. A close study reveals an intact fighter in the background, with a wing showing behind the olive tree in the center.

Groundcrew discuss how best to clear up the mess in the aftermath of the Republican bombing raid on the Legion Condor's base at La Cenia on 16 December 1938. Little of this Bf 109 remains to be salvaged. Note the Mercedes-Benz 320WK Kfz 12 car in the background.

Good detail of the VDM metal propeller and undercarriage of this Bf 109B. The comet on the fuselage of the Heinkel He 111B, 25-16, of 1.K/88 can be seen streaking across the background.

This is a front view of Bf 109B-1 6-15 after it was captured intact by the Republicans when *Oberfeldwebel* Otto Polenz of 2.J/88 landed it near Bujaraloz. It is seen here repainted with Republican red stripes, and undergoing testing by Konstantin Rozanof, who was a member of a French technical mission in Spain. Note the wide red bands wrapping around the wing leading edges.

This is the prototype Messerschmitt Bf 109V-5, alias 6-3 in Spain, undergoing serious maintenance at Tablada in early 1937. Noticeable is the chamois-topped funnel plugged into the oil supply aperture. This aircraft seems not to have been destroyed in Spain but as it was a prototype it could have been returned to the factory for examination after use.

In July 1937 on Vitoria airfield, 2.J/88 waits for the first great offensive sustained by the unit since its conversion onto the Bf 109. Right is 6-3, otherwise the prototype V5. The crews laze comfortably in the shade, and all is still calm. Note the great thickness of the wing disc's white crosses, at a time when the 109 was still not very well known by the aviators on its own side.

A view of Bf 109B-1 numbered 6-7, before the bad landing performed by its usual pilot, Norbert Flegel, the first time he landed on La Albericia airfield, recently captured from the Republicans after the surrender of Santander. The aircraft appears to be finished in a mixture of natural metal panels and grey paint. Note the wooden propeller.

And this is Bf 109B-1 6-7 after the bad landing performed by its usual pilot, Norbert Flegel, the first time he landed on La Albericia airfield. Although serious, the damage was repairable and the machine later flew in the hands of Werner Mölders of 3.J/88.

Messerschmitt Bf 109B 6-10 was allocated to *Unteroffizier* Ernst Mratzek in March 1937 while he was with VJ/88. He was killed, however, in a Ju 52 crash on 30 April 1937, so those kill markings cannot be his. There are fourteen such markings on the fin and only one pilot in the Legion got that many: Werner Mölders. However, the machine also carries the top hat emblem of 2.J/88, in which Mölders never served, but Günther Lützow did and probably flew this aircraft and was credited with five victories. But why so many kill markings?

This port side view of Bf 109B 6-10 clearly shows that the kill markings were applied to both sides of the fin, as well as the top hat of 2.J/88. The only pilot of *2 Staffel* to gain kills in double figures was Peter Boddem with ten official victories. Did he score more? Or are the markings the work of an over-optimistic crew chief? Note the name on the nose, *Altertum* (*Antiquity*). What significance does that have? Perhaps it had been relegated to training on account of age, yet it appears to be in pristine condition.

A closer view of the nose of Bf 109B 6-10 showing the shadow-style name. It is apparent that the aircraft is finished in the early grey-green and light blue finish. Despite being one of the earliest Bf 109s to enter service, it survived to be passed on to the Spanish air force after the civil war. That perhaps is the clue to the name and the tail markings, the aircraft may have just been "bulled up" prior to handover.

The Messerschmitt Bf-109B-1 6-10 in flight. This is the first period of markings, with the whole registration painted behind the fuselage disc, and the big white crosses on the wing. Later, the Legion Condor received a batch of B-2 aircraft, equipped with a two-blade variable pitch metal propeller. This aircraft and 6-16 may have been the longest lasting B series 109s as both survived until 1944.

The new Bf 109B-1s ready for a period of flight testing on Seville-Tablada airfield. Behind 6-13 is clearly visible 6•11, otherwise prototype V4.

An excellent side view of *Oberfeldwebel* Otto Polenz's Bf 109B-1 shortly after its capture by the Republicans. Note that it still retains the wooden propeller.

View into the cockpit of a Bf 109B-1, number 6-15, showing the instruments and the manual gun cocking handles.

This shows the cowling guns of a later Bf 109B-2 or D model which differs in various details with the B-1. The most important is the change from manual gun cocking from within the cockpit to an electrical system.

This closer view of the guns of a Bf 109B-1 shows that the early models used manual cocking to load their cowling machine guns, just as in the Great War. The rod to one of the handles can be seen protruding from the tube in the bottom left corner. These no longer appeared on the B-2 and subsequent models with the introduction of an electrical system.

This Bf 109B-2 is probably 6-19, which arrived in Spain in July 1937 and was assigned to 3.J/88. It was one of the first Messerschmitts of the Condor to use the VDM metal propeller.

Bf 109B 6-38 was one of the last of the July 1937 batch. The white cross in the fuselage cockade identifies it as a 1.J/88 aircraft at the time under Harro Harder's command, and it is known that it was flown in 1937 by *Unteroffizier* Ernst Terry. This was a lucky aircraft, as it survived its time with the Legion and was transferred to the 1st Escuadrilla of the Spanish *Grupo 5-G-5*.

This 1.J/88 aircraft, coded 6-42, was one of the few which got to Spain wearing a green livery, probably in the haste of the transfer. Its color scheme adapted rather well to the northern provinces of Spain, but once the Legion got back to the central area, it had to be repainted in classic RLM grey.

A blurred in-flight shot of Bf 109B 6-42, apparently now wearing its new grey camouflage.

An indifferent picture but one of few known of Bf 109 6-47. This may be one of the extremely rare "C" variants. It carries a single white "kill" bar on the fin.

A rather better known aircraft, this is Bf 109D 6-51 flown by twelve-victory ace Wolfgang Schellmann of 1.J/88. This might explain why he received the first "D" model to be delivered to the Legion.

Ground crew pose in front of a Bf 109, alleged to be that of Werner Mölders during repairs at the Legion depot in León towards the end of 1938. The aircraft sports seven victory bars on the fin and a dark rudder, possibly a replacement in the then standard *Luftwaffe* dark green.

6-52 of 2.J/88 tucked in close. The pilot appears to be wearing a side cap and has opened the sliding panel in the canopy and stuck his head out to get a better view. No other details known.

Feverish activity for 1.J/88 between two sorties on the Northern front. In the foreground is 6-50, with 6-44 and 6-38 visible in the background. Note the very clean condition of the aircraft.

A worn Bf 109 6-53 of 2.J/88 awaits the next mission.

Bf 109 6-56 was used by in combat by both Handrick and Schellmann, yet survived to be handed over to the Spanish air force at the end of the war, as shown by the emblem of 5-G-5 on the fin. Spanish officers are in the foreground.

A close view of probably the best known nose in Spain, that of Bf 109 6-56 while being used by *Major* Gotthard Hendrick, who had won the gold medal in the pentathlon in the Berlin Olympics of 1936. The extreme front of the spinner is painted in bands of red, yellow and red, the Spanish colors. On the opposite face was a similar Olympic device but with the date 1940 and a well-judged question mark.

Bf 109 6-60 attempts to find some shade among the olive trees at La Cenia in summer 1938. This was the favored mount of *Unteroffizier* Herbert Schob, a six-victory ace with 2.J/88. 6-56 sits in the background.

This view of Bf 109 6-60 being flown by Schob shows that unit and personal emblems were mostly confined to the port side. Three white victory bars are just visible on the fin, suggesting that the date is beween 16 November and 30 December 1938, the dates on which Schob scored his third and fourth kills. Location is probably Sanjurjo.

This Bf-109D, 6-74, was most probably being scrapped (the wings and tailplane are already off) after major structural damage to the fuselage spine which has been broken, probably due to a combat overstress. The place seems to be La Cenia, the time being summer 1938. The dark areas of paint left where the flying surfaces have been removed are noteworthy.

This 109D seems to be 6-76. Notice two victory bars on its tail fin. Date and location unknown.

Over the Ebro front, a *Kette* from 3.J/88 is flying what would now be called a CAP (combat air patrol). Aircraft are number 6-82 (formerly Bertram's aircraft in 1.J/88), 6-83, 6-84 and 6-??. This loose four- aircraft formation was introduced in Spain by the great Werner Mölders and revolutionized air warfare.

Mölders's Bf 109D, 6-79, named *Luchs* (*Lynx*), sometime between 19 July and 19 August 1938 when he scored his third and fourth kills.

Messerschmitt Bf 109D 6-84 at dispersal, with two others faintly visible, the one on the left being an "E" model with a three-bladed propeller. The service tent is not far away on the right. Date and location not confirmed.

An almost anonymous Messerschmitt Bf 109E, 6-88, trundles out for takeoff. This was the second such type delivered to Spain, so it may be under test before delivery to the front line.

A close-up view of the Mickey Mouse emblem of 3.J/88. There is a small legend *Grazi* to the left which may give a clue to the identity of the pilot. Note the sliding panel in the canopy. Overall color seems to be a light grey, heavily weathered about the joints in the fuselage skinning.

Bf 109E-3 6-107 of 2.J/88 is put back on its legs after what appears to be a typical landing accident with the type, where the aircraft has veered to starboard and collapsed the leg on that side. The apparently unrepentant pilot (?) adds his weight on the port wing. The spinner appears to be yellow with a red tip—the Spanish colors. Note the natty black panel to disguise the exhaust stain applied by a proud ground crew.

Bf 109E 6-119 was the second aircraft of *Oberleutnant* Siebelt Reents, commander of 1.J/88. The official *Holzauge* ("wooden eye") insignia relating to a Spanish gesture meaning "look out" was applied under the canopy. This plane flew until the end of the 109's service in Spain, 9 September 1951.

A detail view of the "wooden eye" emblem of 1.J/88. Applied in black and white, apparently by means of a stencil, the position of the badge varied from aircraft to aircraft. Usually, it was under the canopy sill as here, but was sometimes applied farther back, below the handgrip.

A retouched picture of Bf 109E 6-117, probably under test at about the time it was handed over to 3.J/88 or soon afterwards when it went to the Spanish air force in April 1939.

Bf-109 number 6-126 was one of the last to arrive in Spain, and representative of the E-3 sub-model. It was still flying in Prat de Llobregat near Barcelona during World War II; 6-107, on the left, was an E-1. Both are seen just a few days after the end of the war in Spain.

This is Bf 109E-3 6-126 at Prat de Llobregat during World War II, in immaculate condition and wearing a slightly different finish to which it was delivered. The main difference between the E-3 and earlier models was the pair of 20-millimeter machine-gun FF wing cannons.

Two of the last E-3s undergoing maintenance, at Prat de Llobregat as the war winds down. The ground crews are obviously under no great pressure. 6-127 is in the background.

An unidentified Bf 109E-3, probably also taken at Prat de Llobregat, as the pilot checks over his guns. The white disc of 1.J/88's emblem can just be made out below the cockpit sill.

A mechanic of 2.J/88 admires "his" Bf 109E-3 at La Cenia at the end of 1938. It was common for many ground crew to think of their charges in this way; the aircraft was only loaned to the pilot. Note the interesting spinner markings.

La Cenia, summer 1938. A mechanic replces the upper cowling panel after work on this Bf-109B-2. The white spinner could mean it is Oesau's aircraft, which was often photographed by the propaganda system, yet oddly enough did not record the actual aircraft number.

In front of a dark-camouflaged Bf-109B-2, Legion Condor personnel and North African troops have gathered for a souvenir picture. Most of the latter appear to be recovering from the loss of an arm, so this visit may be part of the rehabilitation.

Although in most aspects a better aircraft than the Heinkel He 51, the Arado Ar 68 was slightly later in arriving with the *Luftwaffe*. Experience in Spain rapidly convinced the RLM that the day of the biplane was over and sent just three Ar 68Es for trials as night fighters. This unmarked version (no. 1?) is probably seen just after arrival and erection in Spain at Sanjurjo.

# The Arado Ar 68E in Spain

## Type code 9

Though easy to fly, the Arado 68 was no match for the I-15, and its narrow wheel track made night operations trickier than the norm. After some ground attack trials in German hands, the aircraft were passed on to the Spaniards, who did not like them much. This is 9-2.

Here is 9-1, well wrapped up against the elements, which seems to have enjoyed a long career within the Ejercito del Aire, as it was still in service in 1948.

Another view of 9-2. Finish is probably RLM 63 (L40/52) overall. The cockpit cover is in place; this aircraft is not set to fly for a while. Location is probably Sanjurjo.

# Kampfgruppe K/88

## Organization and Operations

**STAB K/88**

In the beginning, the staff formation was led by *Major* Robert Fuchs. In March 1937, it was comprised of a Ju 52 (22-79) whose crew consisted of *Oberleutnant* Wolfgang Riedinger (pilot), *Leutnant* Hans-Joachim Dittler (observer), *Unteroffizier* Max Bleesen, and *Unteroffizier* Josef Traut. There were also two He 70s under the direct command of the *Kampfgruppe* (14-31 and 14-32). The crews consisted of, respectively, *Unteroffizier* Karl-Heinz Oldenburg (pilot), *Leutnant* Wilhelm Balthasar (observer), and *Unteroffizier* Arthur Kahl (engineer); and *Unteroffizier* Ehrardt Stahl (pilot), *Leutnant* Rolf Kaldrack (observer), and *Obergefreiter* Walter Wahnberger (engineer). In the end, the reconnaissance weather forecasting, well practiced and understood by the Germans, was carried out by two Junkers W34s (43-1 and 43-2) with civilian crews, pilot August Haep and observer Dr. Nitze on one and Dr. Schulze-Eckart and Dr. Schulz for the other.

Fuchs soon gained the help of an adjutant, *Hauptmann* Josef Kögl, and a radio and navigation officer, *Leutnant* Ernst König. Later came two new radio operators, *Oberfeldwebel* Werner Eichler and *Unteroffizier* Herbert Schlick. The pair of He 70s was reinforced by another aircraft crewed by *Gefreiter* Alfred Füllgrabe, *Leutnant* Gottfried Thilo, and *Obergefreiter* Willy Wachholz. Upon his departure from Spain, Fuchs was replaced by *Major* Carl von Wechmar, who came from the *Luftkriegsschule* (Air War School), and Kögl by *Leutnant* Hermann Weeber. Then Riedinger and Dittler went back to Germany, being replaced by *Leutnant* Helmut Dennewitz and *Leutnant* Manfred Michaelis.

In turn, *Major* von Wechmar was replaced by *Major* Karl Mehnert, who eventually passed command of K/88 to *Major* Friedrich Haerle on 10 September 1938. No other group leaders were foreseen before the end of the conflict, but when *Major* Haerle's He 111 blew up in flight on 12 March 1939, several days before the end of the war, von Richthofen was obliged to replace him with *Major* Nielsen, who then led the group for the last three weeks.

A well-detailed view of the nose of Heinkel He 111B, 25-15, flown by *Leutnant* Fuhrhop of 1.K/88. This is possibly the most highly decorated Heinkel in the Legion Condor, for not only did it have the semi-official name *Pedro 15*, it was called by its crew *Hümel-Hümel*, which suggests that some of them at least hailed from Hamburg, as well as *Holzauge* (*Clog*). In addition to all this, it had elaborate tail art commemorating the crew's unlucky mascot.

## 1.K/88

At its creation, *1 Staffel* of K/88 was commanded by Heinz Liegnitz, who was sadly shot down and killed on 8 December 1936. By mid-March 1937, the *Staffel*, commanded by *Oberleutnant* von Knauer comprised nine Ju 52s (22-100, 22-94, 22-98, 22-99, 22-84, 22-97, 22-91, 22-90, and 22-95) with the following crews (pilot/observer/radio mechanic):

22-100: *Oberleutnant* Karl von Knauer, *Leutnant* Christian Segnitz, *Oberfeldwebel* Kurt Müller, *Unteroffizier* Heinrich Kost.

22-94: *Unteroffizier* Erick Deckert, *Leutnant* Heinz Schröder, *Feldwebel* Lehmann, *Unteroffizier* Otto Stüber.

22-98: *Unteroffizier* Wienzek, *Leutnant* Rolf Leuchs, *Unteroffizier* Martin Härtel, *Unteroffizier* Emil Pomplun.

22-99: *Leutnant* Hajo Herrmann, *Leutnant* Horst Röbling, *Unteroffizier* Max Witzke, *Unteroffizier* Karl Schorr.

22-84: *Unteroffizier* Willy Dous, *Unteroffizier* Walter Bradel, *Unteroffizier* Fritz Thumser, *Unteroffizier* Richard Günther.

22-97: *Unteroffizier* Edgar Albrecht, *Unteroffizier* Hermann Weeber, *Unteroffizier* Fritz Nüber, *Unteroffizier* Otto Ziesing.

22-91: *Unteroffizier* Herbert Hampe, *Unteroffizier* Ernst Nitsche, *Unteroffizier* Bruno Lange, *Unteroffizier* Bernhard Knobelspiess.

22-90: *Unteroffizier* Alexander Chilla, *Unteroffizier* Hans Hossenfelder, *Unteroffizier* Herbert Schlick, *Unteroffizier* Erich Linke.

22-95: *Unteroffizier* Ewald Rasche, *Unteroffizier* Heinrich Richard, *Unteroffizier* Reinhold Brinner, *Unteroffizier* Gerhard Schneider.

In April, some new crews arrived to allow a rollover of the personnel who were at the expeditionary base. These were observers *Leutnant* Manfred Michaelis, *Leutnant* Siegfried Plate, and *Leutnant* Siegfried Schweinhagen; pilots *Leutnant* Helmut Dennewitz and *Leutnant* Wilhelm Spies (pilots); radio operators *Unteroffizier* Otto Bohnsack and *Unteroffizier* Hans Weng; flight engineers *Unteroffizier* Hans Johansen and *Unteroffizier* Josef Kowatsch. May saw the arrival of *Unteroffizier* Fritz Wiemer (pilot), *Unteroffizier* Gerhard Altmann, and *Oberfeldwebel* Paul Völzer. The changes during June were less intense, with the arrival of a new pilot, *Unteroffizier* Franz Deuerling, and *Unteroffizier* Otto Hesse to reinforce the radio section. At the end of the month, the only new arrival was *Oberfeldwebel* Gottfried Thorley, a radio operator. In July the changeover was more intense, with the arrival of new pilots *Unteroffizier* Alois Link, *Unteroffizier* Johannes Remling, *Unteroffizier* Max Röhring, and *Unteroffizier* Oskar Schmidtke; observers *Leutnant* Dietrich Marwitz, *Leutnant* Kurt Meinecke, *Leutnant* Rolf Pirner and *Leutnant* Andreas Siemens; while the radio operators were reinforced by *Unteroffizier* Heinz Birschel, *Unteroffizier* August Heyer, *Unteroffizier* Walter Spring, and *Unteroffizier* Bruno Thielbein. New navigators arriving were *Unteroffizier* Georg Mayer, *Unteroffizier* Walter Schellhorn, and *Unteroffizier* Gerhard Träber.

During one of the first nighttime engagements in the Spanish war, *1 Staffel* lost an aircraft shot down by a Soviet I-15 on the night of 26–27 July. Remling, Pirner, Schellhorn, and the two radio operators, Heyer and Thielebein, were lost with the aircraft. Replacements continued to arrive regularly, and in the personnel reports, new names were *Leutnant* Gerhard Richter, *Oberfeldwebel* Werner Paul, *Feldwebel* Heinz Harries, and *Unteroffizier* Heinrich Kämper as pilots; Alfred Borchelt and Hermann Sasse as observers; *Oberfeldwebel* Johannes Elster, *Oberfeldwebel* Willy Gau, *Unteroffizier* Gustav Gebel, and *Obergefreiter* Gerhard Endrigkeit as radio operators; and *Unteroffizier* Gerhard Hobbis, *Unteroffizier* Willy Krone, *Gefreiter* Heinz Grune, and *Gefreiter* Willi Sembach as flight engineers.

*Hauptmann* von Knauer handed over command to newcomer *Hauptmann* Heinz Trettner (observer), who, along with *Oberleutnant* Bernhard Staerke (pilot), *Leutnant* Heinrich Fahrenberg, *Oberfeldwebel* Herbert Fenski, and *Unteroffizier* Martin Thomas (observers), *Unteroffizier* Heinz Uhlich (radio), and *Unteroffizier* Herbert Eckstein (flight engineer), constituted the principal crew changes during the month of October. The only new arrival in November was *Unteroffizier* Werner Stechard, a radio operator. By mid-December, new pilot *Unteroffizier* Kurt Schlicht had arrived, along with *Unteroffizier* Bruno Ehm, an observer. New flight engineers were *Unteroffizier* Alfons Welzel and *Obergefreiter* Werner Ensslin and *Obergefreiter* Werner Bremer as reinforcements. Two new radio operators arrived at the end of the month: *Unteroffizier* Gustav Gotto and *Unteroffizier* Hans Baur at the same time as the new *Staffel* commander, *Hauptmann* Hans Schulz, who was an observer.[29]

Thanks to the arrival of *Unteroffizier* Oswald Kroschbersky, *Unteroffizier* Herbert Okelmann, and *Unteroffizier* Günther Hoffman, the year 1938 saw the *Staffel* with ten pilots on the roster. Additional observers to arrive were *Leutnant* Egon Stein and *Leutnant* Erich Langguth, accompanied by flight engineer *Unteroffizier* Helmut Hanisch and radio operators *Unteroffizier* Rudolf Spieler and *Unteroffizier* Franz Gruendges. At the beginning of March, the unit had grown to a dozen complete crews thanks to reinforcements in the shape of *Unteroffizier* Franz Hermann, *Unteroffizier* Gerd Ritter, and *Unteroffizier* Walter Bruenn (pilots); *Leutnant* Joachim Hanebutt, *Leutnant* Fritz von Wuthenau, and *Leutnant* Rolf Hirschberg, and *Unteroffizier* Hans Heinrich (observers); *Unteroffizier* Artur Hildebrandt, *Unteroffizier* Richard Wagner, *Unteroffizier* Willi Fischer, *Unteroffizier* Bruno Laenger, *Unteroffizier* Hans Gloe, and *Obergrefreiter* Eugen Jehlen (flight engineers); and *Unteroffizier* Franz Resch, *Unteroffizier* Walter Schuster, *Obergefreiter* Werner Niemann, and *Obergefreiter* Georg Schweizer (radio operators). By the end of March, yet another new pilot, *Oberleutnant* Kurt Brandt, had been posted in, as well as new observers *Leutnant* Rudolf Strassert and *Unteroffizier* Walter Ostertag. *Unteroffizier* Max Zieringer and *Obergefreiter* Erich Frielingsdorf were additional flight engineers. *Unteroffizier* Fritz Weidenhauer was a radio operator.

Turnover of personnel was surprisingly rapid; the month of April saw the unit with only ten crews. *Oberleutnant* Heinz Lonicer swelled the ranks of the pilots; *Obergefreiter* Bernhard Hintze those of the observers, whereas the radio section received the reinforcement of *Unteroffizier* Bruno Franz. There was a lull in May when only *Unteroffizier* Erich Fettback (flight engineer) arrived. In June *Unteroffizier* Gerhard Nickutt (pilot), *Leutnant* Helmut Wolff and *Leutnant* Hermann Sasse (observers, the latter for his second tour of operations) took up their postings. In addition *Unteroffizier* Heinz Lutter (flight engineer) and radio operators *Unteroffizier* Artur Thiele and *Feldwebel* Hans Keppler were all integrated into the Staffel.

July saw a revolution for *1 Staffel* of K/88: a new leader, new aircraft, and yet more new crews. The unit converted to the Heinkel He 111B-2 and came under the command of *Hauptmann* Karl-Heinrich Heyse, who had been in Spain since April. To fly the Heinkels, there were thirteen complete crews, with pilots *Oberleutnant* Friedjoff von Sichart, *Oberleutnant* Heinz Lonicer (the only survivor from the former unit), *Leutnant* Friedrich Podbielski, *Leutnant* Erich Thiel, *Feldwebel* Bruno Kamsties, *Unteroffizier* Gustav Heinrichs, *Unteroffizier* Johannes van Beckum, *Unteroffizier* Gerhard Schubert, *Unteroffizier* Josef Blase, *Unteroffizier* Günther von Kretowicz, *Unteroffizier* Heinz Schmitz, *Unteroffizier* Alfons Bulach, and *Unteroffizier* Erich Ortlepp. Other than Heyse, the observers included *Leutnant* Walter Ribbeck, *Leutnant* Friedrich Koch, *Leutnant* Helmut Fuhrhopp, *Leutnant* Karl-Ernst Wilke, *Leutnant* Walter Schott, *Leutnant* Fritz von Wuthenau (also a survivor from the Ju flyers), *Leutnant* Rüdiger Thiemann, *Unteroffizier* Helmut Engelke, *Unteroffizier* Gerhard Weinert, and *Unteroffizier* Josej Kozubeck. New radio operators were *Feldwebel* Friedrich Paul, *Unteroffizier* Heinrich Beckmeier, *Unteroffizier* Heinz Wickhorst, *Unteroffizier* Alfred Wittke, *Unteroffizier* Hermann Drees, *Unteroffizier* Max Bassmann, *Unteroffizier* Helmut Matz, *Unteroffizier* Hans Bremer, *Unteroffizier* Walter Cramer, *Unteroffizier* Heinrich Pippig, *Unteroffizier* Ugo Zimmermann, and *Obergefreiter* Johann Graf. Finally, the ranks of the flight engineers were augmented by *Feldwebel* Herbert Hetzel, *Unteroffizier* Friedrich Lange, *Unteroffizier* August Kaiser, *Unteroffizier* Otto Marx, *Unteroffizier* Edgar Warzecha, *Unteroffizier* Helmut Plate, *Unteroffizier* Johann Weger, *Unteroffizier* Fritz Gundlack, *Unteroffizier* Bruno Laengner, *Unteroffizier* Fritz Weigel and *Unteroffizier* Paul Hätzel.

In August, *Unteroffizier* Hans Bleich (a pilot), *Leutnant* Hermann Rosenthal (observer), *Unteroffizier* Ernst Grützmacher (radio) and flight engineers *Unteroffizier* Otto Pichard, *Unteroffizier* Walter Börner, and *Obergefreiter* Erich Quesdorf arrived in the *Staffel*. The unit then numbered just ninety-nine members. New pilots arrived in September: *Leutnant* Gerhard Czernik, *Leutnant* Hermann Hogeback, *Feldwebel* Rudolf Kollenda, *Unteroffizier* Heinrich Waschkowski, *Unteroffizier* Fritz Tertel, *Unteroffizier* Walter Klaue, and *Obergefreiter* Karl Detlefsen. New observers were *Leutnant* Max Pröbst, *Leutnant* Albrecht Otto Schmoelder, *Leutnant* Otto Harms, *Feldwebel* Rudolf Henkel, *Feldwebel* Herbert Poppenhagen, *Unteroffizier* Rudolf Deicke, and *Unteroffizier* Wolfgang Grunert. The radio operators also changed for the most part with the arrival of *Unteroffizier* Albert Hein, *Unteroffizier* Kurt Heinze, *Unteroffizier* Otto Leyk, *Unteroffizier* Georg Adam, *Unteroffizier* Gerhard Pach, and *Obergefreiter* Adolf Düring. The engineers absorbed *Unteroffizier* Robert Spies, *Unteroffizier* Martin Schwarzer, *Unteroffizier* Rolf Heilbronner, *Unteroffizier* Leo Klawunn, *Unteroffizier* Josef Spreng, *Obergefreiter* Kurt Herrmann, and *Gefreiter* Gerhard Hentschel.[30]

In October, *Unteroffizier* Johannes Reinirkens and *Gefreiter* Josef Bisping arrived as radio operators. In November, it was the turn of *Oberleutnant* Ernst Püttmann, an observer, and in December came pilot *Leutnant* Erich von Werthern, the observer *Feldwebel* Willi Hübner, the radio operator *Unteroffizier* Edwin Eisermann, and the engineer *Unteroffizier* Hans Schrödel. By then, the unit was under the command of *Oberleutnant* Püttmann. Since the conversion to the He 111, there had been fewer flying personnel changes, and even towards the end of the war, the rhythm of these altered little.[31]

At the end of January 1939, there was a new pilot, *Unteroffizier* Anton Hörwick; a new observer, *Leutnant*. Werner Lemme; a new radio operator, *Unteroffizier* Max Schott; and four new engineers, *Unteroffizier* Kurt Herrmann, *Unteroffizier* Gerhard Hentschel, *Unteroffizier* Peter Müller, and *Unteroffizier* Helmut Hetzel. Three new pilots, *Unteroffizier* Hans Czekay, *Unteroffizier* Helmut Peterheit, and *Unteroffizier* Herbert Knaebel, were present at the end of February, even though the *Staffel* had no more than

Currently undergoing an overhaul in the Tablada workshops, Ju 52 22-86 is an aircraft from 1.K/88. It was later used on the Kleinbahn transport shuttle service between Spain and Germany. It was on such a flight that it went missing on 24 October 1938. Note the large St. Andrew's cross which was applied to the fuselage of many of the Ju 52s. The purpose of this is unclear. It could be a misinterpretation of markings orders, or it may only relate to the early period of activities and was to identify the still relatively few "friendly" aircraft, or possibly, it could have identified the bomber versions of the Ju 52.

eight crews. On the side of the observers, there were *Oberleutnant* Eberhard Bertelsmann, *Oberleutnant* Erich Schlecht, and *Leutnant* Otto Köhnke. Among the radio operators were *Oberfeldwebel* Walter Menzel, *Unteroffizier* Edmund Puhl, and *Unteroffizier* Günther Schmidt, while *Feldwebel* Walter Scheller, *Unteroffizier* Johann Ludzinski, and *Unteroffizier* Hans Salzsieder joined the flight engineers.

Even as the end of the war came into sight in March 1939, new arrivals continued to arrive, including pilots *Oberleutnant* Otto Reimers, *Feldwebel* Josef Rederer, *Unteroffizier* Erich Caspari, *Unteroffizier* Kurt Bitterlich, and *Unteroffizier* Hermann Veit; observers *Oberleutnant* Siegfried Langer, *Leutnant* Paul-Georg Schrader, *Leutnant* Erich Seebode, and *Leutnant* Ernst Schifferings. New radio operators were *Feldwebel* Bruno Falkenhagen, *Feldwebel* Fritz Jakobsmeier, *Unteroffizier* Alfred Waldmann, *Unteroffizier* Kurt Wacker, and *Unteroffizier* Johannes Bredtmeyer. *Unteroffizier* Gerhard Häntsch, *Unteroffizier* Anton Lamm, *Unteroffizier* Hans Rösl, and *Unteroffizier* Johann Weyer were the last flight engineers.

## 2.K/88

At the creation of K/88, the second *Staffel* was commanded by *Oberleutnant* Brasser. In mid-March 1937 it comprised nine Ju 52s numbered 22-88, 22-89, 22-87, 22-83, 22-80, 22-86, 22-85, 22-70, and 22-81 with the following crews (pilot/observer/radio operator/navigator-flight engineer):

22-88: *Unteroffizier* Rump, *Leutnant* Bodenberger, *Unteroffizier* Walter Schulze, *Unteroffizier* Kurt Huth.

22-89: *Unteroffizier* Franke, *Leutnant* Klauss, *Unteroffizier* Bohnhoff, *Feldwebel* Hurst.

22-87: *Unteroffizier* Frey, *Leutnant* Siehe, *Oberfeldwebel* Wolff, *Unteroffizier* Bendrich.

22-83: *Unteroffizier* Alfred Dreher, *Leutnant* Otto-Heinrich Wildau, *Unteroffizier* Albert Markgraf, *Unteroffizier* Friedrich Götze.

22-80: *Oberleutnant* Graf zu Castell, *Leutnant* Savade, *Unteroffizier* Komp, *Unteroffizier* Eckert.

22-86: *Unteroffizier* Heinz Laschinski, *Leutnant* Fritz Aufhammer, *Unteroffizier* Ernst Köster, *Unteroffizier* Ludwig Trageser.

22-85: *Unteroffizier* Ernst Eggert, *Leutnant* Erwin Jäger, *Unteroffizier* Fritz Hey-mann, *Unteroffizier* Ernst Köhne.

22-70: *Oberleutnant* Hans-Henning von Beust, *Leutnant* Schweinhagen, *Unteroffizier* Stützel, *Unteroffizier* Deutschmann.

22-81: *Oberleutnant* von Nordeck, *Hauptmann* Brasser, *Unteroffizier* Dahmann, *Unteroffizier* Hessler.

The last aircraft on the list suffered a disastrous accident on 9 March at Bejar. Dahmann was killed, the rest of the crew, including the *Staffel* commander, Brasser, were out of action for several months. Consequently, *Oberleutnant* von Beust took over command of the *Staffel*. For once, a pilot commanded a bomber unit, whereas normally the responsibility was entrusted to an observer, although there had already been an exception with von Moreau.[32]

A little while afterwards, two new pilots arrived, *Unteroffizier* Walter von Felde and *Gefreiter* Engelbert Heiner, as well as two new observers, *Leutnant* Wolfgang von Poellnitz and *Leutnant* Julius Rauchenberger; two new radio operators, *Unteroffizier* Arthur Tenz and *Unteroffizier* Werner Zorn; and two new navigator/flight engineers, *Unteroffizier* Albert Mayn and *Unteroffizier* Adolf Reuter. There were then only six aircraft available in the unit.

In November 1937, things began to improve, with the imminent arrival of a better aeroplane, the Heinkel 111 and the integration into the *Staffel* of a new pilot, *Leutnant* Rudi Westhaus. Also arriving were two new observers, *Leutnant* Friedrich-Diethelm von Eichel-Streiber and *Unteroffizier* Hugo Jacob; a new radio operator, *Unteroffizier* Erich Lucke; and three new engineers, *Unteroffizier* Rudolf Lödel, *Unteroffizier* Karl Müller, and *Unteroffizier* Alfred Paulsberg. In December 1937, von Beust passed on command of the *Staffel* to another pilot, *Oberleutnant* Rolf Schroeter, just as some new crews arrived: pilots *Leutnant* Wilhelm Spiess, *Oberfeldwebel* Kurt Bartel, *Feldwebel* Friedrich Meyer zu Düte, *Unteroffizier* Wilhelm Walter, and *Unteroffizier* Walter Dünnebier; the observers *Leutnant* Joachim Bismarck, *Leutnant* Hans-Horst Graf, *Leutnant* Bernhard Granicky, *Leutnant* Helmut Schüttke, *Leutnant* Rudolf Strasser, and *Feldwebel* Hans Seidel; radio operators *Feldwebel* Heinz Krutzki, *Oberfeldwebel* Gerhard Schulz, *Unteroffizier* Kurt Haase, *Unteroffizier* Karl Haugg, *Unteroffizier* Paul Henze, *Unteroffizier* Heinz Vogler, *Unteroffizier* Franz Peters, and *Unteroffizier* Paul Schick; and the flight engineers *Unteroffizier* Friedrich Carlsen, *Unteroffizier* Anton Janowski, *Unteroffizier* Heinrich Abbetmeyer, *Unteroffizier* Karl Goldmann, *Unteroffizier* Arthur Weyers, and *Obergefreiter* Walter Ziehmer. Shortly before the end of December, pilot *Obergefreiter* Erwin Hoster and observers *Feldwebel* Bernhard Köberich and *Unteroffizier* Fritz Selzer arrived.

With the delivery of the new He 111s in January 1938, 2 *Staffel* saw its personnel roster grow with the addition of new crews: *Leutnant* Sighart Dommer, *Leutnant* Peter Lehwess-Litzmann, *Oberfeldwebel* Wilhelm Oppitz, *Unteroffizier* Helmut Bremicker, and *Unteroffizier* Alexander Stegen (all pilots); *Leutnant* Gerhard Stauch, *Leutnant* Karl-August Petersen,

*Leutnant* Christian Koebrich, and *Leutnant* Erwin Wienroth (observers); *Unteroffizier* Alois Kagermeier, *Unteroffizier* Ewald Lange, *Obergefreiter* Rudolf Engel, and *Obergefreiter* Hans Fickmann (radio operators); and *Unteroffizier* Walter Stemmler (an engineer). In February, the following arrived: *Unteroffizier* Hermann Giesen (pilot); *Hauptmann* Karl Wolfien; and observers *Leutnant* Alexander von Blomberg and *Leutnant* Karl Köstlin. *Unteroffizier* Richard Hahne and *Obergefreiter* Hans Zitzmann were radio operators while *Unteroffizier* Rudolf Bronitzki and *Obergefreiter* Hubert Wörz were both engineers. Once again, it should be noted that, as in the case of von Moreau's command, the *Staffelkapitän* (*Oberleutnant* Rolf Schröter) was temporarily lower in rank than his chief observer (*Hauptmann* Karl Wolfien). Also noteworthy is the active part members of certain illustrious families took in the war, such as the son of *General* von Blomberg. Nonetheless the exception did not last long, and at the end of March 1938, Wolfien was the leader of the unit with two new pilots, *Leutnant* Horst von Besser and *Leutnant* Albrecht Wichmann; two new observers, *Leutnant* Wilibald Liebech and *Unteroffizier* Karl Dräger; two new radio operators, *Feldwebel* Hans Gauweiler and *Unteroffizier* Walter Gietz; and three new navigator/flight engineers, *Unteroffizier* Wilhelm Tenninger, *Unteroffizier* Willi Fisher, and *Unteroffizier* Heinz Burkhart.

A single new crew arrived in April 1938: *Feldwebel* Ernst Kröner, *Leutnant* Rudolf Anders, *Unteroffizier* Erich Blüher, *Obergefreiter* Karl Warmuth. Meanwhile, *Freiherr* (Baron) von Blomberg was promoted to *Oberleutnant*. In May, the turnover of crews remained at a trickle with the renewal of only a single one (*Unteroffizier* Walter Hasenbein, *Oberleutnant* Willy Henke, *Unteroffizier* Hans Kempmann, and *Unteroffizier* Hans Ahrens). In June, the unit only possessed nine aircraft, Wichmann was promoted to *Oberleutnant*, and only one new pilot arrived, *Leutnant* Karl Bechhaus.

On the battlefields, the course of events began to accelerate, and in July, *2 Staffel* found itself with no fewer than fifteen complete crews plus several reserves. In this manner, the following personnel arrived: *Oberleutnant* Rolf Jung, *Feldwebel* Rudolf Kollenda, *Unteroffizier* Heinrich Behne, *Unteroffizier* Franz Hermann, *Unteroffizier* Gerd Ritter, and *Unteroffizier* Gerhard Nickutt (pilots); *Leutnant* Fritz Kuechle, *Leutnant* Hans Pawelcik, *Leutnant* Erich Langguth, *Leutnant* Helmut Wolff, *Leutnant* Rolf Hirschberg, *Unteroffizier* Walter Ostertag, and *Unteroffizier* Gerhard Mueller (observers). *Unteroffizier* Bruno Franz, *Unteroffizier* Walter Schuster, *Unteroffizier* Arthur Thiele, *Unteroffizier* Werner Niemann, *Unteroffizier* Fritz Weidenhammer, and *Obergefreiter* Max Pfeiffer were all radio operators, while *Unteroffizier* Kurt Stengel, *Unteroffizier* Hans Gloe, *Unteroffizier* Georg Kahle, and *Unteroffizier* Heinz Lutter were flight engineers. In

August, new crews arrived with the following: pilots *Leutnant* Walter Fläming and *Unteroffizier* Hans Heinz; observers *Leutnant* Ernst Süss and *Unteroffizier* Horst von Prondzynski; radio operators *Oberfeldwebel* August Leicht, *Unteroffizier* Alfred Meisel, and *Unteroffizier* Franz Repke; and navigator/flight engineers *Unteroffizier* Werner Le Bret and *Unteroffizier* Bruno Albrecht.

In September 1938, 2 *Staffel* gained a new chief, the observer *Hauptmann* Kurt-Eckhard Allolio at the same time as some new crews: *Leutnant* August Speckmann, *Feldwebel* Heinrich Meier, *Feldwebel* Heinz Domack, *Unteroffizier* Karl Riemschneider, *Unteroffizier* Max Raith, *Unteroffizier* Josef-Rudolf Jansen, and *Obergefreiter* Hans Kopf (pilots); *Leutnant* Heinz Gehrke, *Leutnant* Wilhelm Lazarus, *Leutnant* Paul Zimmermann, *Leutnant* Heinz Axe, *Leutnant* Joachim Kleinfeldt, *Unteroffizier* Peter Matz, and *Gefreiter* Wilhelm Gernhold (observers); *Unteroffizier* Erich Maar, *Unteroffizier* Ernst Eichelbaum, *Unteroffizier* Hans Auracher, *Unteroffizier* Georg Engel, *Unteroffizier* Gustav Stöver, *Obergefreiter* Georg-Heinrich Gass, and *Gefreiter* Walter Janowitz (radio operators); *Unteroffizier* Friedrich Manske, *Unteroffizier* Karl-Heinz Rauschert, *Unteroffizier* Karl Marschler, *Unteroffizier* Adolf Strasser, *Unteroffizier* Werner Vedder, *Unteroffizier* Willi Weisse, and *Obergefreiter* Paul Meyer (engineers). After so many new arrivals, there were few changes in the composition of the crews up until December 1938.

In December, two new pilots arrived, *Oberleutnant* Hans-Joachim Gabriel (who had been in Spain since October) and *Unteroffizier* Heinz Paech, as well as two new observers, *Leutnant* Walter Meister and *Unteroffizier* Hans Schwarz; two new radio operators, *Feldwebel* Herbert Pauli and *Unteroffizier* Gustav Kollig; three new navigator/flight engineers, *Unteroffizier* Fritz Cellarius, *Unteroffizier* Rudolf Hacker, and *Unteroffizier* Willi Steidel. On 4 January 1939, the *Staffel* lost an aircraft shot down over Tarragona, which resulted in the deaths of *Unteroffizier* Albrecht and *Unteroffizier* von Prondzynski; the last days of the war were decidedly no picnic. Then, on the twenty-fifth, the *Staffel* lost another He 111, shot down by flak over Barcelona, *Leutnant* Meister being killed in the battle. In the course of the month of January, 2 *Staffel* acquired several more aircrew replacements: pilots *Unteroffizier* Helmut Pliefke, *Unteroffizier* Ernst Müller, and *Unteroffizier* Hans-Karl Schröder; observers *Oberleutnant* Reinhard Günzel, *Leutnant* Karl Laudenbach, and *Leutnant* Hans Bröcker; radio operators *Unteroffizier* Eugen Zimmermann, *Unteroffizier* Walter Magerhans, and *Unteroffizier* Helmut Posselt; and navigators *Unteroffizier* Helmut von Borstel, *Unteroffizier* Anton Sebald, *Unteroffizier* Erich Schmidtke, and *Unteroffizier* Friedrich Koletzko.

The General Staff of the Legion already knew that the war was virtually finished, and that to profit from the occasion, above all for training officers and NCOs, it was necessary to accelerate the rate of rotation of personnel. Therefore, in February 1939, the following air crews were posted to the unit: pilots *Oberleutnant* Gottfried Buchholz, *Unteroffizier* Heinz Wolpers, *Unteroffizier* Anton Besendorfer, *Unteroffizier* Hans Bartesch, *Unteroffizier* Werner Herschenröther, and *Unteroffizier* Günter Wagner (this latter had been in Spain since November 1938); observers *Oberleutnant* Helmut Rammig, *Oberleutnant* Hans Delinsky, and *Oberleutnant* Bruno Davids, *Leutnant* Karl Brandt, and *Leutnant* Hans Bröcker; radio operators *Feldwebel* Werner Thalmann, *Unteroffizier* Johannes Reinirkens (in Spain since October), *Unteroffizier* Heinz Franke, *Unteroffizier* Georg Milbradt, and *Unteroffizier* Albert Dietl; and engineers *Unteroffizier* Franz Kyrich, *Unteroffizier* Willi Woczyns, and *Unteroffizier* Walter Hanke. On the ninth, the He 111 of *Hauptmann* Allolio suffered an engine failure and was forced to make an emergency landing resulting in an aircraft 100 percent destroyed and a *Staffel* commander painfully (although lightly) injured in a most delicate part of his anatomy.

The last days brought the last changes, and 2 *Staffel* changed command, with *Hauptmann* Freiherr von Buttlar-Brandenfels, an observer, taking over. Replacement pilots arriving were *Feldwebel* Adolf Schied, *Unteroffizier* Hans-Karl Schröder, *Unteroffizier* Friedlieb Blauert, and *Gefreiter* Gerhard Seemann. Replacement observers were *Leutnant* Günter Helm and *Leutnant* Fritz Kunkel; radio operators to arrive were *Unteroffizier* Walter Ruff, *Unteroffizier* Bruno Schlesiger, and *Unteroffizier* Franz Eggert, and finally, the last navigator/flight engineers were *Unteroffizier* Erich Bläser and *Unteroffizier* Ferdinand Jürgens.

## 3.K/88

When the *Gruppe* was first formed, 3 *Staffel* was under the command of *Hauptmann* Kraft von Delmensingen. In mid-March 1937, 3 *Staffel* comprised eight aircraft numbered 22-77, 22-76, 22-71, 22-73, 22-93, 22-92, 22-82 and 22-75, which were crewed as follows (pilot/observer/radio operator/flight engineer):

22-77: *Hauptmann* Kraft von Delmensingen, *Leutnant* Walter von Keisenberg, *Feldwebel* Leonhardt Dirschner, *Gefreiter* Heinrich Nothaft.

22-76: *Unteroffizier* Fritz Berndt, *Leutnant* Leo Falk, *Unteroffizier* Walter Brötzmann, *Unteroffizier* Gerhard Dörfel.

22-71: *Unteroffizier* Edmund Riebel, *Leutnant* Erich Laszig, *Unteroffizier* Georg Lisczik, *Unteroffizier* Horst Streit.

22-73: *Unteroffizier* Rudolf Göpfert, *Leutnant* Rolf Altenmüller, *Unteroffizier* Georg Schwenzer, *Unteroffizier* Hans Clausen.

22-93: *Unteroffizier* Friedrich Pfeiffer, *Leutnant* Herbert Mosbach, *Unteroffizier* Paul Remmlinger, *Unteroffizier* Hans Moritz.

22-92: *Oberleutnant* Adolf Koch, *Leutnant* Willy Gockel, *Unteroffizier* Hans Freund, *Oberfeldwebel* Heinz Böttcher.

22-82: *Unteroffizier* Josef Schimpel, *Leutnant* Georg Pfeiffer, *Feldwebel* Alfred Burghadt, *Unteroffizier* Arthur Scheich.

22-75: *Unteroffizier* Werner Kühnle, *Leutnant* Fritz Engelke, *Unteroffizier* Fritz Ziegler, *Unteroffizier* Erich Emhardt.

Having one aircraft less than the other units, *3 Staffel* had a reserve of personnel in the form of *Unteroffizier* Ferdinand Schmitt (pilot), *Leutnant* Treumund Engelhardt (observer), and *Obergefreiter* Oskar Lösch (mechanic). In May, an additional pilot, *Unteroffizier* Paul Ziep, arrived, along with an observer, *Leutnant* Karl-Gustav Schmidt; a radio operator, *Feldwebel* Herbert Barowski; and two flight engineers, *Oberfeldwebel* Adolf Hermann and *Unteroffizier* Bernard Sohl. Profiting from the arrival of a number of new He 111s, the *Staffel* was the second unit (after VB/88) to convert to the new bomber.

In June, Gockel was detached to Stab/88 in exchange for observer *Leutnant* Oskar Schmidt. At the same time, *Oberleutnant* Adolf Koch assumed command of the unit, as the following new personnel began to arrive: new pilots *Unteroffizier* Heinz Finke, *Unteroffizier* Rudolf Dedlow, and *Feldwebel* Kurt Herzog; new observers *Leutnant* Hann-Jost Hüttenhain, *Leutnant* Rudolf Krochmann, and *Leutnant* Willy Peters; new radio operators *Unteroffizier* Willy Knopf, *Unteroffizier* Heinz Meyer, *Unteroffizier* Hans Vick, and *Unteroffizier* Helmut Wolf; and flight engineers *Oberfeldwebel* Otto Blank, *Unteroffizier* Werner Heuer, *Unteroffizier* Horst Streit, and *Obergefreiter* Heinrich Schreyer. Heinrich Nothaft was in the meantime promoted to *Unteroffizier*. In July 1937, two pilots arrived, *Oberleutnant* Wolfgang Schlenkhoff and *Unteroffizier* August Sasse, as well as two observers, *Leutnant* Ullrich Steffen and *Leutnant* Heinrich Stallbaum; a new radio operator, *Unteroffizier* Emil Freek; and a new mechanic, *Unteroffizier* Egon Ahrens. On the night of 25–26 July, the *Staffel* lost a Ju 52 shot down by Republican night fighters. All of the crew of Falk, Berndt, Böttcher, Brötzmann, and Ubelhack were killed.

In August 1937, *Oberleutnant* Schlenkhoff took over command of *3 Staffel*; new air crew arrived comprised of pilots *Oberfeldwebel* Willy Leppin and *Feldwebel* Erwin Niederer; observers *Leutnant* Ottmar Hollmann and *Leutnant* Paul Waechter; radio operators *Unteroffizier* Walter Löwe and *Unteroffizier* Paul Schmidt; and flight engineer *Obergefreiter* Günter Stahlberg. *Leutnant* Georg Pfeiffer joined Gockel at Stab/88.

There were few staff movements noted in September 1937. New among the pilots was *Leutnant* Peter Lehwess-Litzmann; new among the observers were *Leutnant* Ulrich Knauth, *Leutnant* Ernst Heinrich, and *Leutnant* Peter-Heinz Nolte; new among the radio operators was *Unteroffizier* Joachim Winter; and new among the flight engineers were *Unteroffizier* Wilhelm Maack, *Unteroffizier* Heinrich Manck, and *Gefreiter* Herbert Mücke. In October, the unit was reduced to seven aircraft. Just two new observers arrived, *Leutnant* Kurt Geisler and Edmund Sorg, and one mechanic, *Unteroffizier* Erich Ebert, while *Leutnant* Krochmann was detached to Stab/88. The month of November saw no change at all except for the departure of *Leutnant* Pfeiffer to Stab/88.

The end of 1937 saw the arrival of some new names at *3 Staffel* at the same time as the first He 111s of the unit. Among the new pilots were *Oberleutnant* Bernhard Mielke, *Leutnant* Peter Litzmann, *Feldwebel* Martin Winter, *Unteroffizier* Wilhelm Bokeloh, *Unteroffizier* Hans Seewald, *Unteroffizier* Erich Slotosch, *Unteroffizier* Herbert Streicher, and *Gefreiter* Wilhelm Volke. New observers were *Leutnant* Heinz Krahl, *Leutnant* Hans Wolf, *Leutnant* Joachim Gerstenmeyer, and *Feldwebel* Walter Müller. Replacement radio operators were *Feldwebel* Herbert Burian, *Unteroffizier* Karl-Heinz Becker, *Unteroffizier* Paul Walter, *Obergefreiter* Paul Knappe, and *Obergefreiter* Thomas Wartner, while new engineers were *Unteroffizier* Wilhelm Holzkamm, *Unteroffizier* Hans Nielsen, *Unteroffizier* Heinrich Nicklaus, *Unteroffizier* Gerhard Payenberg, and *Unteroffizier* Walter Schütz.

1938 started with a new chief, Schlenkhoff only just having settled in before he handed over command to *Hauptmann* Heinz Fisher. Also three new pilots arrived: *Leutnant* Georg Teske, *Leutnant* Werner tum Suden, and *Capitán*[32] Ricardo Guerrero, who was to form the first Spanish crew on He 111s. As always, there were new aircrew. Among the observers there were *Unteroffizier* Hans Schönemann and the Spaniard *Alférez*[33] Alejandro Fernández. New radio operators were *Unteroffizier* Hubert Ziermann, *Unteroffizier* Helmut Maaz, *Unteroffizier* Friedrich Plückelmann, and *Teniente*[34] Alfonso Garcia Quintano. New flight engineers were *Unteroffizier* Konrad Rieder, *Unteroffizier* Heinrich Heidt, and *Sargento*[35] Ervigio Gamazo. In February, the following arrived: *Unteroffizier* Hermann Janzik (pilot); *Leutnant* Rolf Richter and *Leutnant* Siegfried Lamprecht (observers); *Unteroffizier* Hans Retzko and *Unteroffizier* Herbert Steiner (radio operators); and *Unteroffizier* Werner Grahmann and *Unteroffizier* Alfred Tschage (flight engineers). The Spanish crew had already left after having tried the He 111 in action. In March, *Feldwebel* Martin Ziegler, a pilot, arrived, as did *Obergefreiter* Kurt Goldau (a radio operator). In April, it was the turn of *Unteroffizier* Willi Winkler (pilot) and *Leutnant* Kurt Zecher (observer) and of *Unteroffizier* Karl Heber and

*Unteroffizier* Wilhelm Lutz (flight engineers). In May, yet another new crew was posted in: *Leutnant* Emil Rödel, *Unteroffizier* Rudolf Deicke, *Oberfeldwebel* Walter Lange, and *Unteroffizier* Martin Schwarzer.

Two new pilots arrived in June, *Unteroffizier* Heinz Kühme and *Unteroffizier* Günther Dorn, as well as two new observers, *Leutnant* Joachim Schwarz and *Leutnant* Gottfried Hager; two radio operators, *Unteroffizier* Herbert Tittel and *Unteroffizier* Fritz Schackert; and two flight engineers, *Unteroffizier* Wilhelm Augustin and *Unteroffizier* Paul Henkel. July saw yet more personnel changes, with the arrival of pilots *Oberleutnant* Günther Hoffmann, *Oberleutnant* Kurt Brandt, *Leutnant* Heinz Willer, *Unteroffizier* Walter Brünn, and *Obergefreiter* Heinz Grothe. New observers were *Oberleutnant* Thilo von Janson, *Leutnant* Ludwig Braun, *Leutnant* Joachim Hanebutt, *Leutnant* Gottfried Hager, *Leutnant* Joachim Schwarz, and *Unteroffizier* Hans Heinrich. These were accompanied by radio operators Fw Hans Keppler, *Unteroffizier* Hans Bauer, *Unteroffizier* Franz Resch, *Unteroffizier* Karl Frischling, and *Obergefreiter* Fritz Bautzmann. Flight engineers rotated in were *Feldwebel* Rudolf Ernst, *Unteroffizier* Arthur Hildebrandt, *Unteroffizier* Erich Fettback, *Unteroffizier* Erich Neumann, and *Obergefreiter* Reiner Wilde.

In August, new arrivals were *Unteroffizier* Heinrich Opper (pilot), *Leutnant* Werner Kanther (observer), *Unteroffizier* Georg Birkmeier (a radio operator), and *Unteroffizier* Karl Baeuerle (flight engineer). September was also a month of numerous arrivals, including the change of command in the person of *Oberleutnant* von Janson. Others to arrive were *Leutnant* Ernst Mueller, *Leutnant* Artur Wiesemann, *Unteroffizier* Willi Hoffmann, *Unteroffizier* Anton Hoerwick, *Unteroffizier* Heinrich Hoevener, *Unteroffizier* Guenther Hoelscher, and *Obergefreiter* Walter Schoen, all pilots. *Leutnant* Hermann Braune, *Leutnant* Walter Broecker, *Leutnant* Dietrich von Buttlar, *Leutnant* Werner Morich, *Leutnant* Robert Kalischewski, *Feldwebel* Heinz Schwar, *Feldwebel* Peter Heldt, and *Unteroffizier* Hermann Kessler were all observers, while *Feldwebel* Gustav Schade, *Unteroffizier* Heinrich Henseler, *Unteroffizier* Fritz Wiessmann, *Unteroffizier* Walter Lemke, *Unteroffizier* Max Schott, *Unteroffizier* Hans Scholven, and *Unteroffizier* Willi Cryns were all radio operators. New flight engineers included *Unteroffizier* Rudolf Schnabel, *Unteroffizier* Friedrich Altstaedt, *Unteroffizier* Helmut Hezel, *Unteroffizier* Hans Mann, *Obergefreiter* Günther Briebsch, *Obergefreiter* Gustav Bohnekamp, and *Gefreiter* Willi Klause. On 20 August, however, while flying He 111 25-41, *Leutnant* Willer was shot down and killed over Gandesa by *4ª Escuadrilla* of Republican Moscas. The rest of the crew, among them *Unteroffizier* Schwarz and *Unteroffizier* Frischling, succeeded in parachuting to safety.

After this vigorous injection of new blood, October 1938 passed without any change in personnel, but on 16 October, the aircraft of von Janson, Roedel, Keppler, and Ernst exploded in flight, leaving no chance for its crew. In November, however, when *Hauptmann* Friedrich Winkler took over command of the unit, the following personnel arrived: *Unteroffizier* Leonard Etzel and *Unteroffizier* Günther Wagner (pilots); *Feldwebel* Heribald Ruppert (radio operator); and *Unteroffizier* Johann Wagner (flight engineer). November also saw the arrival of *Leutnant* Herbert Hilberg and *Unteroffizier* Heinrich Kropp (pilots); *Leutnant* Karl von der Fecht and *Unteroffizier* Herbert Woelber (observers); *Unteroffizier* Friedrich Luebbing and *Unteroffizier* Wilhelm Schmeiss (radio operators); and *Unteroffizier* Walter Roell and *Unteroffizier* Anton Kalisch (flight engineers).

Two new pilots arrived in February 1939, *Unteroffizier* Hans-Joachim Rihsel and *Unteroffizier* Richard Kuke, as well as one observer, *Leutnant* Günther Erbs; four radio operators, *Unteroffizier* Wilhelm Schmeiss, *Unteroffizier* Albert Dietl, *Unteroffizier* Hans Fiedler, and *Unteroffizier* Herbert Hoffmann; and two flight engineers, *Unteroffizier* Herrmann Limburg and *Unteroffizier* Peter Kazmierczak. On 5 February, aircraft 25-65 was shot down over Borjas Blancas, killing *Leutnant* Bröcker and *Unteroffizier* Hoffmann and *Unteroffizier* Schnabel. The losses of the last remaining weeks of combat left *3 Staffel* understrength with only six aircraft. In March, the only arrivals in the unit were *Oberleutnant* Helmut Neubert (observer); *Unteroffizier* Edmund Klumb (radio operator); and Albert Dürr (flight engineer). Winkler stayed in command until the Nationalist victory. A last effort in March brought the number of effective aircraft to a dozen. Then the following arrived: *Oberleutnant* Bernhard Jope[36], *Leutnant* Hilmar Bott, *Unteroffizier* Helmet Libuda, *Unteroffizier* Hans Weck, *Unteroffizier* Willi Neubert, and *Unteroffizier* Helmut Hoffmann (pilots); *Oberleutnant* Wolrad Harseim, *Leutnant* Karl Matthaeus, *Leutnant* Rolf Tappen, *Leutnant* Hans Fisher, *Unteroffizier* Fritz Bluhm, and *Unteroffizier* Henry Wendt (observers); *Unteroffizier* Henry Hoppe, *Unteroffizier* Hubertus Sturmhöfel, *Unteroffizier* Richard Koch, *Unteroffizier* Heinrich Schilling, *Unteroffizier* Gustav Babbe, and *Gefreiter* Kurt Weigang (radio operators); *Feldwebel* Philipp Haisch, *Unteroffizier* Rudolf Schneider, *Unteroffizier* Karl-Heinz Pissyk, *Unteroffizier* Reinhard Lütke, *Unteroffizier* Walter Siegmund, *Unteroffizier* Herbert Merzhäuser, and *Unteroffizier* Kurt Hauck (flight engineers).

## 4.K/88

In July 1937, the original crews of VB/88, led by *Oberleutnant* von Moreau, left to set up a new regular *Staffel*, 4.K/88, equipped with newly delivered He 111s. The unit started its career with a *Schwarm* of four aircraft (25-11 to 25-14) with pilots *Oberleutnant* Hans-Henning von Beust, *Oberleutnant* Rudolf Jöster, *Leutnant* Hajo Herrmann[38], *Unteroffizier* Rudolf Henne, *Unteroffizier* Hans Immel, *Unteroffizier* Walter Meier, *Unteroffizier* Josef Schmitz, and *Unteroffizier* Adolf Zober; observers *Leutnant* Clemens von Detten, *Leutnant* Max Graf Hoyos, *Leutnant* Georg Piecha, and *Leutnant* Oskar Schmidt; radio operators *Feldwebel* Hermann Kössler, *Feldwebel* Alfred Mantwitz, *Feldwebel* Fritz Messer, *Unteroffizier* Karl Brohammer, *Unteroffizier* Fritz Langbein, *Unteroffizier* Otto Löffler, *Unteroffizier* Werner Steiner, and *Unteroffizier* Fritz Thumser; and navigator/flight engineers *Unteroffizier* Karl Auernhammer, *Unteroffizier* Erich Hempe, *Unteroffizier* Josef Troll, *Unteroffizier* Hans Peckhaus, *Obergefreiter* Heinz Marché, *Obergefreiter* Walter Meyenberg, and *Obergefreiter* Erich Noller.

The evident lack of observers was partly filled by the end of August, when the original crews returned to Germany, by the integration of the crews of the defunct group VB/88, namely *Leutnant* Wolfgang Schiller, *Leutnant* Juergen Bartens, *Leutnant* Rolf Kloeppel, *Leutnant* Kurt von Leutsch, *Leutnant* Wilhelm Stemmler, and *Leutnant* Otto Bodenmeyer. Pilots from VB/88 were *Leutnant* Sigmund von Gravenreuth, *Leutnant* Heinrich Mellmann, *Oberfeldwebel* Karl Haefele, *Unteroffizier* Gottlob Beilharz, *Unteroffizier* Heinrich Bohne, *Unteroffizier* Kurt Bucholz, *Unteroffizier* Wolfgang Harder, *Unteroffizier* Anton Lenzen, and *Unteroffizier* Albert Schreiweis. The radio operators from the defunct unit, *Feldwebel* Kurt Geerdts, *Feldwebel* Werner Steiner, *Feldwebel* Willi Kruse, *Unteroffizier* Gerhard Goering, *Unteroffizier* Georg Hiebl, *Unteroffizier* Willi Kasten, *Unteroffizier* Karl Kleih, and *Obergefreiter* Herbert Süsse, and the flight engineers, *Oberfeldwebel* Hans Best, *Unteroffizier* Gerhard Berndt, *Unteroffizier* Helmut Dube, *Unteroffizier* Anton Kenn, *Unteroffizier* Herbert Leppin, *Unteroffizier* Josef Wallburger, and *Obergefreiter* Kurt Gruenig were also all posted to 4.K/88. On 18 August, a Heinkel was destroyed at Reinosa in the course of a bad landing, a second aircraft being seriously damaged in the same circumstances. During the last days of August, the entire *Gruppe* K/88 proceeded to the front at Aragon, and there, on the twenty-ninth, there were sixteen He 111s operating together against Medina de Ebro.

In October, pilots Willy Hesse and *Obergefreiter* Erich Jordan arrived at *4 Staffel*, as did *Leutnant* Kurt Kettner, *Leutnant* Joachim Spielmann, and *Unteroffizier* Herbert Brugmann (observers); *Feldwebel* Karl Schütt, *Unteroffizier* Theo Kowollik, and *Unteroffizier* Kurt Kondziela (radio operators); and *Oberfeldwebel* Georg Feiertag, *Unteroffizier* Kurt Aurin, *Unteroffizier* Herbert Lehmann, *Obergefreiter* Karl Hofmeister, and *Obergefreiter* Walter Klemm (flight engineers). In reserve was *Unteroffizier* Gerhard Bernd.

**Kampfgruppe K/88**

In November 1937, *Hauptmann* Wolfgang Neudörffer took over command of the unit as the following personnel were brought in: *Feldwebel* Hans Peetz, *Unteroffizier* Alfred Katzberg, and *Unteroffizier* Herbert Schmid (pilots); *Leutnant* Selmar Huke, *Leutnant* Heinrich Meyer, and *Leutnant* Oskar Otolski (observers); *Unteroffizier* Josef Luxen, *Unteroffizier* Ernst Pietruska, and *Unteroffizier* Werner Steiner (radio operators); and *Unteroffizier* Willi Dietsch, *Unteroffizier* Martin Hinterberger, *Unteroffizier* Josef Kahlert, *Unteroffizier* Franz Niebuhr, *Unteroffizier* Rudolf Kleff, and *Obergefreiter* Kurt Grünig (observers). At year's end, pilots *Leutnant* Friedjof von Sichardt and *Feldwebel* Arthur Vetter arrived along with *Oberleutnant* Kurt Stein, *Leutnant* Hans Dölling, *Leutnant* Kurt von Leutsch, *Unteroffizier* Helmut Engelke, and *Unteroffizier* Jakob Jacobs (observers); *Feldwebel* Paul Friedrich, *Unteroffizier* Waldemar Dettmann, *Unteroffizier* Theo Schwarz, *Unteroffizier* Karl Weyand (radio operators); and *Feldwebel* Herbert Hetzel and *Feldwebel* Erich Wacker (flight engineers).

In January 1938, the unit received *Leutnant* Armin Hoyer (a pilot); *Hauptmann* Dietrich von Zielberg (observer), who took over command of the unit; *Unteroffizier* Heinrich Beckmeier (radio operator); and *Feldwebel* Walter Hoyer and *Unteroffizier* Friedrich Lange (both flight engineers). Yet more replacement aircrew arrived in February: *Leutnant* Friedrich, *Leutnant* Freiherr Podbielski, *Unteroffizier* Gustav Heinrichs, *Unteroffizier* Johannes van Beckum, and *Obergefreiter* Gerhard Schubert, all pilots. New arrivals among the observers were *Leutnant* Heinrich Fahrenberg, *Leutnant* Walter Ribbeck, *Leutnant* Friedrich Koch, *Unteroffizier* Gerhard Weinert, and *Unteroffizier* Fritz Selzer, with *Unteroffizier* Heinz Wickhorst, *Unteroffizier* Alfred Wittke, and *Unteroffizier* Heinz Clavery as radiomen and *Unteroffizier* August Kaiser, *Unteroffizier* Otto Marx, and *Unteroffizier* Edgar Warzecha as flight engineers.

March was a quiet month as far as staff movements were concerned, with only the appearance of *Feldwebel* Bruno Kamsties (pilot), *Leutnant* Eduard Jacob (observer), and *Unteroffizier* Hermann Drees and *Obergefreiter* Otto Pickard (flight engineers). In contrast, at the operational level, the month saw the loss of one aircraft, 25-10, with *Leutnant* Kettner and *Unteroffizier* Hofmeister both being made prisoner. April was similar; the regular rhythm of rotation brought to the unit *Unteroffizier* Josef Blasé (pilot), *Leutnant* Helmut Kinder (observer), *Unteroffizier* Max Passmann (radio operator), and *Unteroffizier* Helmut Plate (mechanic). On 2 April, the *Staffel* lost two aircraft, which ran into each other at take-off while being bombed by a group of Republican SB-2s. One of the German aircraft succeeded in landing; the other was destroyed in a crash into the town of Alfaro. In May, *Unteroffizier* Günther von Kretowicz (pilot) arrived, as did *Hauptmann* Karl-Heinrich Heyse (observer), who then inherited the command of *4 Staffel*. Others posted to 4./88 in May were *Leutnant* Helmut Furhop and *Leutnant* Karl-Ernst Wilke (observers) and *Unteroffizier* Helmut Maaz, *Unteroffizier* Johann Weger, *Unteroffizier* Hans Bremer, and *Unteroffizier* Walter Cramer (radio operators).

In June, *Leutnant* Erich Thiel, *Leutnant* Wolfgang Schink, *Unteroffizier* Heinz Schmitz, and *Unteroffizier* Alfons Bulach (pilots); *Leutnant* Walter Schott and *Unteroffizier* Josej Kozubcek (observers); *Unteroffizier* Heinrich Pippig and *Unteroffizier* Hugo Zimmermann (radio operators); and *Unteroffizier* Fritz Gundlack and *Obergefreiter* Erich Quesdorf (flight engineers) were all posted into the unit.

By July, the Legion had been weakened by continual combats and K/88 was therefore obliged to reduce its strength to three *Staffeln*. The crews of *4 Staffel* who had not yet done their time in Spain were therefore dispersed to relieve or reinforce the other units in order to reestablish a theoretical strength of a dozen aircraft for each *Staffel*.

**THE OPERATIONS**

In contrast to the fighter units, the *Staffeln* of K/88 nearly always stayed together during the course of the war in Spain, carrying out operations in a joint manner for obvious reasons: requiring more ground space and more sophisticated installations than the fighters, they had little choice considering the limited number of major bases in a country without a great deal of aeronautical infrastructure. Another factor was that the effectiveness of an attack by, and the defense of, a unit of conventional bombers of the time depended directly on the number of them.

It has already been seen that the first twenty Ju 52s, which arrived at the end of October 1936, were diverted to bombing, by reason of circumstances. Once the Legion Condor was officially created on 7 November, the *Fulda* left from Stettin, the first of a convoy of twenty-five steamers that would follow one another heading for Spain from 7 to 29 November. But it was by air, thanks to a supplementary fuel tank of 1,000 liters in the fuselage, that the thirty-one Ju 52s, which were going to equip the three *Staffeln* of the bomber group K/88, were delivered. For the voyage, the rudder was painted yellow, all other marks having been effaced. The transfer commenced on 15 November from Greifswald to Lechfeld, continuing towards Rome on the seventeenth, then to Melilla on the eighteenth (in eight hours of flying), and finally Seville on the nineteenth. The *Gruppe* arrived at Salamanca on the twenty-first, but *2 Staffel* and *3 Staffel* were to return to Seville by the twenty-third and to Melilla on the twenty-fifth.

1.K/88, 2.K/88, and 3.K/88 thus scraped together ten aircraft each, a single Ju 52 staying with the General Staff flight. The aircraft were numbered 22-70 to 22-100, 1.K/88 receiving the 90s, 2.K/88 the 80s, and 3.K/88 the 70s. The three units were then placed under the command, respectively, of Heinz von Lignitz, Brasser, and *Hauptmann* Kraft von Dellmensingen, *Major* Fuchs having overall command of the *Gruppe*. *3 Staffel* was based for a while at Seville-Tablada, but quickly rejoined the other two at Salamanca–San Fernando. The new aircraft were equipped with a supplementary weapon in the "dustbin" ventral turret, which was only extended at the time of passing over the target—the least time possible given the consequent drag. This fitting imposed a reduction in load-carrying capacity from 1,500 to 1,250 kilograms, but the need to improve the protection of the Ju 52 was already evident.

On 23 November, *2 Staffel* and *3 Staffel* were to bomb the port of Cartagena, where the unloading of cargo boats bringing Soviet war matériel was in full swing. For this, the aircraft, leaving from Seville, had to make a detour with a stop at Melilla, the Spanish enclave in Morocco. The attack took place on the twenty-fifth at an altitude of 2,500 meters and the return was effected by the same route, without loss, despite heavy but as yet inaccurate flak. The first mission of K/88 in Spain therefore went well. In December, the German crews were more than happy to pass on the five remaining Ju 52s of the *Pedro* and *Pablo* units to the Spanish. The aircraft in question were certainly already very tired by the operating conditions.

At the start of December, the three *Staffeln* found themselves at the Madrid front attacking, in particular, the aerodrome of Alcalá de Henares. But the tide had already turned for the slow three-engined aircraft, and come the eighth, the Legion lost two of its bombers. One was being flown by von Lignitz, *Leutnant* Werner Hornschuh, *Unteroffizier* Josef Ullmann, and *Obergefreiter* Johann Seitz and fell at Arenas de San Pedro, while that of *Unteroffizier* Wilhelm Harjes and his crew came down at Alcalá de Henares. By the end of the month, the three *Staffeln* were on the Andalusian fronts of Asturias and Santander.

On 4 January, two of the *Staffeln* were surprised above Torrijos by Republican I-15 fighters, and the Germans of *3 Staffel*, who attacked the Campsa fuel depots, lost one of their aircraft over Bilbao. *Oberfeldwebel* Adolf Hermann and Karl Schmidt succeed in parachuting, but the former, who tried to defend himself with his pistol from an armed mob, was rapidly overpowered once upon the ground. His body was dragged through the streets of Bilbao, provoking a demand for reprisals by the Legion which were, however, refused. *Feldwebel* Herbert Barowski, *Unteroffizier* Paul Ziepek, and *Gefreiter* Hans Schüll were unable to escape from the burning aircraft.

Probably at Alfaro while they await the next attack on the docks at Cartagena, these Heinkel bombers, mostly from 2.K/88, display the transition in *Luftwaffe* camouflage from overall RLM 63 (L40/52) grey (aircraft 25-15 and 25-30) while 25-46, 25-50, 25-52, and 25-53 are all painted in the newer splinter-type 61/62/63 scheme. Note that there are subtle variations between each aircraft.

On 6 January, fourteen aircraft operated against Madrid and were intercepted by Republican I-16s; the He 51s paid with two aircraft shot down. Then, on 17 January, an aeroplane crashed into a mountain in the Sierra de Gredos, fortunately killing only one of its crew, *Flieger* Alfred Jentsch. It was the fourth Ju 52 lost in two months.

On 13 February, ten aircraft operated to the south of Madrid. The *Staffel* operating in Andalucia lost one of its aircraft on 23 February, shot down at Andujar. The crew of *Leutnant* Rudolf Kaufmann, *Unteroffizier* Gerhard Bowitz, and *Unteroffizier* Heinrich Siefken were all killed. By the end of March, for the offensive against Bilbao, the three *Staffeln* of K/88 had only sixteen total aircraft. The campaign began badly, when the unit bombed a friendly sector in error, wounding the chief of the General Staff of the 4th Navarre Brigade and just missing killing Sperrle himself. Nonetheless, on 1 April, twenty-two aircraft were available to attack the front in the Murubain and Oleata sector. The Ju 52s participated as principal protagonists in the bombardments against Ochandiano on the fourth and, above all, against Guerricaíz and Guernica on the twenty-sixth, destroying 25 percent of the town in in a single mission, destruction which rose to 70 percent that same evening by the aid of fires started by incendiary bombs.[37] In the meantime, they also intervened in the course of the battle of Guadalajara, but only at night.

On 29 May, twenty-one Ju 52s operated jointly with the prototypes of VB/88 against Amorebieta and Gorbea. The Ju 52s particularly distinguished themselves by their resolute action on 11–12 June, which provoked the collapse of the "Iron Ring" around Bilbao.[38] The Basque capital finally fell on 21 June, as a precursor to the final collapse of Republican resistance in the northern zone, which had been able replenish supplies only in small amounts from across the French frontier.

On 5 July 1937, the Republicans opened operations at Brunete, to the south of Madrid, in order to relieve the pressure of the rebels on the northern front. This provoked a general transfer of assets. Consequently, on 7 July, all the bombers of A/88, K/88, and VB/88 were reunited, the Legion Condor then operating together at the front. For the battle of Brunete, K/88 spread out between Salamanca and Avila. The first missions of this campaign took place on the eighth, more precisely on the sector between Brunete, Villanueva de la Cañada, and Valdemorillo, which each received two visits from units of the Legion Condor. The following day, K/88 carried out two joint missions with VB, and had to land back at night. Already there was intense Republican flak, which, according to the crews' accounts, "proliferated" on the front. In addition, the presence there of large numbers of I-16s, capable of both intercepting the He 111s and combating on equal terms at least with the Bf 109s at the preferred altitude of the bombers (from 600 to 1,850 meters) forced K/88 to operate principally at night.

On 16 July, the Republicans claimed the destruction of two Ju 52s. For K/88, the day was, above all, marked by the special mission for one of its trimotors which left for Germany at 16.00 hours to carry back the remains of *Unteroffizier* Guido Höness, the first Bf 109 pilot to be killed in combat. On the afternoon of the seventeenth, all the available bombers of the Legion regrouped on the front of Brunete.

On 21 July, a total of fifty-nine Ju 52s had arrived in Spain (plus a floatplane dedicated to transport and liaison with the Balearic Islands).

During the night of 25–26 July, K/88 lost one of its aircraft, shot down by the Russian, Yakushin, in an I-15. At the time, this was one the first experiences of night fighting in Spain. *Leutnant* Leo Falk and his crew—*Feldwebel* Georg Ubelhack, *Unteroffizier* Fritz Berndt, *Unteroffizier* Walter Brotzmann, *Unteroffizier*, and *Unteroffizier* August Heyer—were all killed in the action. Attributed at first to bad luck, the affair became more serious the following night with the loss of another aircraft, shot down under the same conditions by Serov. On this occasion, the crew were made prisoner, but the lesson was clear: the Ju 52s were condemned to disappear from the ranks of the Legion.

For the campaign against Santander, K/88 had at its disposal eighteen Ju 52s and fourteen He 111s, since *3 Staffel* had profited from the arrival of a new batch of He 111s that enabled it to convert onto the new model at the end of April. The two modern units were then based at Herrera de Pisuerga and Calahorra de Boedo. At 03.00 hours on 14 August, the offensive began, but it started rather badly, since in the afternoon a Ju 52 exploded in flight, assumed to have been the victim of a direct flak hit in the bomb bay. On the eighteenth, K/88 carried out a large-scale night-bombing mission on the base of Santander, announcing the destruction of a dozen aircraft on the ground. Some twenty He 111s participated in the operation, one being hit by a fighter and having to make an emergency landing at Reinosa. K/88 intervened en masse again on the twenty-third before Santander fell (on 25 August), but that same day, the Legion lost two of its precious He 111s, shot down by the last I-16s based in the Asturias, over the bridge at El Musél.

The bomber *Gruppe* linked up for the campaign against Gijón, last bastion of the Republic in the northern zone. For this the Heinkels were based on the recently captured territory of La Albericia, the only Republican base in the sector with tarmac and hangars. From 1 September, the principal objectives of the group were the ports of Gijón and Avilés and, despite a desperate opposition by the remainder of the Republican fighters, they soon very seriously damaged the destroyer *Ciscar*. On the second, however, an He111 was shot down above Gijón by one of the surviving Chatos. On the thirtieth, another aircraft was lost due to an engine failure, which could have have been the result of an interception. Moreover, on the same day, two other Heinkels were obliged to make emergency landings in the country. On 21 September, another Ju 52 of K/88 was lost when it crashed into a mountain at Reinosa, near Santander, killing its crew of *Unteroffizier* Claus Held, *Obergefreiter* Bruno Ness, *Obergefreiter* Franz Nokler, and *Obergefreiter* Egon Marting. On the twenty-fourth, the Ju 52s were intercepted by Republican fighters and lost *Obergefreiter* Willi Sembach, who was mortally wounded in flight, while another aircraft was obliged to make a violent forced landing at Pontejos, in which the crew lost their lives (*Leutnant* Ernst König, *Leutnant* Heinrich Meyer, *Unteroffizier* Franz Niebuhr, and *Obergefreiter* Karl Brettmeier).

On 7 October, a Ju 52 of K/88 was destroyed at Gijón by flak, and as a result, *Leutnant* Heinrich Stallamann, *Unteroffizier* Rudolf Hartig, and *Unteroffizier* Karl Uhrmeister perished. The series of bad events was not yet finished, for two more accidents destroyed an He 111 on the twenty-first and another on the twenty-second of October. By the end of October 1937, K/88 under *Major* Mehnert could field three *Staffeln* of He 111s, the last Ju 52s having by then being confined only to specific night missions on relatively quiet fronts. Nine of the trimotors had already been passed on to the Spaniards.

For K/88, based at Burgo de Osma, on the road from Soria to Aranda, the campaign of Teruel started at the beginning of December. On the fourth, the *Gruppe* released thirty tons of bombs on Bujaraloz. The aircraft of the unit were principally tasked to attack the Republican bases of Candasnos, Sariñena, Puebla de Hijar, Selgua, Pomar, Lérida Bujaraloz, and Balaguer. K/88 lost an aircraft (of an undetermined type), which crashed into a mountain and killed *Unteroffizier* Paul Schick and *Obergefreiter* Erwin Hoster on 8 December. On the tenth, an He 111 exploded in flight for reasons unknown during a mission against the aerodrome of Candasnos, killing in one blow the crew of *Leutnant* Friedrich-Karl Beucke, *Leutnant* Heinrich Klein, *Feldwebel* Anton Bergmann, *Unteroffizier* Fritz Brühl, and *Obergefreiter* Alois Ehlen. On the fifteenth, the Republicans decided to launch an offensive on the Teruel front in order to impede a new Nationalist attack against Madrid. Two days later, twenty-three He 111s attacked Teruel, and one of them (25-32)

Spanish ground crews manhandling German SC 50 bombs. Each He 111 could carry twenty of these, plus a bigger bomb weighing 250 kilograms and four packs of incendiaries. The work of loading a single machine can be imagined. Behind them is a 1.K/88 aircraft, 25-93, which flaunts the unit emblem of a bomb-carrying eagle on the fin. This became the official emblem of *I Gruppe* of KG 53 in World War II.

was forced to land in Republican territory, where its crew was made prisoner. The aircraft was thoroughly tested by a French technical mission (Cdt de Bray, Cne Rozanoff) of the STAé before being taken to pieces and sent to the USSR.[39] In rapid succession, the aircraft of K/88 were based at Avila, Escalona, Burgo de Osma, and Talavera. On the twenty-ninth, the whole *Gruppe* attacked Teruel. On the thirty-first, seven aircraft attempted to attack concentrations of troops at Alfambra, Perales, and Argote but were dispersed by a blizzard before seeing their target.

On the twenty-sixth, an He 111 was shot down above Teruel by Republican fighters. This was the only loss during the campaign, which took place in abominable weather. Certain sources, however, indicate that the aircraft, although badly hit, was able to put down at Alcocer. By 31 January 1938, the *Gruppe* was at Alfaro. There was intense activity on 6 February, with a total of 120 tonnes of bombs being dropped. On the twenty-third, K/88 was installed at Burgo de Osma in preparation for the offensive towards the Mediterranean coast.

The Nationalists were not going to wait before launching their first real strategic movement in the direction of Valencia in order to cut the Republican territory in two anew. On 6 March, sixteen He 111s attacked the aerodrome of Caspe, while eighteen others took on the base at Bujaraloz; at 12.00 hours, nine aircraft carried out a surprise attack on the General Staff of a Republican division to the south of Teruel. At 13.00 the following day, all of A/88 and K/88 bombed the station at Puebla de Hijar. On 8 March, two *Staffeln* of He 111s attacked the bridges on the Ebro at Sastago, repeatedly missed by the Ju 87s on the sixth and seventh of the month. The aircraft bombed from an altitude of fifty meters but had no more success against the stated objective but, by pure chance, two hits were made against a power station which was not even listed. The two other *Staffeln* attacked a munitions factory and the station at Puebla de Hijar.

On 10 March, K/88 carries out three missions. During the first, the four *Staffeln* joined to attack Candasnos; 25-7 was taken apart from below by an I-15 and forced to make a lucky landing in the area of Bujaraloz, sending *Leutnant* Kurt Kettner, *Feldwebel* Willi Hesse, *Unteroffizier* Theo Kowollek, *Unteroffizier* Karl Hofmeister, and *Obergefreiter* Heinz Clacery to prisoner of war camp. The latter, having been invited on the trip for the day, had made an unfortunate choice for his aerial promenade. From this time on, K/88 began systematic attacks against towns and stations at regular intervals.

On 12 March, the He 111s attacked Albalate and Hijar, and at 17.00 hours, thirty-one aircraft operated against Azaila and Hijar, five of them limping back to base after having been badly hit by Republican flak. The following day, thirty-three aircraft attacked the aerodrome at Caspe at 09.30 hours. On the sixteenth at 15.00 hours, a single *Staffel* attacked enemy lines at Maella.

On 27 March, the four *Staffeln* were commanded respectively by *Hauptmann* Hans Schultz, *Oberleutnant* Rolf Schröter, *Hauptmann* Heinz Fischer, and *Hauptmann* Dietrich von Ziehlberg. The priority objectives at the end of March were the enemy positions of Fraga and the aerodromes in the sector of Lérida. It was at about this time that a flight of I-15s, engaged in a strafing sortie, surprised a formation of Heinkels without escort and forced one to land in Republican territory between Candasnos and Fraga. The crew managed to set fire to the aircraft before giving themselves up. During a mission against the aerodrome at Lérida, the He 111s hit several aircraft stationed along the length of the runway, sweeping up four I-16s in course of taking off. On the thirtieth, the *Gruppe* bombed Barbastro at night. On 2 April, two aircraft crashed into each other on take-off when Republican SB-2 s and I-15s attacked Alfaro, one of these falling onto the town killing the crew (*Leutnant* Herbert Hoyer, *Feldwebel* Walter Hoyer, *Feldwebel* Herbert Brüggemann, and *Unteroffizier* Kurt Kondziela). The other aircraft was able to land although damaged. Five other He 111s were hit on the ground.

On 16 April, when new arrivals of matériel were being discharged at Cartagena, the Legion Condor decided to deliver a massive strike and sent its forty available He 111s from Sanjurjo to Seville-Tablada via Avila. One aircraft tried to make a forced landing at Villafranca de los Barros, thirteen kilometers to the west of Monasterio, the entire crew being killed in the attempt (*Leutnant* Andreas Siemsen, *Feldwebel* Oswald Kruschbersky, *Feldwebel* Rudolf Spieler, and *Feldwebel* Albert Matz, as well as two invited passengers, *Obergefreiter* Fritz Schmalfuss and *Obergefreiter* Erich Frielingsdorf). Two other machines were damaged when landing at Seville. This was a bad period for K/88, and the following day, only thirty-four aircraft could attack the port of Cartagena under an intense barrage of flak. During the second mission of the day at 12.00 hours, twenty-five aircraft hit the Republican cruiser *Jaime 1°* and sank an MTB (motor torpedo boat) in the harbor. The aircraft of *1 Staffel*'s leader, 25-27, was hit but was able to stay with the formation to go on to attack the secondary target of Almeria. There it was again hit by more flak and had to ditch in the sea off the coast of Motril. 25-15, first hit by flak and then by I-15s, struggled back to base. Thus, Operation "Neptune" finished with rather mediocre results; of the forty aircraft that left Sanjurjo, only twenty-five returned on the eighteenth, with five getting back later in the following days. In total, sixteen aircraft were damaged by the dreadful weather conditions encountered en route, and apart from the two aircraft lost, six others had to be scrapped as irreparably damaged.

On the twenty-fifth, K/88 took off from Alfaro to attack Castellón de la Plana and the port of Sagunto. A battle above the aerodrome of Castellón ended with no loss according to the Legion; the Republicans, however, claimed three aircraft shot down into the sea off the coast of Valencia. On 5 May, the *Gruppe* carried out two missions against Vinaroz. On 14 and 29 May, Republican communiqués announced the destruction of two other He 111s, which the Legion did not respond to. Nevertheless, in Legion records, 29 May was given as the date of the death of *Leutnant* Karl Kostlin, shot down by flak over San Jorge. More serious, however, was the general state of the aircraft of K/88, which were beginning to suffer from the infernal rhythm of four to six missions daily. Happily, a new batch of He 111s, of the latest "E" model, arrived at the start of July, in time for the Ebro offensive that the Republic unleashed on 25 July. Faster and capable of carrying a larger weapons payload, the He 111Es assured the superiority of the Nationalist camp in the months that followed.

On 7 July, K/88 operated to the south of Castellón. The following day, thirty-seven He 111s flew a mission over the Sierra de Espadán, registering good results from their bombardment. During a second sortie, they encountered strong flak both light and heavy, without loss, at the station of Sagunto. On the ninth, the *Gruppe* set itself up at Saragossa, where the aircraft had to land carrying their bomb loads, ready to bomb the port and the station of Sagunto. On the tenth, thirty-nine machines bombed the enemy lines at Sierra de Espadán and Vall de Uxo. The weather was very bad. K/88 then operated in company with A/88 over the sector of Adzaneta. On the eleventh, the group attacked the roads to the south of Castellón. Two days later, over the same sector, a big aerial combat took place during which six He 111s were hit, two of which had to carry out forced landings in the countryside. On the sixteenth, nine aircraft attacked enemy batteries near Ayedar. The following day, twenty-one aircraft bombed the stations of Segorbe and Soñeja, then, during a second sortie, attacked the road from Segorbe to Sagunto. The following day the same bombers attacked enemy positions at Algimia de Almonacid. On the twenty-first, there were thirty aircraft available to flatten roads and bridges in the sector of Segorbe in support of the Valiño Army Corps. The next day, twenty-one aircraft bombed the Republican positions at Algimia de Almonacid again, starting numerous fires on the ground, in the face of heavy flak. Operations recommenced on the twenty-third and

A formation of Heinkel He 111Bs drones overhead, probably during the victory parade at the end of the Spanish Civil War. The distinctive mismatched beat of their engines was to become all too familiar to citizens of Europe in just a few months from when this picture was taken. At the time, only the Spaniards and the Legion Condor knew it well.

twenty-fourth. On the twenty-fifth, the *Gruppe* operated against Sagunto jointly with A/88. The day after, three sorties saw the operation, respectively, of thirty, twenty-seven, and twenty He 111s, first against Benifallet and Mora la Nueva, then against Ginestar, Miravet and Rasquera, and finally against Corbera. In each case, the flak was very serious.

The twenty-seventh was a very busy day for the group, with no fewer than six sorties. First, nine aircraft attacked the crossing points on the Ebro between Mora la Nueva and Rivarroja, while twelve others bombed the enemy positions between Pinell and Corbera; next another formation of nine He 111s smashed the sector between Fatarella, Corbera and Venta de Camposines, where an intense flak barrage shook the formation at 11.25 hours. Another *Staffel* bombed the roads on the axis Flix-Camposines, and a third the pontoon bridges on the Ebro to the north of Ginestar. Finally twelve He 111s operated against the roads between Gandesa and Pinell and concentrations of troops to the north of Ginestar and to the west of Asco. On the twenty-eighth, a seized engine (after only 202 hours of service) caused an He 111 to land outside the airfield at Sanjuro, the machine being 80 percent destroyed but without loss to the crew. The next day, thirty aircraft attacked the crossings of the Ebro between Asco and Miravet, destroying fuel reserves. The operation was repeated a little while afterwards with the same number of aircraft against the bridges between Vinebre and Ginestar, hitting at least one bridge and a flak battery. On the twenty-ninth, the same formation succeeded in breaching one of the bridges at Flix. The thirtieth was again an intense day with six missions occupying from nine to twenty-one aircraft against the same type of targets. The month ended with only two sorties on the thirty-first.

Much of the rest of the Ebro campaign was carried out at a similar intensity. It would be repetitive and perhaps boring to describe it in detail. It can, however, be noted that the principal actions of the He 111s of K/88 were interdiction missions against the bridges of the Ebro and road intersections, stations, troop concentrations, and ammunition depots—nearly always against much flak, heavy and light, and generally in formations of twenty-one aircraft. On 6 August, K/88 received for the first time some operational Spanish crews, nine men taking their places in aircraft two and three of the *Kette*[40] of the staff formation. On 14 August, *2 Staffel*, then commanded by *Hauptmann* Wolfien, left to attack the sector of Gandesa in the company of the *Führungskette*[41] of the Staff HQ, also called "5.K/88." It is noted that the aircraft of *2 Staffel* were numbered 25-26, 25-42, 25-46, 25-47, 25-49, 25-50, 25-51, 25-52, and 25-53, and that those of 5.K/88 were 25-3, 25-24, and 25-28. During this time, *1 Staffel*, under the command of *Hauptmann* Heyse, attacked the bridges at Mora de Ebro with aircraft 25-1, 25-2, 25-6, 25-9, 25-10, 25-12, 25-15, and 25-22. 25-17 was under repair after a forced landing. During this mission, 25-9 was hit and returned with a dead engine, while 25-6 suffered damage to the fuselage but arrived at Sanjurjo. At the time of this campaign, the normal load of the He 111s was a bomb of 250 kilograms and twenty of 50 kilograms, plus four packets of incendiary bombs (BSK 36), a well-mixed load capable of "treating" any target.

The principal objectives of the He 111s during the battle of the Ebro were the crossing points, notably the bridges to the north of Flix, at Mora de Ebro, and to the north of Ginestar; the footbridges launched across the river to the west of Ginestar, at Miravet, and Benifallet; and the ford at Asco. But the defense was desperate, and on 20 August, 25-41 of *3 Staffel* was shot down by flak at Gandesa. The crew baled out, but *Leutnant* Heinz Willer crashed into the tail unit of the aircraft and was dead upon reaching the ground. *Unteroffizier* Schwarz and *Unteroffizier* Frishling fell wounded in their parachutes, and *Unteroffizier* Naumann was made prisoner. On 3 September, another aircraft flying at 2,600 meters was hit close to the cockpit by a round of 37-millimeter ground fire over a bridge on the Ebro; it got back to base only to be scrapped.

It is interesting to note that certain targets become "classics" little by little: the bridge at Mora de Ebro was attacked thirty-four times between 25 July and 18 September. It thus received in the course of the campaign 671 tons of bombs, being cut five times. The bridge situated to the north of Ginestar was a good second, with thirty-two attacks between 26 July and 6 September, receiving 545 tons of bombs and eight breaks, whereas a simple infantry footbridge, such as that of Miravet, merited six visits by He 111s and thirty-two tons of bombs, to be cut three times. But the Republican engineers and bridge-builders worked quickly and well, using the nights to repair the damage made during the days.

On 5 September, a machine gunner from an He 111 claimed the destruction of an I-16. On the tenth, *Major* Mehnert passed command of *Gruppe K/88* to *Major* Haerle. On 18 September, an aircraft that had been hit in the wing by flak came back over the base but, probably because it was incapable of dropping either its flaps or its undercarriage, the pilot ordered the crew to bale out, without problem, and the aircraft crashed into the ground. On 1 October, the first flight of *Leutnant* Hogeback with *1 Staffel* finished rather badly; having left with the rest of the flight to attack the positions at Mora and Ebro, he found himself first with his starboard engine on fire, hit by the Republican flak, which was formidable during the course of the battle of Ebro. He attempted to return to Saragossa-Sanjurjo, but finally had to give the order to abandon the aircraft. He landed in no-man's-land between the two camps with a fractured skull and lung damage. The observer, Poppenhagen, and the flight engineer, Hermann, managed to get away from the mess, but the radio operator, *Unteroffizier* Gerhard Pacht, was wounded by flak and was unable to escape from the aircraft.

On 16 October, a new He 111 exploded in flight to the southwest of Fatarella, the presence of I-16s in the area leaving them to suppose a surprise victory. *Feldwebel* Kepler and *Oberfeldwebel* Ernst (radio operator and flight engineer respectively) parachuted out and were made prisoner. Later, it was discovered that they were in a hospital in Barcelona, but *Oberleutnant* Thilo von Janson, *Leutnant* Emil Rodel, and *Unteroffizier* Heinrich Hoevener all perished in the accident. On the eighteenth, the very bad weather imposed a welcome truce. An He 111 was claimed destroyed by the Republicans on 31 October. Another aircraft was destroyed in a forced landing at Pinell on 2 November after the nose was shot off by the flak of his own side.

For the offensive against Catalonia, K/88 took up quarters at the comfortable base of Sanjurjo with the complete establishment of forty He 111s. For K/88, the campaign of Catalonia constituted a repetition of that of the Ebro, with regard to both to the intensity of the sorties and to the type of targets attacked. The only differences were the presence of numerous Republican airfields in the region and a defense which became more relentless as the Republican hopes evaporated. On 4 December, an aircraft of unknown type but belonging to K/88 was shot down at sea, taking with it *Unteroffizier* Gustav Achade. On 8 December, K/88 attacked the station at Tamarit, to the north of Lérida. On the twenty-third at 12.30 hours, the *Gruppe* struck against the lines of Mayals and Granadella, returning at 16.00 and pursuing the action up to Llardecona. K/88 then had only twenty-five He 111s available.

On 4 January, an aircraft of K/88 piloted by *Unteroffizier* Bruno Albrecht was shot down over Tarragona, taking to their deaths both the pilot and *Unteroffizier* Horst von Prondzynski. On 9 January 1939, the targets were the port and station of Tarragona, from where fresh arrivals of matériel coming from the USSR were distributed. On the seventeenth, the Heinkel of *Leutnant* Horst Meiling was shot down over Ocejo. Eight days later, that of *Leutnant* Claus Bötker crashed at night into the flank of the mountain at Arrens, killing all the rest of the crew (*Unteroffizier* Fritz Seiler, *Unteroffizier* Armin Möller, and *Unteroffizier* Otto Adler). At 09.00

The result of a carpet-bombing mission. Some bombs are just beginning to explode, on the left. This is Spain; in a few months, it would be Poland, Holland, France, Britain, Germany . . .

hours on 27 January, seventeen He 111s attacked the station at Massanas and the road intersections of Tordera from 3,800 meters altitude. The next day, they operated against the port of Palamós at 08.20, then at 13.30 against the enemy lines to the northwest of Tossa.

On 3 February, three complete *Staffeln* of K/88 bombed the station at Figueras four times. On the fourth, forty-six He 111s struck the port of Puerto de la Selva under the protection of J/88, then the sector of Sabadell. The weather was so bad that aircraft 25-65 crashed into a mountain in the region of Cervia, in the fog. *Leutnant* Walter Brückers, *Unteroffizier* Willi Hoffmann, and *Unteroffizier* Rudolf Schnabel perished in the crash, but *Unteroffizier* Wissmann, the radio operator, miraculously walked away from the accident with only light wounds. K/88 at this time had a problem with the resupply of bombs: there were no more than 500 remaining at Sabadell, and the 10,000 bombs on order needed to arrive by sea at Palma before the seventh in order to be able to be transferred in time to Barcelona.

On 8 and 9 February, the whole of K/88, at last fully supplied, launched itself against the roads and road intersections of the sector Figueras-Navata-Rosas-Llansa, in order to prevent Republican reinforcements and supplies entering via the French frontier. On the ninth, the He 111 of *Hauptmann* Allolio, leader of *3 Staffel*, suffered an engine failure and had to land heavily, destroying the aircraft completely. The following day, fourteen aircraft left at 11.15 hours to bomb the port of Valencia. Two crashed into each other at take-off, resulting in one suffering 75 percent damage, the other 30 percent. In the sortie of 16.30 hours against the same objective, an aircraft was hit by Republican flak and had to belly-land at La Cenia, very damaged. At this time, thirty-one He 111s were based at Lérida. On 21 February 1939, a long time since the dice were first cast so to speak, K/88 participated in the first grand victory parade organised by the Francoists at Barcelona, symbol of the Catalan resistance. By the twenty-eighth, the group was back in action, this time against the roads around Madrid (Torre Baja and Salvacañete), accomplishing no fewer than six sorties, but with formations of from two to five aircraft. The same objectives were taken apart in the same way on 2 March and then the third, with an extension to Villanueva and Huélamo. The protection offered by J/88 was already unnecessary.

On 4 March, K/88 carried out seven sorties by small groups of aircraft. Five He 111s attacked the road intersections to the west of Torre Baja; 25-61 was hit by flak but got back to base. On the seventh, thirty-three He 111s struck the sector Viver-Segorbe-Sagunto and, in particular, the port of Sagunto, flying at an altitude of between 2,000 meters and 6,000 meters in order to avoid as much of the flak as possible. The next day, twenty-seven aircraft bombed the bridges and roads to the southwest of Teruel to disorganize the Republican rearguard. On 9 March, twenty-nine aircraft set off to attack the airfield at Alcalá, the stations at Colmenar and Collado, and the bridges at Salvacañete and Moncofar. Another explosion in flight on the twelfth put K/88 into mourning, this time it was the leader of the *Gruppe* who disappeared along with *Major* Friedrich Haerle (replaced by *Major* Nielsen for the last days of operations), *Oberleutnant* Pawelcik, *Oberfeldwebel* Rudolf Kollenda, *Oberfeldwebel* Walter Lange, *Unteroffizier* Hans Schrödel, and *Unteroffizier* Harry Buttner.

The sixteenth of March saw the last aerial combat for the He 111s, which came out of it without mishap. At 11.00 hours, they attacked the road intersections to the north of Arganda, as well as the road going from Las Rozas to Escorial. At 11.30, other aircraft took on infantry positions to the northwest of Quijorna and, at 15.00, similar objectives at Valdemorillo. In all, twenty-eight He 111s operated on this day. Finally, on 18 March at 13.00 hours, they returned to Quijorna, recording excellent results. At 14.30, a *Kette* of three He 111s went to bomb an artillery battery at Titulcia. The last mission of K/88 in Spain took place on 27 March 1939, in a clear sky, devoid of all opposition.

For most of the Legion bomber crews, the greatest enemy was flak. Civilian personnel from the Heinkel factory are examining the results of what seems to have been a couple of direct hits from the Republican flak on He 111B-1, 25-1. It is a miracle that the aircraft could land in this condition with its undercarriage down, and it proves at the very least the sturdiness of the Heinkel design. Observe that the champagne bottle was painted on both sides of the fuselage.

A pristine He 111B-2 of 2.K/88 at the end of the war. The location is most likely at Sanjurjo.

Even on their airfields, the bombers were not entirely safe. This He 111 appears to have lost its nose as the result of a ground collision between it and 25-24 in the background. This latter aircraft belonged to the *Stabskette* of K/88, the so-called *5 Staffel*, so the date could be some time in August 1938. So far as is known only one He 111 was lost due to a collision on the ground, this taking place on 10 February 1939. If this is the occasion, then the place is probably Sabadell, but neither of these aircraft looks beyond repair.

An He 111B lifts off at the start of a mission. It appears to carry an emblem on the fin, so it may be in Spanish hands.

Another He 111 appears to have ground-looped. Damage is minimal.

Another *Unteroffizier* of the Legion at the end of the war in parade uniform. 25-78 is in the background.

# The Junkers Ju 52/3M in Spain

## Type code 22

| Code | Type | Unit | Arrived | Crew | A/C Name | Fate |
|---|---|---|---|---|---|---|
| 22-47 | 6E22 | | | | | |
| 22-48 | | | | | | |
| 22-49 | 2E22 | | | | | Destroyed on ground 15.09.37, Sanjurjo |
| 22-50 | Pedro | | | | | |
| | 6E22 | 12.36 | | | | |
| 22-51 | Pedro | | | | | |
| 22-52 | Pedro | | | | | |
| 22-53 | Pablo | | | | | |
| 22-54 | 4E22 | 10.36 | | | | |
| | 2E22 | | | | | Destroyed on ground 15.09.37, Sanjurjo |
| 22-55 | 4E22 | 09.36 | | | | |
| | 2E22 | | | | | |
| 22-56 | | 09.36 | von Moreau | | | |
| | 4E22 | 09.36 | | | | |
| | 2E22 | | | | | |
| 22-57 | Pablo | | von Moreau | | | |
| | 1E22 | 09.36 | | | | |
| 22-58 | Pablo | | | | | |
| | 2E22 | | | | | |
| | 3E22 | | | | | |
| 22-59 | Pablo | | | | | |
| | 2E22 | | | | | |
| | 3E22 | | | | | |
| 22-60 | 1E22 | | | | | |
| 22-61 | 2E22 | | | "Maria de la O" | | |
| | 4E22 | | | | | Shot down 14.09.37 |
| 22-62 | 1E22 | | | "Maria Magdalena" | | Destroyed on ground 15.09.37 |
| 22-63 | 1E22 | | | | | |
| 22-64 | 2E22 | | Cn E.Ruiz de Alda | | | Shot down 26.09.36 |
| 22-65 | 2E22 | | | | | |
| | 3E22 | | | | | |

| Code | Type | Unit | Arrived | Crew | A/C Name | Fate |
|---|---|---|---|---|---|---|
| 22-66 | | 2E22 | | | | |
| | | 3E22 | | | | Exploded 26.07.37 |
| 22-67 | | 3E22 | | Cn Guerrero | | |
| | | 4E22 | | | "Maria" | Flak 02.09.36 |
| 22-68 | | 3E22 | | Cn Rute, Atienza | "Maria de la O" | Flak 03.09.36 |
| | | 4E22 | | | | |
| | | 6E22 | | | | Destroyed on ground |
| 22-69 | | 3E22 | 09.36 | | "Maria" | |
| | | 1E22 | | | | |
| | | 3E22 | | | | |
| | | 4E22 | | | | |
| | | 6E22 | | | | Destroyed on ground |
| 22-70 | | 3K/88 | | | | |
| | | 2K/88 | | | | Written off |
| 22-71 | | 3K/88 | | | | |
| 22-72 | | 3K/88 | | | | |
| | | 2G22 | | | | Shot down |
| 22-73 | | Pedro2 | | | | |
| | | 3K/88 | | | | |
| | | Kleinbahn | | | | |
| 22-74 | | 3K/88 | | | | Shot down |
| 22-75 | | 3K/88 | | | | |
| 22-76 | | 3K/88 | | | ex-DLH | |
| 22-77 | | 3K/88 | | | | |
| 22-78 | | 3K/88 | | | | Shot down |
| 22-79 | | 3K/88 | | | | |
| | | St/88 | | | | |
| | | Kleinbahn | | | ex-DLH | |
| 22-80 | | 2K/88 | | | | |
| 22-81 | | 2K/88 | | | | Shot down |
| 22-82 | | 2K/88 | | | | |
| | | 3K/88 | | | | |
| | | Kleinbahn | | | | |
| 22-83 | | 2K/88 | | | | |
| | | 1E22 | | | "Arganda" | |
| 22-84 | | 2K/88 | | | | |
| | | 1K/88 | 03.37 | | | |
| 22-85 | | 2K/88 | | | | |
| 22-86 | | 2K/88 | | | | |
| | | Kleinbahn | | | | MIA 24.10.38 |
| 22-87 | | 2K/88 | | | | |
| 22-88 | | 2K/88 | | | | |
| 22-89 | | 2K/88 | | | | |
| | | 2E22 | | | | 03.39 |
| 22-90 | | 1K/88 | | | | Accident, Sabadell |

# The Junkers Ju 52/3M in Spain

| Code | Type | Unit | Arrived | Crew | A/C Name | Fate |
|---|---|---|---|---|---|---|
| 22-91 | | 1K/88 | | | | 03.39 |
| 22-92 | | 1K/88 | | | | |
| | | 3K/88 | 03.37 | | | 03.39 |
| 22-93 | | 1K/88 | | | | |
| | | 3K/88 | 03.37 | | | 03.39 |
| 22-94 | | 1K/88 | | | | |
| 22-95 | | 1K/88 | | | | |
| 22-96 | | 1K/88 | | | | Shot down |
| 22-97 | | 1K/88 | | | | |
| 22-98 | | 1K/88 | | | | |
| 22-99 | | 1K/88 | | | | |
| 22-100 | | 1K/88 | | | | |
| 22-101 | | 6E22 | 12.36 | | | |
| 22-102 | | 6E22 | 12.36 | | | |
| 22-103 | | | | | | |
| 22-104 | | | | | | |
| 22-105 | | | | | | |

## OTHER JU 52 LOSSES

| Date | A/C | Crew | Unit | Location | Fate | Cause |
|---|---|---|---|---|---|---|
| 09.37 | | | K/88 | | | Accident |
| 09.37 | | | K/88 | | | Accident |

The "Three Marys" made up the 3rd Squadron of Spanish-flown Ju 52 bombers, formed at about the same time as the Legion Condor itself in 1936. The pictures serves to show the use of the ventral gun position. 22-62 is *Mary Magdalena*.

The Junkers 52 was not the first three-engine Junkers in Spain; several G-24 and K-30 had been sold to Spain, and some of them were still flying in 1936. This one seems to have just received some basic rebel markings.

The rain in Spain falls heavily in Madrid as Lufthansa Ju 52/3m D-AKYS *Emil Thuy* unloads its freight; the passengers have already taken cover. This is one of the last official flights between Madrid and Germany. Emil Thuy was a First World War fighter ace; many of the Lufthansa fleet Ju 52s were named after such pilots.

Refuelling under the Moroccan sun for D-ALYL which made several lifts between there and Spain in the markings of Lufthansa carrying Franco's troops.

Yet another Lufthansa Ju 52 to participate in the general airlift of matériel to Spain was D-ARAM, WNr 4041, named after one of the most famous of German fighter aces of World War One, Werner Voss.

Newcomers have just alighted from Ju 52 D-ATRN, probably in Burgos. It was not listed as a DLH aircraft so it may be a *Luftwaffe* bomber in mufti.

Two Legion Condor soldiers pose in front of Ju 52, D-AVIA. This also was not officially a Lufthansa aircraft, but it may have belonged to the RLM or German State Railways. Perhaps this was the origin of the nickname *Eisenbahn* for the regular shuttle flights used by Legion members.

D-AVAE was yet another of the many Ju 52s operated on the airlift by DLH on behalf of the RLM. This one appears to be in overall light grey with the glossy black bands and cowlings which were more or less standard on all Junkers civilian aircraft.

D-AXAP came to grief as a result of pilot error while landing at Bonete in Spain late in 1938. Damage looks fairly extensive, requiring a new wing and undercarriage. The scale of the German effort in Spain can be appreciated by the large number of "civilian" Ju 52s used for trooping duties.

As early as December 8, 1936, K/88 lost two bombers near Madrid. Here, Republican militiamen are examining the wreck of the one that fell in Arenas de San Pedro, flown by *Oberleutnant* Heinz Liegnitz and *Leutnant* Werner Hornschuh, both of whom were killed.

León airfield was the main maintenance base of the rebel air force, which explains the motley collection of aircraft in front of the hangars: two Ju 52s, one DC-2, one Ro 43, one Miles, and even a Fokker F-VIIa.

A grainy picture of *General* Hugo Sperrle, alias "Sander," wearing his broad-brimmed hat aboard a Ju 52 during an official visit to one of the Condor units. Note the complete absence of any soundproofing on the walls of the Ju 52 fuselage. Noise levels over a long journey must have been extremely tiring. Later, Sperrle was probably one of the first German generals to recognize the true war position of Germany, which led to his forced retirement in 1944.

Whoever is sitting behind the last (prime choice) window must be top brass, as this Condor Legion officer is already at attention. The aircraft could be 22-79 from K/88's Stab. Note the light blue cross; the specific conditions which required its application to some aircraft and not others remain unknown.

The imposing bulk of the energetic and brusque Hugo Sperrle during a tour of inspection at a Legion Condor base during his period of tenure as the Legion Condor's commander between November 1936 and 31 October 1937. Arguably his was the most difficult task of putting the operating systems in place and establishing ground rules for dealing with the notably recalcitrant Franco.

This ex-DLH aircraft has obviously been carrying high priority cargo, as the two men behind the tailpane are carrying a case with much care to the BMW motorbike side-car on the left. The splinter scheme appears to be interrupted by a black area behind the engines.

Junkers Ju 52/3, 22-79, awaits its next cargo. It is unusual in having what appear to be very light gray (63?) engine cowlings. The wing in the foreground belongs to an Heinkel He 70. Date and location unknown.

Flights between Spain and Germany were often enough fraught with danger, not only from enemy action but also the weather. This *Kleinbahn* aircraft crashed on the French side of the Pyrenees (note the French *gendarmes* in the center of the picture) on 24 February 1939. There were no survivors. Among those killed was Wilhelm Peter Boddem, a ten-victory ace with 2.J/88, on his way home to Germany after his last tour.

Extracted from actual film footage taken on operations by propaganda crews. This shows 22-87 of 2.K/88, another dedicated bomber, over the target with its ventral gun tub extended. The drag was so significant that it was the custom only to use the device when enemy fighters were expected.

Taken during the painting of markings, this picture shows 22-73, assigned to 3.K/88 and easy to identify by reason of the exceptionally wide camouflage areas; it wears a white *Pedro 3* on the nose.

*Pedro 3* in flight somewhere over the sea. The lower defense bin was not extended when away from the front, as it created very severe aerodynamic drag. This aircraft was eventually assigned to 3.K/88, and finally to the *Kleinbahn* services.

Two militarized Ju 52s stand in Seville between two of their Lufthansa colleagues, D-ATRN and D-AVIA. The number of windows on aircraft 22-79 shows it is obviously an ex-civilian transport converted to bomber duties. This particular aircraft was operated by Stab/88 (HQ) of the Legion Condor and flown by *Oberleutnant* Riedinger and *Leutnant* Dittler.

Taken from another Ju 52, 22-79 of the Stab/88 is flying to the front in murky weather conditions. Easily recognized are the wide camouflage bands. The flying formation is close and could be an indication that this is an actual combat scene. The dorsal gun position can just be made out.

22-80 was assigned to 2.K/88 and was flown for a long time by one of the German bomber pilots who was to enjoy an exceptional career: *Leutnant* Hajo Herrmann, assisted by *Leutnant* Röbling. Date and location are both unknown.

Lunch al fresco for the crew of this all-RLM grey Ju 52 of 2.K/88, 22-86, and their guests, who are probably enjoying a lull in operations. The aircraft is a dedicated bomber, as most of the airline windows have been blanked out on the production line. It was later transferred to *Kleinbahn* duties after it was phased out of first line operations, but disappeared on 24 October 1938, while on an aborted flight between Saragossa and Mallorca. It was forced to return to the mainland, where it crashed, the fact not being reported until the following day. All the crew were injured to some degree.

Last ceremonies before this aircraft from 1.K/88 flies back to Germany with a rather macabre load: the coffins of four Legion Condor members who had been killed in action. 22-84 was a dedicated bomber, but all the Ju 52/3 family could carry greater or lesser loads of freight. Flight times for the period were Berlin-Rome-Seville, two days; Berlin-Milan-Palma, one day. Allowing for airport delays, these may not be so different from today.

Junkers Ju 52/3 22-90 is a dedicated bomber-transport and wears the diving falcon emblem of 2.K/88 under the canopy. It appears freshly painted in a style resembling that of many of the Italian bombers which were a familiar sight to the Legion Condor airmen. It was later lost in an accident at Sabadell. Note that it has retained the enormous wheel spats which were usually removed in later service as they were prone to clogging with mud.

In front of 22-92 from 3.K/88, this mechanic shows two of the bombs that could fit in the Ju 52's bays. Left is an SC 250, right an SC 50. Bombs in a Ju 52 were stored vertically and dropped tail first. Not very accurate.

Ju-52 22-100 had a long career, as it was first assigned to 1.K/88 before flying the shuttle route with the *Kleinbahn* ("light railway") from mid-1937. The badge on the nose represents an eagle with a letter in its claws. Date and location of the picture are unknown.

Approaching the Basque coast from the sea, in order to avoid being intercepted at an early stage of their attack, these aircraft from 1.K/88 are flying at less than 300 feet above sea level; 22-100 was the machine of the unit's commanding officer, *Oberleutnant* Christian von Knauer. It was later assigned to the *Kleinbahn* service.

Ju 52 22-101 being salvaged after a difficult situation. It is an ex-DLH aircraft, and the time seems to be early in the war, as it is still in RLM grey overall. It was eventually transferred to the Spanish *Escuadrilla 6-E-22*.

This is 22-101, still in Legion Condor service, but repainted in camouflage appropriate for a combat zone. A mechanic is visible over the wing, refilling the wing fuel tank from the bowser.

22-102 is another auxiliary bomber of the Legion Condor. A pale blue cross is just visible on the fuselage while a Junker W34, 43-4, lurks in the background.

This seemingly all-RLM grey Ju 52 wears the highest known registration number in Spain, and in spite of being a dedicated bomber, it still sports the DLH-like black nose trim, which could mean it stayed as a Stab aircraft, excluded from active front duties. On the right is Bf 109 6-60, flown by Herbert Schob of 2.J/88 taxies past. As it has three victory tallies on its fin, the time is probably somewhere between 16 November and 30 December 1938, the dates on which Schob made his third and fourth kills. Location is probably Sanjurjo.

An unusual view by the other side. Seen from the air by a Republican Potez 54 aircrew, this Ju 52 has been dispersed among the trees, probably for maintenance, as two ladders seem to appear against the nose engine. The operational difficulties (no maps, half-trained crews of different nationalities) met by the Republicans in trying to keep these large French bombers useable meant that they were obliged to fly most missions at this kind of altitude.

A sample of the damage suffered by Ju 52s during combat and forced landings. Here an entire propeller blade has been shot off.

Flak damage to the fuselage.

The Junkers factory badge on this propeller blade indicates that this wreckage was once a Ju 52, shot down near Madrid in December 1936. On account of the date this could be the aircraft flown by the first commander of 1.K/88, Heinz Liegnitz, who perished with his entire crew.

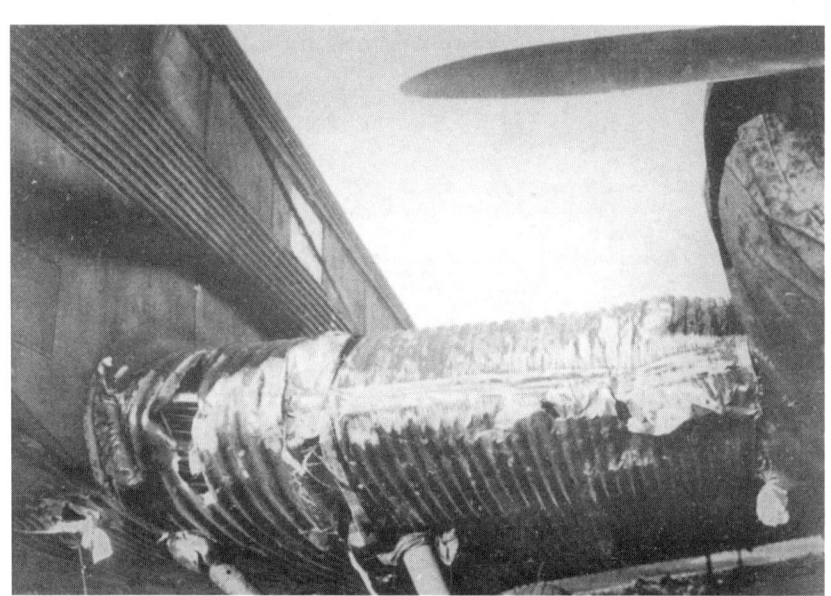

"Auntie Ju" was a strong lady. The corrugated construction of the Junkers Ju 52 meant that it could survive impacts like this (a midair collision?) and still get home.

An unidentified Ju 52 which appears to have either bogged down in soft ground, with the ground crew trying to haul it out with the aid of the central engine, or lost its middle propeller and force-landed.

The whole personnel of 3.J/88 (and their dogs) have gathered around the *Kleinbahn* aircraft to wish their popular *Staffelkapitän* Werner Mölders a safe trip back home. Ironically, it was on such a trip that Mölders was eventually to meet his death—not in air combat but travelling back to Germany for Ernst Udet's funeral as a passenger.

Members of 3.J/88 show off their Legion Condor uniforms to advantage as they wait to say good-bye to their colleagues returning to Germany. The men nearest the aircraft are all of the rank of either *Leutnant* or *Oberleutnant*. The detail of the corrugated skinning to the Junkers double flaps is very clearly seen.

Having attended to a last-minute call, going back to Germany with Mölders is *Leutnant* Hans Asmus, seen here walking towards the ex-DHL *Kleinbahn* aircraft. To preserve the fiction of German noninvolvement in Spain, personnel on rotation were required to wear civilian dress while travelling.

A Spanish pilot has also come to say good-bye and probably proceed to the traditional gift exchange. He is examining a *Luftwaffe* summer-weight flying helmet. The corrugated tail plane of the Ju 52 is clearly evident, as is the three-tone camouflage.

In front of 22-52, an ex-DLH aircraft which first saw service with the *Pedro* flight, those fortunates in civilian clothes leaving for home enjoy a last-minute joke with their comrades who are to remain in Spain.

Underneath the cabin of this Ju 52 is an emblem which identifies it as belonging to the Stab of J/88. If the "little fish" are the fighters, then presumably this must be the big fish.

This aircraft from the Spanish *Escuadrilla 1-E-22* is 22-57, formerly one of the *Pablo*s of von Moreau's flight. It is seen here after its pilot, Ananías Sanjuan, here posing with his aircraft, defected to the Republican side with its full bombload.

The badge on the tailfin of this Ju 52 speaks for itself: this is a hack and cargo aircraft, hence the furniture wagon emblem, assigned to 1.K/88 after the unit converted to the He 111. The Spanish *Teniente* (lieutenant) seems to be amused.

# The Heinkel He 111 in Spain

## Type code 25
## Nickname *Pedro*

| Code | Type | Unit | Arrived | Crew | A/C Emblem | A/C Name |
|---|---|---|---|---|---|---|
| 25-1 | B-1 | VB/88 | | | Champagne | Pedro 2 |
| | | 1.K/88 | | | | Pedro 2 |
| 25-2 | B-1 | VB/88 | | Uffz Zoben | | Pedro 3 |
| | | 1.K/88 | | | | Pedro 3 |
| | | 2.K/88 | | | | Pedro 3 |
| 25-3 | B-1 | VB/88 | | | Eagle & bomb | Pedro 1 |
| | | 1.K/88 | | | | Pedro 1 |
| | | '5.K/88' | | | | |
| 25-4 | B-1 | VB/88 | | | | Pedro 4 |
| | | 1.K/88 | | | Champagne/Old lady | Castelo Branco |
| 25-5 | | VB/88 | | | | Pedro 5 |
| 25-6 | B-1 | VB/88 | | | Das Hab ich Gern | Pedro 6 |
| | | 1.K/88 | | | | |
| 25-7 | | VB/88 | | | Glitzer Marys 4.Grad | Pedro 7 |
| 25-8 | B-1 | VB/88 | | | | Pedro 8 |
| 25-9 | B-1 | 1.K/88 | | | Champagne/Witch | Pedro 9 |
| 25-10 | | 1.K/88 | | | | Pedro 10 |
| 25-11 | | | | | | Pedro 11 |
| 25-12 | | VB/88 | | | Champagne | Pedro 12 |
| | | 4.K/88 | | | Clover | |
| | | 1.K/88 | | | | |
| 25-13 | | | | | | Pedro 13 |
| 25-14 | B-1 | | | | | Pedro 14 |
| 25-15 | B-1 | 4.K/88 | | | Holzauge/Hümel Hümel | Pedro 15 |
| | | 1.K/88 | | Lt Fuhrhop | Peter the Scottie | |
| 25-16 | | 1.K/88 | | | | |
| 25-17 | B-2 | 1.K/88 | | | Lucky Sweep | |
| 25-18 | | | | | | |
| 25-19 | | | | | | |
| 25-20 | | 10-G-25 | | | | |
| 25-21 | | | | | | |
| 25-22 | B-1 | 1.K/88 | | | | |
| 25-23 | B-1 | | | | Comet | |
| 25-24 | | '5.K/88' | | | | |
| 25-25 | | | | | | |
| 25-26 | B-1 | 2.K/88 | | | | |
| 25-27 | | | | | | |
| 25-28 | B-1 | 1.K/88 | | | Lucky Sweep | |
| | | '5.K/88' | | | | |

259

| Code | Type | Unit | Arrived | Crew | A/C Emblem | A/C Name |
|------|------|------|---------|------|------------|----------|
| 25-29 | B-1 | 1.K/88 | | | | Comet |
| 25-30 | | | | | | |
| 25-31 | | | | | | |
| 25-32 | | | | | | |
| 25-33 | | | | | | |
| 25-34 | | | | | | |
| 25-35 | | | | | | Viva Mickey |
| 25-36 | | | | | | |
| 25-37 | B-1 | | | | | |
| 25-38 | | | | | | |
| 25-39 | | | | | | |
| 25-40 | | | | | | |
| 25-41 | | | | | | |
| 25-42 | B-2 | | | | | |
| 25-43 | | | | | | Baron Münchausen |
| 25-44 | | 2.K/88 | | | | |
| 25-45 | | 2.K/88 | | | | |
| 25-46 | B-2 | 2.K/88 | | | | |
| 25-47 | | 2.K/88 | | | | |
| 25-48 | | | | | | |
| 25-49 | | 2.K/88 | | | | |
| 25-50 | | 2.K/88 | | | | |
| 25-51 | | 2.K/88 | | | | |
| 25-52 | | 2.K/88 | | | | |
| 25-53 | | 2.K/88 | | | | |
| 25-54 | | | | | | |
| 25-55 | | | | | | |
| 25-56 | B-2 | | | | | |
| 25-57 | B-2 | 1.K/88 | | | | Lucky Sweep |
| 25-58 | | | | | | |
| 25-59 | | | | | | |
| 25-60 | | | | | | |
| 25-61 | | | | | | |
| 25-62 | | | | | | |
| 25-63 | E | 3.K/88 | | | | |
| 25-64 | | | | | | |
| 25-65 | | | | Brücker | | |
| 25-66 | | | | | | |
| 25-67 | | | | | | |
| 25-68 | | | | | | |
| 25-69 | | | | | | |
| 25-70 | | | | | | |
| 25-71 | | | | | | |
| 25-72 | | | | | | |
| 25-73 | | | | | | |
| 25-74 | | | | | | |
| 25-75 | | | | | | |
| 25-76 | E | | | | | |
| 25-77 | | | | | | |
| 25-78 | E | | | | | |
| 25-79 | | | | | | |
| 25-80 | | | | | | |
| 25-81 | E | | | | | |
| 25-82 | | | | | | |

## HEINKEL HE 111 LOSSES IN CHRONOLOGICAL ORDER—49 TOTAL

| Date | A/C | Crew | Unit | Location | Fate | Cause |
|---|---|---|---|---|---|---|
| 23.08.37 | 25-5? | | | El Musel | Shot down | |
| 23.08.37 | 25-11? | | | El Musel | Shot down | |
| 02.09.37 | | | | Gijón | Shot down | |
| 30.09.37 | | | | | Accident | Engine failure |
| 30.09.37 | | | | | Accident | Crash-landing |
| 30.09.37 | | | | | Accident | Crash-landing |
| 21.10.37 | | | | | Accident | |
| 24.10.37 | | | | | Accident | |
| 10.12.37 | | | | Candasnos | Shot down | I-15 |
| 17.12.37 | 25-32 | | | Guadalajara | Pris | |
| 07.01.38 | | | | Teruel | Shot down (4/26) | |
| 26.01.38 | | | | Teruel | Shot down | 3.K/88 |
| 25.02.38 | | | | Alfaro | | |
| 10.03.38 | | Lt Kettner | 4.K/88 | Bujaraloz | Shot down | |
| 29.03.38 | | | | Candasnos | Shot down | I-16 (Tte Guirán) |
| 02.04.38 | | | | Alfaro | Bombed on ground | SB-2 |
| 02.04.38 | | | | Alfaro | Bombed on ground | SB-2 |
| 02.04.38 | | | | Alfaro | Accident | Collision with He111 |
| 16.04.38 | | | | Sierra Morena | Accident | Weather |
| 17.04.38 | 25-27 | | 1.K/88 | Motril | Shot down | Flak |
| ??.04.38 | | | | Written off | | |
| ??.04.38 | | | | Written off | | |
| ??.04.38 | | | | Written off | | |

## HEINKEL HE 111 LOSSES IN CHRONOLOGICAL ORDER—49 TOTAL (continued)

| Date | A/C | Crew | Unit | Location | Fate | Cause |
|---|---|---|---|---|---|---|
| ??.04.38 | | | | Written off | | |
| ??.04.38 | | | | Written off | | |
| ??.04.38 | | | | Written off | | |
| 25.04.38 | | | | Valencia | Shot down | I-16 (21/3) Tarazona |
| 25.04.38 | | | | Valencia | Shot down | I-16 (21/3) Fierro |
| 25.04.38 | | | | Valencia | Shot down | I-16 (31/3) Yuste |
| 14.05.38 | | | | | Shot down | |
| 29.05.38 | | Köstlin | | Vinaroz | Shot down | Flak |
| 28.07.38 | | | | Sanjurjo | Accident | Engine failure |
| 20.08.38 | 25-41 | Lt Willer | 3.K/88 | Gandesa | Shot down | (21/4) |
| 03.09.38 | | | | Ebro | Written off | Flak |
| 18.09.38 | | | | Sanjurjo (?) | Shot down | Flak |
| 01.10.38 | | Lt Hogeback | 1.K/88 | Mora de Ebro | Shot down | Flak |
| 16.10.38 | | Lt Rodel | 3.K/88 | Fatarella | Destroyed | Mid-air explosion |
| 31.10.38 | | | | | Shot down | |
| 02.11.38 | | | | Pinell | Shot down | Flak |
| 04.12.38 | | G. Schade | 3.K/88 | Vinaroz | Accident | Icing |
| 25.12.38 | | Lt Störer | 2.K/88 | Pineda de la Sierra | Shot down | |
| 04.01.39 | | Uffz Albrecht | 3.K/88 | Tarragona | Shot down | |
| 17.01.39 | | Lt Meiling | | Ocejo | Accident | |
| 25.01.39 | | Lt Botker | | Arrens | Accident | |
| | | Lt Meister | | Barcelona | Shot down | Flak |
| 04.02.39 | 25-65 | Uffz Brückers | | Cervia | Accident | |
| 09.02.39 | | Hptmn Allolio | 2.K/88 | | Shot down | Flak |
| 10.02.39 | | | | | Accident | Collision at take-off |
| 12.03.39 | | Maj Härle | | Madrid/Vicalvaro | Destroyed | |

This close-up of the nose of an unidentified Heinkel He 111E gives graphic evidence of the impact of a flak shell which has obviously penetrated the bomb-aimer's compartment before exploding outwards through the starboard side. Apart from the immediate damage, the aircraft appears to be in mint condition. Note that the nose machine gun has been removed from its socket in the rotating Ikaria mounting. Underneath the nose the fairing over the external bombsight is clearly visible. As the spinners appear to be red, this may be a machine of 2.K/88. Three Junkers Ju 87Bs can just be made out in the far distance, so the picture probably dates from late 1938 to early 1939, and the location is most likely Sanjurjo.

In order to be able to stop at the Balearic islands bases, the first Heinkel He 111Bs received this very conspicuous fuselage marking, which corresponded to that of the Nationalist air units based in Majorca.

Civilian personnel from the Heinkel factory are examining with great interest the effects of Republican ground fire on this He 111B-1, 25-1. It was originally flown by *Unteroffizier* Henne and *Leutnant* Graf von Hoyos. Note the spurting champagne bottle just visible on the fuselage black disc, and some serious damage below the wings. The unpainted propeller blades are of interest.

A closer view of the damage sustained by 25-1 which has almost torn away the undercarriage fairing but has miraculously hardly affected the undercarriage itself. The presence of Heinkel civilian technical specialists suggest that the aircraft was then with VB/88.

A close view of the fuselage of He 111B-1, 25-1, but sporting the diving eagle emblem, probably during the time it was used by 4.K/88.

For some reason, the fuselage and *Pedro* numbers did not match, on the early He 111s at least. 25-3 was *Pedro 1* possibly because it had been chosen by von Moreau as his personal machine and von Moreau himself was *Pedro 1* (his observer then being *Leutnant* von Detten). As seen here, the aircraft came to grief while landing with only minor damage. The eagle with a bomb appears to have been a personal motif for Rudolf von Moreau, and then by association briefly that of VB/88 and later still 4.K/88.

Aircraft 25-42 of 2.K/88 in flight, seen from a dorsal gun position. It is an early He 111B-1 model.

Portrait of a Heinkel 111E, registered in the -40 series. Location is most likely Sanjurjo.

The first aircraft in the line is 25-4, shortly after arrival. This was the aircraft flown by *Unteroffizier* Meier and *Leutnant* Oskar Schmidt.

*Leutnant* Oskar Schmidt (left) poses with a Spanish *Teniente* in front of 25-4, which carries a bursting champagne bottle emblem on the fuselage and is probably now in service with 1.K/88.

It is a pity that the artwork has been messed up by what appears to be an oil leak from an engine which has sprayed oil all down the fuselage side. This is He 111B-1 25-4, now known as *Castelo Branco*, with perhaps the most accomplished artwork in the entire Legion Condor on the fin. The symbolism of the name and the little old lady with a dog and suitcase is not known, but it makes a fine subject for modellers.

A final look at He 111B-1 *Pedro*, 25-4, showing the cavernous radiators and "organ pipe" exhausts of this model. The spinners appear to be white.

This is *Pedro 8* (serial number 25-8), which was the last aircraft of those of the second batch of He111B-1s.

*Pedro 8*, otherwise known as Heinkel He 111B-1 25-8, trundles in to land with everything down. The DB 600C engines gave a landing speed of 115 kilometers per hour.

*Pedro 9* was the first of the third batch of He 111s to arrive in Spain, and its decoration included the now famous champagne bottle and a pretty witch flying on a broom with a propeller. This third batch of He111Bs arrived painted light grey overall, perhaps because it was thought that they had no real opposition, or in order to test the operational utility of the splinter camouflage. Note the extended ventral gun position.

This close view of the fin of *Pedro 8* carries what is about as close to "girlie" art that the *Luftwaffe* ever got. It is a pity that color film had not yet arrived in Spain in the 1930s. Note the rudder trim tab and the detail of the antenna lead in, also the marking on the tailplane, possibly exhaust staining or the footmarks of the artist.

In this dispersal scene, the nearest aircraft to the camera is 25-12, identifiable by the clover leaf on the tail fin. Sanjurjo, date unknown.

A closer view of the fin of He 111B, 25-12 of 4.K/88, with the four-leafed clover. Obviously the crew were not leaving much to chance. Was RLM 70 or 71 the official color for clover leaves? Note the Polish-supplied RWD 13 in the background, one of four acquired by the Nationalists and used for liaison purposes.

A distant view of 25-14 which has no fin art, but has the champagne bottle on the fuselage. Two other overall grey He 111s can be seen in the background, but the machine in the foreground has a very light splinter pattern above and a pile of SC50 and SC 250 bombs under its starboard wing. Sanjurjo-Saragossa.

Saragossa-Sanjurjo air base seen from the lefthand seat of an arriving He 111. There are at least sixteen bombers in the picture, including the one flying. Note the different camouflage schemes.

A major flak burst has torn away the starboard wing root and perforated wing of this He 111, but it has returned to base. Or is it the premature detonation of one of its own bombs which has caused this? Several aircraft were lost due to mysterious explosions.

The Republican propaganda machine went into overdrive when the wreck of the first He 111 to be shot down was exhibited in Madrid under this sign reading "This is a Heinkel of the German military aviation, it was shot down by the Spanish aviation. It bombed Spanish cities and villages, flown by German airmen who assassinated women and children. In front of the wreck of the killer plane, every Spaniard, man or woman, promises to defend his fatherland and triumph over the criminals who come to steal our land."

Overall grey Heinkel He 111 25-14 was probably called *Pedro 14*, although no document proves it. The picture is too indistinct to say with certainty which subvariant it is, but it is most likely an early B-1.

What seems to be left of 25-14 after having had a hard time with the Republican fighter arm. Faintly visible on the forward part of the fuselage is a flying comet, also to be found on other bombers of K/88. The ground crew are probably trying to salvage something of value from the wreck.

Aircraft 25-15, in service with 1.K/88, was flown by *Leutnant* Fuhrhop and his crew. Their lucky mascot was a black Scotch terrier, who was apparently not so lucky as the crew, as he was killed over Sagunto on 13 June 1938. Every owner of this aircraft seems to have added to the artwork; note the diving eagle badge of VB/88 on the fuselage.

A close-up for modellers showing the memorial to the unfortunate Peter on the tail of He 111 25-15. There are a number of details worth closer study, notably the rudder lock, the tailplane hinge structure, and the trim tabs. The two shades of paint may represent fresh and weathered paint or perhaps RLM 02 and the lighter 63.

An inflight view of 25-15 showing the overall appearance of the machine while it was in service with 1.K/88. The dorsal gunner is apparently at his post.

This picture of 25-15 at an earlier period in its life shows it as it looked while it was with VB/88. Already called *Pedro 15*, it has the Hamburg slang *Hümel-Hümel* below the 15, and the name *Holzauge* (*Clog*) just behind the cockpit side window. It does not wear the diving eagle badge of VB/4.K/88, nor has Peter yet made his last fateful flight. The exhausts show clearly that it is a B-1 model. Note also that the spinners here appear to be red.

On 25-17, the chimney sweep on the tail fin attracts all the attention, but note the comet of 1.K/88 running along the upper flank of the fuselage. Apparently, the *Pedro* calls ended at 15 or 16. This aircraft must have been one of the earliest to receive the modified exhaust outlets of the late production B-1 model.

He 111B-1 25-22, of 1.K/88, shows off its comet insignia on the overall RLM 63 grey livery.

A member of the Legion Condor clowning for the camera with an SC50 bomb. Heinkel He 111B-1 25-23 of 1.K/88 (note the comet high on the fuselage) sits in the background ready to swallow some at least of the rest of the bombs in the foreground. There is what appears to be a quill pen or feather on the fin. This may be a visual pun on the pilot's name.

He 111B-1 25-26 has made it back home, but the result of the forced landing is obvious: promotion to the scrapyard. A good number of He 111s were lost this way, without being officially shot down. Visible on the nose is the eagle badge of 2.K/88.

Air and ground crew NCOs resting by their all-grey He 111B 25-28, also marked with the chimney sweep. The oil drums are marked "Aeronautica."

This front view of He 111B-1, 25-29 (?), on the ramp gives a good view of the front part of the two-color comet of 1.K/88, including a quite convenient swastika on a big eight-point star. It also allows a clear view of the modified exhausts fitted to the later B-1s in Spain and the white spinner fronts.

A comet bearer, He 111B-1, 25-29, of 1.K/88 flying towards enemy territory, as seen from a wingman's pilot's point of view. Note that the exhausts are of the first "organ pipe" style and the ventral gun tub is retracted. The overall effect is of a very clean grey machine. The picture is believed to have been taken on 17 December 1937 when the aircraft, based at Burgo de Osma, were attacking troop concentrations at Teruel.

Tucked in close for mutual protection, He 111B-1 25-29 of 1.K/88 as seen from the lefthand seat of another aircraft in the formation. Although out of focus, the pilot's steering wheel can be seen.

Actual combat footage from Spain is rare, but here we have He 111B-1 25-29 over the target at the point of bomb release. The dorsal gunner can be clearly seen and the ventral gunner's tub has been extended and manned. This was the most vulnerable phase of the flight when it was necessary to fly straight and level to allow the bomb aimer to carry out his job, but this also presented a good target to enemy fighters. An SC50 bomb has just left the bomb bay, tailfirst, and is aligning itself into the correct position.

Heinkel He 111 25-34 at rest while a crew member inspects the tailwheel. Notice the parachute left on the horizontal tail surfaces and that the ventral gun position is extended. This is probably an early B-2 model but there are no distinguishing markings to say which *Staffel* it belongs to.

A detail of the lowered machine-gun ventral "bin"—the exposed and rudimentary seating position guaranteed great excitement in flight! Note the small black dots on the fuselage are photo defects, not bullet impacts.

This is He 111 25-35 seen from an almost identical viewpoint to 25-34 on the previous page. The markings, camouflage, and lack of unit markings make them virtually indistinguishable.

Heinkel He 111B-2 25-42, as seen from the dorsal gunner's position of an accompanying aircraft. The sweep of the curved leading edge of this machine, which was found to be too complex in production, can be clearly seen.

A tail-end view of He 111, 25-43, of an unidentified *Staffel*, which carries another striking example of Legion Condor tail art. This one is Baron Münchausen, a notorious eighteenth-century German nobleman who was prone to telling fanciful tales of his exploits, perhaps the most outrageous being of his ride on a cannonball.

German and Spanish groundcrew pose for posterity at León in front of Heinkel He 111 25-43, which wore this spectacular and very German insignia on the tail: Baron von Münchausen himself, with the convenient small variation that exchanged the cannonball for a bomb.

Port side view of Baron Münchausen on the fin of 25-43.

Unusually, 25-43 carried its artwork on both sides of the fin.

Heinkel He 111 25-49 has landed without wheels, an all-too-common experience for German bomber crews in Spain; the I-15 and I-16s were often unable to shoot down the aircraft over the front, but the efficient sharpshooting generally damaged many systems inside, including the hydraulics. The damage to the port wing is obvious. A groundcrewman surveys the work he has to repair.

Heinkel He 111B 25-54 drops in at an unidentified Legion base.

Heinkel He 111 25-56 is a B-2 model, with the revised exhaust outlets and cowlings. Apart from the fact that it appears to have yellow spinners, there are no other individual markings visible.

Heinkel He 111B 25-56 rumbles in to land, probably at Sanjurjo. Note the exotically camouflaged DKW car.

Photocall on a cool day at Armilla for aircrew of K/88 in front of He 111B-2, 25-57. All the later He 111s in Spain wore very similar camouflage.

An unidentified member of the Legion Condor shakes the sand out of his boots using the tire of He 111 25-75 as a convenient seat.

Aviation humor on the nose of an unidentified He 111. It is probably from 2.K/88 as 25-76 to the rear wears the eagle on a shield. 25-76 appears to be one of the last B-2 models.

Heinkel He 111E 25-78 at the head of a long line of bombers, probably from 2.K/88, whose badge can just be made out.

Some ten Heinkel bombers, including He 111 E-1, 25-79, are visible in this picture, which allows us to study the splinter scheme on the wing of the nearest aircraft.

Heinkel He 111 25-80 at the point of touchdown. Most of the elaborate artwork seems to have been applied to the early batches only; the later machines in Spain all have a great and dull similarity.

This is Heinkel He 111E, coded 25-81, showing the drag-producing ventral bath tub. The 2.K/88 badge is visible on the nose. The unit was also distinguished by its red propeller spinners.

At the end of the war, the newest aircraft received their unit badge on the fin instead of the fuselage disc. This is He 111E 25-92, of 1.K/88, dropping its load over Republican positions.

This close-up of the starboard Jumo engine of an unidentified Heinkel He 111E of the Legion Condor right at the end of the war. In the background is another example, 25-96, with the highest known number for an He 111 in Spain. Camouflage remains RLM 62/63/64.

A bad Christmas for *Leutnant* Störer of 3.K/88, whose Heinkel 111 suffered from severe icing and crashed at Pineda de la Sierra on 25 December 1938.

This belly-landing by an unidentified He 111B-1 of 2.K/88 seems to be a source of amusement to the Spanish groundcrewman near the propeller spinner. Note the letter "K" on the fin, almost identical to that on *Leutnant* Störer's aircraft. As that belonged to a different *Staffel*, it is not known whether this is an earlier crash by the same machine or if the letter has some other meaning.

A view forward into the bomb-aimer's compartment of a Heinkel He 111B or E. The transparent Ikaria rotating gun mounting gave an unparalleled view.

The bomb-aimer of an He 111B moves to his station while the pilot scans his instruments. The main interior finish appears to be RLM 02.

Another view of the main instrument panel of an Heinkel 111B or E showing the throttle quadrants. Note the subtle differences between this and the panel seen in the previous photo.

A close-up of the port undercarriage assembly of a Heinkel He 111B or E. This proved to be both rugged and reliable in service.

A close-up on the lower defense "bin," open to the air, from which a courageous gunner could use an MG 15 against attacking fighters. Not a place for the fainthearted. Notice the trailing antenna mast on the right.

A selection of the nose art on several Heinkel He 111s seen at Saragossa in autumn 1938. *Annaliese*, an He 111E, has the propeller blade tips painted in the red/yellow/red Spanish colors.

Another has an unreadable inscription and a cartoon which looks as though it may have originated in a newspaper.

What the meaning of this torch on an He 111B-1 might be is unknown, except to the crew.

A close view of the lucky chimney sweep borne on the fin by a number of He 111s of 1.K/88. (This may be 25-17.) They must have worked since sweeps were later used by several other *Luftwaffe* bombers in World War II.

Mickey Mouse was not exclusively dedicated to the fighter aircraft: one all-RLM grey He 111B, 25-35, also sported him on its tail. The question mark behind the slogan "Viva Micky" suggests a degree of uncertainty about Mickey's fate.

No, this He-111B-1 from 2.K/88 will not carry all these bombs. Notice there is name below the unit's badge, but it is unfortunately illegible. The carefree manner in which these bombs have been left in the open suggests that there was little to fear from enemy aircraft.

A typical Spanish town of the 1930s, seen from the 3.K/88 leader's aircraft. Note the Plaza de Toros, down at the left. The glazed nose of the He 111 made such views commonplace.

Where there are bombers, there must be bombs. A Legion Condor bomb dump with a weather service Junkers W34 close by.

A paradoxical message if ever there was: "Happy Easter, Spain, 1939—the war is finished," all neatly delivered on a handy 250-kilogram bomb.

28 May 1939 and the Legion Condor is going back to Germany, but not without a last parade. Two *Oberleutnants* act as escort for the *Unteroffizier* carrying the Legion standard, as was the custom in the *Wehrmacht*.

# The Stuka Adventure in Spain

## Birth of a Legend

It is easy to confuse the phenomenon of the Stuka (*Sturzkampfflugzeug*) with the celebrated Junkers Ju 87, but in fact, events showed another story. The first Stuka arrived in Spain in October 1936 and had been quickly forgotten. It was an He 50G biplane which was tested at Seville-Tablada but which did not impress anyone and was never used in operations. Its ultimate fate is unknown, possibly it was sent back to Germany, but who knows if anyone actually took the trouble? The type later served quite successfully in the Russian campaign but in the very distinct role of night harassment. A little after the arrival of the He 50, three Henschel Hs 123s arrived in Spain, shortly to be joined by two more.

In November 1936, a first pre-production Ju 87A-0 followed the same itinerary with a crew consisting of *Unteroffizier* Herrmann Beurer and *Unteroffizier* Zitzewitz, but it was not until 15 January 1938 that the first operational aircraft arrived. In the event three Ju 87As were set aside for trials in December 1937 upon the establishment of I/StG 163 "Immelmann," later called StG 163. Having eventually arrived at La Cenia, they were numbered 29-3 to 29-5 inclusive, the correlation probably taking account of the two prototypes tested at Seville thirteen months before. Identical on the exterior, the A-0 was numbered 29-2; it has not been possible to determine if number 29-1, which clearly existed, was attributed to the He 50 (which seems questionable) or if there had actually been two Ju 87A-0s of the pre-series. On balance, this seems the likelier possibility; after all, if the German authorities had not hesitated to send to Spain three of their precious Messerschmitt Bf 109V prototypes, there seems no reason for them not to send two of the ten Ju 87s then available. Be that as it may, by 7 February, the *Kette* of Ju 87As was based at Calamocha. The abnormal techniques of the Stuka pilots quickly provoked incredulity among the Spanish aviators who in the beginning called them *Estupido*s.

After the usual hand-over, the small unit—composed of *Leutnant* Hermann Haas, *Leutnant* Gerd Weyert, and *Unteroffizier* Ernst Bartels (pilots of 29-4, 29-3, and 29-2, respectively); *Feldwebel* Kramer, *Unteroffizier*

Deep maintenance work on one of the Junkers Ju 87As sent for trials with the Legion Condor in early 1938. They look quite clean so the location may be Calamocha in February–March that year. 29-3 sits in the background.

Göller, and *Unteroffizier* Fleisch, all radio operators—was baptized 5.J/88 and then sent in April to the northern front for operational trials. All the members of the crews came from 11./LG1 based at Barth. Operations remained limited as the purpose of the unit was always essentially experimental. By the end of July, 5.J/88 was reequipped with Arado Ar 68s, and the Ju 87s were logically re-assigned to K/88 as bombers.

By the month of March 1937, the new experimental group VJ/88 (*Versuchsjagdgruppe*)[42] included five examples of the great competitor to the Ju 87, the Henschel Hs123, a robust and certainly more conventional sesqui-plane. Numbered 24-1 to 24-5, these aircraft were assigned to *Leutnant* Heinrich "Rubio" Brecker, *Feldwebel* Fritz Hillmannn, *Unteroffizier* Hermann Beurer (who had flown in the first Ju 87A-0 in November 1936), *Unteroffizier* Emil Reckert, and *Unteroffizier* August Wilmsen. On 1 April 1937, however, VJ/88 ceased to exist and passed its machines over to 2.J/88. The Hs 123s were then used to form the first Stuka 88, an experimental unit with limited means, barely fifteen people, including— apart from the three pilots—three mechanics, two armorers, an airframe specialist, an engine fitter, a supervisor, an interpreter, and a driver, plus civilians Werner Busch and Walter Krone on detachment from Henschel.

The first aircraft was lost on 25 March on the Aravaca sector of the northern front during a routine patrol. *Feldwebel* Emil Ruckert parachuted cleanly from the aircraft but was killed by rifle fire as he fell between the two opposing lines. Over the Bilbao front on 11 June 1937, *Unteroffizier* Wilmsen had the dubious honor of being the last German pilot of an Hs 123 to be shot down and killed in Spain. By this time, it was already clear that the Ju 87 two-seater had more potential and more useful load-carrying capacity than the conventional single-seater. The three surviving Hs 123s were therefore passed over to the Spanish who, always demanding, received up to sixteen of the Henschels. There was at least one aircraft numbered 24-17, which served in Spain under the name of *Angelito*.

The activities of the Ju 87s in Spain are less well known than those of the fighter *Gruppe*. Some facts are known, however: it seems that their first actual operation was on 17 February 1938 with bombs weighing 250 kilograms. On 6 March, they attacked the bridges over the Ebro at Sastago, a mission which was repeated the following day. Both missions were unsuccessful. On 8 March, they were able to drop two bombs weighing 500 kilograms on the railway station at Puebla de Hijar and to cut the line from Saragossa to Alcañiz. The following day, two aircraft were sent to break what the Germans referred to as a "hard nut," that is, the concrete fortifications four kilometers to the west of Aguilon; on the day, four missions under escort were necessary. The Stukas also attacked the enemy columns towards Azuara at 12.00 hours, the road systems to the west of Belchite, and the fortifications of Casilta six kilometers to the west of Belchite.

On 12 and 15 March, the same two aircraft attacked the bridges at Sastago and Guadalupe without any decisive result. On 26 April, they were sent to attack pockets of resistance at Cuevas de Viñarona, but from the twenty-seventh, the whole unit systematically attacked all the bridges over the Ebro.

From July 1938, the activity of the Ju 87s increased dramatically. The unit received more manpower and also two new Ju 87As, numbered 29-6 and 29-7. They were then used in a semi-systematic way as single-seaters so as to be able to carry a bomb of 500 kilograms and nearly always in a group of three aircraft. On 7 July, they attacked the encampments at Vall de Uxo; on the tenth, others two kilometers southeast of Torralba; on the seventeenth and eighteenth, the Sierra de Espadan. They were then stood down until the twenty-third, after which they started to attack road junctions: first of all, Rasquera, then four missions against Venta de Camposinos and the bridge to the north of Ginestar on the twenty-sixth, where they scored a direct hit. The road intersection at Venta de Camposinos was also the subject of a major attack on the twenty-seventh, just like the ones against Mera de Ebro and the bridge at Vinebre. On the twenty-eighth, they were in operation against Pinell with some very good results. The twenty-ninth was a hard day, with six sorties of three aircraft against Pinell and, above all, the bridge at Ginestar, which received three visits from them. On the thirtieth, they attacked Corbera and the bridges of Asco and Vinebre, the latter being destroyed. The following day, the month ended with just as much intense activity: attacks against the antiaircraft lookouts to the east of Tortosa, then a tunnel four kilometers to the east of Mora la Nueva, then the flak batteries at Corbera, where they made two direct hits.

On 1 August, they went back to the tunnel, making a direct hit on the southern entrance and two direct hits at the northern entrance, after which they attacked the positions of Rasquera anew with two direct hits again. On the second, it was the turn of the positions around Corbera and of the railway lines to the southwest of Ginestar-Miravet; on the third, it was the positions to the east of Benifallet and Ginestar, then an attack against the streets of Rasquera. On 6 August, there were three sorties against the bridges to the northwest of Ginestar; on the seventh, the railway to the west of Benifallet (twice) and the positions to the south of Mora del Ebro. A series of missions started on the eighth against the breakwater footbridges to the west of Benifallet, which required three sorties again on the ninth despite ever-increasing antiaircraft fire. On the tenth, the usual patrol attacked the positions at Corbera, which they left on fire, and then the footbridges to the west of Ginestar, which suffered renewed attacks. Missions were carried out in the face of intense ground fire on the eleventh, thirteenth, fourteenth, fifteenth, and sixteenth, and, on the last day, Republican fighter opposition. These days, they were alternated with attacks against the bridges to the south of Mora de Ebra, which were hit, and three times to the north against ferocious flak.

On 19 August, artillery batteries and munitions parks in the Corbera sector were attacked three times and seriously damaged. Nonetheless, these recommenced activity on the twentieth. At this time, the road intersections in the sector Venta de Camposinos were very strongly attacked although defended by impressive light-caliber antiaircraft fire. On the twenty-third, it was the same on the intersections to the south of Fattarella with good results, but on the twenty-fifth, the mission against the footbridges to the north of Benifallet was repulsed by the Republican antiaircraft fire. After a forced stand-down due to bad weather, the Ju 87s avenged themselves on the twenty-eighth and twenty-ninth by attacking positions around Benisanet, Miravel, and Pinell, scoring two direct hits at each.

On 4 September, the two airworthy aircraft attacked the northwest exit of Corbera, then hit dead center the road intersection at Venta de Camposinos, which was attacked again on the fifth and sixth, as were battalions of reservists stationed at Pinell. On the seventh and eleventh, it was the turn of reserve units at Fatarella. On the thirteenth, artillery positions to the southwest of Fatarella received three direct hits in two consecutive missions. The attack was repeated successfully on the eighteenth. On the twentieth, the pair fell upon the munitions depot at Paitrosos twice during the day, the pilots noting heavy explosions. The operation was repeated twice the following day. On the twenty-second, two missions of two aircraft pounded the railway station at Ampolla.

As a result of this experiment, which seems also to have directed the Ju 87As against the forces disengaging in the Teruel sector, a report from *Oberst*[43] Plocher, who had come to Spain expressly to make it, indicated a good overall performance with an average error of less than five meters, which represents an interesting achievement but was certainly not ideal against tanks and well-protected artillery batteries. The principal fault noted was an obvious lack of power which limited the load to 250-kilogram bombs when used as two-seater; only if the gunner was left on the ground could a bomb of 500 kilograms be carried.

In October 1938, five of the new Ju 87B-1s were brought to Spain with much more expectation than the aircraft of the "A" series. They were numbered 29-8 to 29-11 (with one aircraft in reserve) and fully integrated into the bomber *Gruppe K/88*, retaining nonetheless their name, Stuka 88. The unit was clearly more imposing, regrouping with thirty-three men, among them five pilots, three gunners, nine mechanics, six armorers, an engine specialist, two radio specialists, an electrician, four drivers, an interpreter, and, surprisingly, two "scribes" to deal with the paperwork. They were based principally on the hard ground of Sanjurjo at Saragossa. It seems that the Ju 87As were sent back to Germany.

The operational state of the unit was well demonstrated by the extreme cohesion of this group of volunteers, of which twenty-three people (including all the aircrew) came from the same unit—in fact, the IV./LG 1 of Barth.[44] The greater part of the technical personnel came from the first Stuka 88 and had been in Spain since June–July 1938.

In December 1938, there were four operational Ju 87s. One of the aircraft had been shot down by Republican flak in April 1938 over the sector of Bujaraloz and the debris had been carefully recovered and sent to Germany. Techniques had evolved and the additional power of the Ju 87B permitted the use of 500-kilogram bombs in a two-seater. Systematic coordination into the operations of K/88 also permitted surprise attacks while the enemy's guard was lowered after the passage of the He 111s.

On 14 January 1939, the Ju 87s attacked the port of Tarragone all day long, aiming for cargo ships during the actual process of being unloaded and sinking three of them. On the twenty-seventh, *Oberleutnant* Fritz Glanser, at the helm since July 1938, passed over the command of Stuka 88 to *Oberleutnant* Heinz Bohne, freshly arrived on 11 January along with *Unteroffizier* Karl Fitzner. On the fourteenth, *Unteroffizier* Hans Ott made up the complement of new pilots; the gunner/radio operators were *Unteroffizier* Hermann Witteborn (who had arrived in October 1938), *Unteroffizier* Albert Conrad, and *Unteroffizier* Werner Schlitterlau. Finally, on 28 January, *Leutnant* Siegfried Trogemann arrived as a pilot. On 8 February, *Unteroffizier* Edgar Tocha replaced Conrad. The last aircrew to arrive were *Unteroffizier* Kräft, *Unteroffizier* Bär, and *Unteroffizier* Carlson.

On 4 March 1939, the Stukas attacked the road bridge at Salvacañete and, on the fifth, that at Villanueva, which they failed to hit. That same day, 29-11 was seriously hit by ground fire during an attack on Teruel and had to force land due to an engine failure, fortunately in friendly territory. On the seventh, everybody attacked the sector Viver/Segorbe/Sagunto. On the sixteenth, it was the turn of the road bridge at Meco to the southwest of Guadalajara and, on the seventeenth, of the railway crossing to the northwest of Arganda. For a change, on the eighteenth, the Ju 87s attacked artillery positions to the southwest of Titulcia.

A record was achieved on the twenty-seventh, with thirteen sorties in all on the roads in the sector of Arges. From then on, the Republican resistance was broken, and even the Ju 87s gave themselves up to the delights of the *Freiejagd* around the vicinity of Madrid.

It appears that the activity of a few Ju 87s in Spain permitted the fine-tuning of "pinpoint" bombing techniques in an environment less dangerous than would have been found in a conflict such as the Polish campaign, thereby stealing a bit of a march on history. The general spirit of the unit is best illustrated by this example of German humor when the members of the squadron baptized themselves the *Jolanthe Kette*. Jolanthe was a comedy character taken from the work *Krach um Jolanthe* (*The Problem with Jolanthe*), which was also made into a cartoon film for the cinema with Jolanthe in the character of a small piglet. Furthermore, the squadron mascot was a charming little piglet who waltzed about with a model of a bomb around its neck.

# The Henschel Hs 123 in Spain

**Type code 24**
**Nickname** *Angelito*—"Little Angel"

Nice shot of 24-5, *Teufel* (*Devil*). The devil insignia is clearly visible below the central struts: it was sported on both sides, though not exactly symmetrical. The fact that the aircraft is seen here without its ventral fuel tank can only be explained by a maintenance operation, as is confirmed by the locked tail surfaces. The crate in the foreground is an ammunition box.

On Alfaro airfield in 1938, 24-3 is bathing in the Spanish sun in company of a transport Ju 52, while a silhouetted Do17 banks away on a lonely mission, probably reconnaissance, showing how it came to be known as the "flying pencil."

The original caption to this German archive picture is quite vague about the date, and the landscape is too inconspicuous to be useful, but there are few in-flight pictures of the Hs 123. Here are two examples of the earlier model, without headrests; the nearer aircraft seems to be 24-2.

Also in Seville, Henschel 24-3 shows the *Angelito* emblem, just below the central struts, which gave the aircraft its Spanish nickname (or was maybe derived from it; nobody seems certain). The photo seems to have been taken just after the end of the war, as the tail vertical fin shows a white circle, typical of several Spanish units.

Hs 123 24-3 stands on the flight line, ready to start, with two fire extinguishers ready nearby in case. Note the design of the numbers on the fuselage, which is much rounder than usual in the Legion Condor.

Hs 123 24-5, complete with devil's head emblem seen in company at Vitoria with another Henschel and a Fiat CR.32 in the background. Devils of all sorts were a favorite theme with the *Luftwaffe* unit artists.

A Legion Condor groundcrewman seems to regard Hs 123 24-5 with a degree of suspicion. The unique style of numbering used on the Henschels is clearly on view here.

*Teufel* waits here, with drop tanks but no bombs, by a carefully covered Ju 86. The wheel spats have probably been removed to avoid mud clogging and the almost automatic *caballito* ("ground loop") which usually followed. Later, the same action would be almost mandatory in Russia.

The second batch of Hs 123s that reached Spain did have the headrest that later made it easily identifiable on the Eastern Front. The aircraft on the left of the picture is 24-12. Note also that the thin style of numbers used by the first batch of aircraft has been dropped in favor of the much bolder style seen here.

An everyday scene in an armorer's life. Checking the SC50 wing bombs of an *Angelito*, probably for the sake of the propaganda photographers, as he would be quite unable to hold it by himself, should the necessity occur. Note the details of the wheel spats and their anti-skid surface for engine fitters at work.

Fine static study of the definitive Henschel 123. The second aircraft, in the background, is proof that not all flyers are superstitious.

# The Junkers Ju 87 in Spain

## Type code 29

Ju 87A-1 29-3 sits amidst a featureless Spanish plain, possibly at Calamocha, in 1938 soon after arrival as there is no exhaust staining. The hinged canopy was soon changed in the next model as was the over-sized undercarriage. No radio antenna is fitted. The three-tone camouflage shows up well in this picture. Note also that the wing gun fairing is sealed, probably meaning that the gun is not fitted.

This front view shows well the under-carriage struts and some detail of the main bomb fork. To many, the Anton was a much finer aircraft to look at than its later brother. What is very rarely seen in pictures of any Ju 87 is the window in the floor of the pilot's cockpit which allowed him to visually acquire his target before beginning his dive.

For a very brief period after their arrival, at least one Ju 87A carried this umbrella and bowler emblem. It was soon replaced by the little pig. Perhaps the seemingly "British" imagery was intended to suggest that the Ju 8 was an aircraft for gentlemen.

Seen in León, where it had flown for repair, Stuka 29-2 is still arousing considerable interest from the ground personnel. The time taken to repair it prevented its being used in the attack against the Republican port of Tarragona. Noticeable is the presence of the twin radio antennae, so typical of the A-0 Anton, as it disappeared from the A-1.

The pristine state of the paint and the curious attention paid by the personnel seem to show that this Ju 87A has only just arrived in Spain. The olive trees in the background are typical of La Cenia airfield, one of the biggest bases of the Legion Condor, from where most of the Ebro campaign was fought from.

Same scene as in the previous photo. One can see the oil can under the nose of the aircraft, and the main bomb lying on the ground, between the undercarriage legs. The cockpit was left open at all times in Spain, in order to limit the excessive heat of the summer.

Something seems to be baffling the ground crew. Note how the upwards hinging canopies restricted access to the cockpit, the non-slip walkways on the wing root, the reinforcing plate over the wing joint and the splinter camouflage.

The war is just over and all the combat aircraft are gathering in Madrid for the final victory parade. Among other types of aircraft (see a He 70 at left, and the spatted undercarriage of a Hs 126 between the Stuka's wheels) is this Ju 87A, which is not 29-2 (no antennae) nor 29-3 or 5 (see different splinter scheme on the nose), from which we may conclude it is 29-4, the usual mount of the leading crew, *Leutnant* Haas and *Feldwebel* Kramer. Note the stain over the engine exhaust and the presence of the little pig emblem.

Fine shot of 29-5. The little pig emblem was painted apparently only on the left wheel spat, and it seems to have appeared after the *Kette* had gone independent from J/88. Note all flaps down and the absence of bombs, which seem to indicate the aircraft is still undergoing flight tests.

A closer view of *Jolanthe*, the pig on the wheel spat of 29-5, and a proud mechanic who gives an idea of the size of the Ju 87. The reinforcing rollover bars can be seen behind the pilot's seat.

Nice detail of the 500-kilogram bomb in place under the Ju 87A's belly. Ground clearance was not very generous in this configuration, until the aircraft could lift its tail from the ground.

Last checks before a mission for this now very tired looking Ju 87A, with a 500-kilogram bomb in place, shortly before it moves out of the olive groves at La Cenia.

A detail study of the Ju 87B's nose and generous radiator, the shutters being open.

The shark-like smile of a Ju 87B revving up before take-off, here with shutters closed.

Nothing would apparently distinguish this Ju 87B from hundreds of its brothers that took part in World War II, but for the hardly visible *Jolanthe Kette* insignia on the left wheel spat, which shows its undeniable presence in Spain.

The frontal aspect of the Ju 87B looked remarkably like a bird of prey.

A classic shot of a classic plane, here it is fully bombed up at La Cenia with one central projectile and four little bombs under the wings. The bomb seen behind the tail tied to the tailwheel is being used just as a weight to prevent the wind from dragging the aircraft. This habit could have originated in the fierce tempest that destroyed several aircraft on the ground on this same airfield during the summer of 1938.

The crew being assisted into Ju 87Bs 29-7 and 29-8 show that a mission is just a few minutes away. There seems to be no sign of the rear gunners. Perhaps enemy air opposition was so limited at this time that the gunners were left behind to save weight. The camouflage is the entirely standard *Luftwaffe* dark greens of the 1939 period, the three-tone splinter type having being abandoned as a result of the experience in Spain.

Cause. A Francoist air force lieutenant is admiring the ETC 500/IX 500-kilogram bomb that constituted the Ju 87's main armament. At that time, no other single-engine combat aircraft could even take it off the ground, though the Anton needed to be flown solo to achieve that.

Means. Seen here from the wingman position, 29-11 is probably the most frequently published Ju 87 in Spain. The landscape appears to correspond to the Ebro campaign and the aircraft are probably on a live mission, as all armament has been fitted. This machine was badly damaged by Republican flak on 4 March 1939, subsequently making a tricky deadstick landing in Teruel.

And effect. Typical targets for the Stukas' pinpoint accuracy were crossroads, bridges, strongpoints, and even enemy tanks. Here a Nationalist soldier stays low and watches the show.

# Versuchsbombengruppe VB/88

## Tempering the Steel

In December 1937, Rudolf von Moreau was recalled to Berlin for discussions with Hermann Göring. The appearance of Soviet-built fighters over Madrid required a radical reappraisal of the German strategy. If the Heinkel He 51 biplane fighters were unable to take on the Polikarpov I-15 and I-16, then the slow and heavy Ju 52 bombers, pride of the *Luftwaffe* only three months previously, would be quickly forced to operate solely by night. The verbal report from von Moreau, one of the most respected German aviators of the period, reinforced the cries of alarm from the fighter pilots of the Legion Condor. The Third Reich was using in Spain its latest machines, some still prototypes or only just entering service. Not only was the prestige of the regime at stake but the opportunity to put German technology to trial by fire was not to be missed.

Returning to Spain before Christmas, von Moreau expedited the transfer of the the cream of K/88, in this case almost the whole of his *Staffel* (1.K/88), to conversion courses onto the three most modern types of bombers available in Hitler's Germany. At the beginning of February 1938, he had posted to his new unit specialists on the Ju 86: *Leutnant* Rudolf Kauffmann, *Leutnant* Oskar Otolski, and *Leutnant* Selmar Huke (observers); *Unteroffizier* Alfred Katzberg, *Unteroffizier* Hans Peetz, and *Unteroffizier* Gerhardt Bowitz (pilots); *Unteroffizier* Harmon Schmid, *Unteroffizier* Ernst Pietruska, and *Unteroffizier* Günther Loehning (radio operators); and *Unteroffizier* Rupert Sieben, *Unteroffizier* Willy Dietsch, and *Unteroffizier* Heinrich Siefken (flight engineers). In mid-February, four Heinkel He 111B-1s, four Dornier Do 17E-1s and four Junkers Ju 86D-1s arrived at Seville. Just as the new ideas and equipment for J/88 were tried out within VJ/88, so the bomber *Gruppe* in the Legion Condor had available its experimental unit, the *Versuchsbomberstaffel* (VB/88), which tested and developed the techniques and tactics used by the *Luftwaffe* during the Second World War.

Coming into existence rather later than VJ/88, the experimental unit developed more slowly; a bomber is heavier, more complicated and a great deal more expensive than a fighter. At that time the German gamble was that a fast, lightly armed bomber carried an operational risk which could only be beaten by well-refined tactics. It is therefore not surprising that an early entry into combat was avoided by von Moreau, even more so after he flew to the aid of the troops of the Italian Expeditionary Corps embroiled in their great offensive against Guadalajara. They had been obliged to dig in so as to resist attacks by Republican "aerial cavalry" in the shape of I-15s and I-16s. His misgivings were confirmed when on the first mission the He 111Bs of VB/88 came under fire—from Italian antiaircraft artillery.

During this time, on 23 February, a Ju 86 (26-1) was shot down over Andujar. Out of the crew, Kaufmann, Bowitz, and Siefken were all killed in action but the radio operator, Loehning, succeeded in escaping by parachute and was made prisoner. The aircraft was immediately replaced by a new machine flown from Germany and numbered 26-5. On 12 March, the Do 17s carried out their first combat mission accompanied by a single Ju 86. They then operated regularly, from Matacán-Salamanca from 20 March, bombing the Republican territory of Barajas and Alcalá de Henares, and outrunning an I-16 which tried to catch them. Two He 111s were unable to complete their mission that day on account of the bad weather but another followed the same route on the twenty-third. On the twenty-fifth, almost the whole of VB/88 was in the air; three He 111s attacked the port of Santander sinking one of the vessels there, while the fourth machine bombed the enemy base at Alcalá de Henares, and claimed the destruction of four aircraft on the ground. A Do 17 and a Ju 86 attacked Ocaña and the station at Aranjuez, which was followed by an attack on this last objective by three more Dorniers which hit the metal railway bridge nearby.

Fortunately, the complete order of battle for VB/88 for mid-March 1937 has survived. The unit then consisted of seventy-five men, of whom fifteen were civilian specialists on detachment from Junkers, Mercedes, Dornier, Heinkel, and BMW, plus the inevitable representative from the RLM. The He 111s were numbered 25-1 to 25-4; the Ju 86s 26-2 to 26-5, and the Do 17Es, 27-1 to 27-4. Using his status as *Staffelkapitän*, von Moreau chose 25-3 as his personal aircraft. The crews of the He 111s were made up as follows (pilot/observer/radio operator/flight engineer): *Oberleutnant* von Moreau, *Leutnant* von Detten, *Feldwebel* Messer, *Unteroffizier* Meyenberg (25-3); *Unteroffizier* Henne, *Leutnant* Graf Hoyos, *Feldwebel* Seebach, *Unteroffizier* Hempe (25-1); *Unteroffizier* Zober, *Leutnant*

Piecha, *Feldwebel* Langbein, *Unteroffizier* Brueningsen (25-2); *Unteroffizier* Meier, *Leutnant* Oskar Schmidt, *Feldwebel* Loeffler, *Unteroffizier* Wagner (25-4).

In mid-March, only two of the four Ju 86s had complete crews: *Unteroffizier* Katzberg, *Leutnant* Otolski, *Unteroffizier* Schmid, *Unteroffizier* Sieben (26-2); and *Unteroffizier* Peetz, *Leutnant* Huke, *Unteroffizier* Pietruska, *Unteroffizier* Dietsch (26-3). Three Do 17s only had the following crews: *Oberleutnant* Joester, *Oberfeldwebel* Koessler, *Unteroffizier* Troll (27-1); *Unteroffizier* Schmitz, *Feldwebel* Mantwitz, *Unteroffizier* Hinterberger (27-2); *Unteroffizier* Immel, *Unteroffizier* Brohammer, *Unteroffizier* Noller (27-3); *Unteroffizier* Steiner, a radio operator, was in reserve. All the crew members of the Ju 86s were drawn from KG 152, 153 and 157. At the end of the month, *Unteroffizier* Kratzert, a flight engineer, arrived to complete the flight crews.[45]

Rumor has it that the first operations by the He 111s of VB/88 consisted of repeated strikes against the headquarters of the Soviets in Spain at Alcalá de Henares as the four aircraft had attacked in line astern formation. This seems doubtful if only because it does seem like the prudent von Moreau to make a direct attack against the largest fighter base in Republican territory. On 25 March, von Richthofen visited Vitoria, the Basque front and various secondary airfields and, after a summit meeting on the twenty-ninth, VB/88 followed the rest of the bomber *Gruppe* to Burgos on 30 March in preparation for the offensive against the northern zone. Their first important contribution was an attack against Ochandiano and positions on Monte Jacinto on the thirty-first. On that date, two other Ju 86s were lost on operations following forced landings caused by the notoriously unreliable diesel engines. The two survivors were handed over to the Spaniards. Throughout April, the new bombers gave priority to attacks on Republican territory at Lamiaco, Sondica and Santander, in the hope of eliminating the meagre fighter forces of the Basque country.

On 1 April, six aircraft (one He 111, two Ju 86s and 3 Do 17s) dropped five tons of bombs on the front. The next day the combats intensified following an attack on second-line positions at Mecoleta, when they dropped eight and a half tonnes. On the fourth, the breakthrough took place and Ochandiano was occupied. The aircraft of VB/88 were then dedicated to attacks on Republican-held territory around Bilbao and Santander. The offensive had clearly ended by the seventh, and the Legion therefore decided to quietly forget the rather difficult exchange of words which had taken place on the evening of the second between the Nationalist General Mola and *Oberst* von Richthofen, who had called the Spaniards both slow and unprofessional.

The new bombers returned all the same on 7 April to destroy a Douglas DC-2[46] and two I-15s at Santander. In the evening, the whole of VB/88 went to Seville to prepare for the following day's Nationalist counteroffensive against Peñarroya. They bombed the airfield at Andujar on the ninth before returning to Burgos the next day to ready themselves for the second phase of the offensive against the northern Republicans. Until the seventeenth, poor weather enforced an unwanted respite on the *Gruppe*, except for a raid on Ochandiano on the thirteenth and an attack on the airfield at Bilbao on the fifteenth, during which they destroyed the I-15 of *Sergento* Juan Rodriguez. On the eighteenth, three He 111s and three Do 17s returned to Bilbao, but this time they were intercepted by half a dozen Chatos from the field at Lamiaco, led by the hero of the Basque country, Felipe del Río, who broke up the VB/88 formation and shot down the Do 17E (27-2) of *Leutnant* Hans Sobotka, *Unteroffizier* Otto Hofmeister, and *Unteroffizier* Friedrich Müller. The last two managed to parachute to safety, but Sobotka, who had only arrived from Germany on 16 April, perished in his aircraft.

The afternoon mission on the twentieth, intended to break the eastern front, did not meet with success. On the twenty-second, VB/88 attacked the airfields of Bilbao with an He 111 formation in the morning and Do 17s in the afternoon. By the twenty-fourth, the new front had been broken and the unit returned to harassing the port and environs of Bilbao. Then, on the twenty-sixth, with little risk, the new bombers gained for themselves a world-wide reputation when a single Do 17 marked an objective for the main body of K/88 by bombing the Rentería bridge in the village of Guernica. This attack was followed by another by an isolated He 111 in the afternoon. Of this mission, the Legion history says little except that the aircraft of VB/88 were not only the first over the target, but also the last, when a second He 111 left Burgos at 19.30, according to Karl Ries, "so as to complete the chaos." Mission accomplished. During the month, VB/88 lost *Leutnant* Schmidt, who was transferred to reinforce 3.K/88.

On 29 April, VB/88 accompanied the rest of K/88 in raids on positions at Amorebieta and the mountain of Gorbea, which were offering much more resistance to the Nationalists than previously, and to the area of Bilbao. At the beginning of May, the bombers of VB/88 had been sent twice to the Bermeo and Sollube sectors to relieve an Italian brigade which had imprudently advanced. On 7 May, the unit began attacks against Santander. These lasted an entire week but gave no respite to Bilbao since, on the twelfth, three He 111s and two Do 17s successfully set fire to the fuel depots of the Campsa. During May, the Do 17 operated five times over the Basque front, principally against Amorebieta. On 15 and 21 May, VB/88 carried out almost routine visited to the areas around Bilbao, Santander, and Reinosa. On the twenty-second, enemy fighters bounced the formation but the bombers were saved by the presence of an easier prey: one of the He 70s of A/88 which had to make a hasty landing at Ochandiano. At last, on 28 May, VB/88 and eight He 70s of A/88 succeeded in catching the remaining Republican fighters on the ground at Santander, burning five aircraft.

The technical difficulties attendant upon the introduction of the Ju 86 condemned them to a much slower ryhthm of action. On 15 May, two had operated to the east of Bilbao; on the twenty-ninth, they managed three missions to the west of Amorebieta, before one of them crashed to the east of Durango after an engine failure. By 15 June, the entire unit struck at a new airfield at Somorrostro, which had been prepared ready to receive a squadron of I-15s from Madrid, damaging several between them. On 11 and 12 June, VB/88 made a significant contribution to the breaking of the "Iron Ring" around Bilbao by making three missions daily. On the thirteenth, they returned to the routine of hitting the bases around Bilbao, then on fourteenth, the unit struck against Santo Domingo and the road from Miravalles to Llodio. The following day, they hit Republican positions to the west of Bilbao three times. On sixteenth, they hit the airfield at Santander and, on the seventeenth, flew three times against San Roque. The next day, it was missions to the south of Bilbao and the road from Bilbao to Santander, followed by operations to the northwest of Valmaseda on the nineteenth.

After the fall of Bilbao on 19 June, VB/88 entered the eye of the hurricane so to speak until the twenty-ninth. On the thirtieth, in preparation for the second phase of the offensive against the central sector of the northern zone, five aircraft from the unit attacked the vicinity of Laredo, then on 1 and 2 July, the airfield at Santander. When the Republicans unleashed their offensive against Brunete, however, this soon delayed any further efforts and obliged the units at the spearhead of the Nationalist forces to return to the central sector.

The arrival of a new batch of four He 111B-1s (25-5, 25-6, 25-7, and 25-8, and the first to be fitted with supplementary radiators) and eight Do 17s (27-5, 27-6, 27-7, 27-8, 27-9, 27-10, 27-11, 27-12) then enabled VB/88 to dispense with the last of the unreliable Ju 86s to the Spaniards and rationalise their type establishment. Operational training was not only necessary in the air, and the ground crews of the Legion fully appreciated both the need for precision and the importance of their maintenance role. On 18 June, two NCO armorers were killed at Burgos by the explosion of a bomb which was mishandled, an event repeated on the twenty-second when a *Feldwebel* was killed in similar circumstances.

It was at this time that *Hauptmann* Wolfgang Neudoerfer (an observer) arrived at the unit to oversee the transition from an experimental unit to that of a regular frontline unit. The unit then consisted of ninety-five men, fourteen of whom were civilians. In between times, the following pilots had arrived: *Feldwebel* Karl Haefele, *Unteroffizier* Wolfgang Harder, *Unteroffizier* Herbert Schmid, *Unteroffizier* Albert Schreiweis, *Unteroffizier* Kurt Buchholz, *Unteroffizier* Gottlob Beilharz, *Unteroffizier* Heinrich Bohne, and *Unteroffizier* Hans Peetz, one of the original members of the unit. Of the observers, only Otolski and Huke remained from the originals, the others being *Leutnant* Heinrich Meyer, *Leutnant* Rolf Kloeppel, *Leutnant* Wolfgang Schiller, *Leutnant* Wilhelm Stemmler, *Leutnant* Juergen Baertens, and *Leutnant* Otto Bodemeyer. As for the original crews, they were sent to reform 4.K/88, with von Moreau at the head. They did not remain there for long, however, for the majority of them returned to Germany in the following month.

As the northern front had quietened down for a time, VB/88 moved to Salamanca with K/88. On 7 July, the eight serviceable aircraft took part in an attack against Valdemorillo and Villanueva de la Cañada in company with seven He 70s; this was a formation which was to be used regularly during the course of the campaign. The next day, in company with the Ju 52s of 1.K/88 and 2.K/88 and the He 111s of 3.K/88, they attacked Brunete, Villanueva de la Cañada, and, for the first time, Valdemorillo. Until 17 July, VB/88 was fully occupied with missions in support of the infantry at the front. On the seventeenth, the unit attacked positions in the Alcalá sector in the morning, in the afternoon in the general effort against Brunete. On the twenty-first, they returned to their original intended task, that of using their modern bombers to harass the Republican airfields of Barajas, Alcalá, and Tembleque. On the twenty-second, they operated twice against Alcalá and, the following day, against Torre de la Alameda. Two days later, however, VB/88 lost one of its new Do 17s, 27-5, but fortunately, the crew were able to parachute to safety over Republican territory.

On the twenty-fifth, the unit worked over a Republican antiaircraft battery, then a formation of tanks two kilometers north of Villanueva de la Cañada. On the twenty-sixth, it was the turn of the road between Villanueva and Valdemorillo, and Republican Headquarters at Torrelodones.

From the twenty-seventh, the aircraft of VB/88 returned to harassing enemy bases as the ground fighting wound down, notably around Alcalá and Guadalajara, with five He 111s on the twenty-eighth and four Do17s on the twenty-ninth. On 30 July, VB/88 returned to the airfield at Burgos in the northern zone in company with A/88 and K/88.

A third delivery of He 111s (numbered 25-9 to 25-20 inclusive) arrived in Spain at this time. The superior load-carrying ability of the He 111 over the "flying pencil" led to the decision by the Legion authorities to use the Heinkel for "heavy" bombing, relatively speaking, and the Dornier for "light" bombing. When the campaign against Santander began on 8 August, VB/88 went into action with eight He 111s against Alcalá and Guadalajara in the morning, and against Casar de Talamanca in the afternoon. By 14 August, there were already fourteen Heinkels available; consequently, the Dorniers were sent to A/88, which was in urgent need of replacements for its worn-out He 70s and which could no longer outrun the Republican fighters. For a time, however, VB/88 still retained 27-3, 27-4, and 27-8 in order to carry out their reconnaissance missions punctually. At the end of August, reorganization of the Legion Condor led to the disappearance of VB/88 in favor of the new 4.K/88, built up by von Moreau and his veterans, who then returned to Germany.

The Ju 86D-1 in flight was little more aerodynamic than the "Tante Ju," most of all with the "morale booster" defensive dust bin it had inherited from her.

Of course, *Pedro 1* was He 111B-1, 25-3. It had been chosen by von Moreau as his personal mount (his observer being *Leutnant* von Detten). It came to grief at landing, as seen here. The port propeller seems to be undamaged and the eagle with a bomb, which appears to have been a personal insignia for Rudolf von Moreau, eventually became the official Legion Condor emblem.

Ground crew gather around *Pedro 1* and start dismantling the engine, which may have been the cause of the crash seen in the previous photo.

This starboard side view of the crashed *Pedro 1* allows a good view of the exhaust arrangement used on the early-production He 111B-1. Clearly, the starboard engine was still turning when the aircraft hit the ground.

For unknown reasons, the aircraft number and names did not correspond on the early He 111s as they did on the Do 17s, and we can see here that aircraft 25-1 was called *Pedro 2*. It was originally flown by *Unteroffizier* Henne and *Leutnant* Graf von Hoyos. Note the spurting champagne bottle on the fuselage black disc, and some serious damage below the wings. This was to be of great interest to the Heinkel technicians in Spain.

Following a none-too-Germanic logic, *Pedro 3* was aircraft 25-2. The activity around the aircraft denotes a flying test period, as there is no danger of a scramble with the nose entirely covered. The He 111B-1 was originally flown by *Unteroffizier* Zober and *Leutnant* Piecha.

He 111B-1 25-7 was from the second batch of aircraft to arrive in Spain. It was surprised over Candsnos airfield by the Polikarpov I-15 CAP and shot down on the airfield itself, where the crew were made prisoners and the aircraft almost entirely burnt out. In these pictures, one can see the "Glitzer Mary's 4.Grad" inscription, as well as the female part of a dancing couple, which included a skeleton and had characterized this aircraft.

A closer view of 25-7 showing the remains of the interesting artwork. However, the man on the wing and those standing around are all in Legion uniform, which suggests that these pictures must have been taken after the airfield was captured by the Nationalists.

This ground-to-air view of a formation of He 111s shows the curved leading edge to the wing, the slender fuselage and the relatively small tailplane, a combination of features which probably led to its nickname of the the "spade" in the *Luftwaffe*.

On-the-job training in Spain was not restricted to aircrews. This view of the MG 15 nose gun and bomb-aimer's position shows evidence of a field repair to the nose glazing of the Ikaria turret, the spares position being what it was in Spain. Those little rivets, however, must have frequently looked like a flock of Moscas to the crew.

A He-111B-1 of 3.K/88 had to make a forced landing when it could not reach Burgos airfield, as a result of heavy hydraulics damage. Here the aircraft is immobilized for a few days. Note the yellow spinner tip that identified the *3 Staffel* in flight.

The first examples of the Do 17E were tried out operationally within the experimental VB/88 *Versuchsbomber Staffel*. Here are 27-2 and 27-3, respectively named *Pablo 2* and *Pablo 3*, names picked up from the many such examples on the false Spanish documents carried by the members of the Legion. The former aircraft was rapidly lost in action over the northern front, shot down by the Republican I-15 ace Felipe del Rio on 18 April 1937.

In the VB/88 in March–April 1937, the two new bombers produced by the German aeronautical industry sit side by side. Note the bombs merrily left unguarded in the open, which speaks highly of the low threat perceived then from the Republican aviation units.

The sleek Do 17E revolutionized A/88, where it replaced an aging He 70. Aircraft 27-3 was one of those which lived longer in Spain: it was to be transferred to A/88 and later to the Spanish 8-G-27 and christened *Comandante Rambaud* before being written off in an accident in October 1938.

Do 17E-1 27-1, *Pablo 1*, has come to grief when landing at Santander-West airfield, its hydraulic system damaged by Republican fire. It is obvious that the propellers were still turning during the crash. Damage does not look too serious as the smooth belly of the Dornier lent itself to relatively smooth landings.

*Pablo 3* also suffered a crash-landing, an illness all too frequent in the first few weeks of service of the Do 17 in Spain. This aircraft was lost in action on 9 October 1937. Note the complete absence of forward firing armament.

A pair of *Luftwaffe* "erks" (they did not wear black overalls in Spain, so probably do not qualify as "black men") from VB/88 while away the time until the *Spiess*, the regimental sergeant major, catches up with them. Unit pride extends also to the truck, a Phänomen Granit 25H.

# The Junkers Ju 86D in Spain

**Type code 26**
**Nickname** *Fumo*—"Smokey"

The relatively "long-lived" 25-3 proved to be the most reliable example of the Ju 86 in Spain, before it went into Spanish hands in mid-1937. Here it is with the engines receiving attention as was usual.

As soon as 25-1 was lost in combat (and that was soon enough), a replacement aircraft was sent from Germany and registered as 25-5. This was as high as it could be for a Ju 86 in Spain.

A group of German and Spanish personnel idle the time away around a Ju 86D, which, as seems customary, is well wrapped up. It seems to be serving as a sunshade for a mechanic.

Operational testing of the competing He 111, Do 17, and Ju 86 bombers in Spain soon showed a fast loser in the Junkers aircraft, which proved both too complex and too unreliable under field conditions. The diesel fuel for its engines may also have proved to be a problem; stocks of any military equipment in Spain were often in short supply.

This is Ju 86D-1, 26-5, soon after its arrival at Tablada. The angular cowlings for the Junkers diesel engines are very obvious. Although found not to be a good bomber (its erratic flight characteristics made aiming particularly difficult), with new engines it eventually proved to be a good trainer.

# Versuchsjagdgruppe VJ/88

## Forging the Blade

Even if the Spanish conflict represented an excellent opportunity to test new types of combat aircraft which Germany then had under development, it was not simply a question of sending precious prototypes directly into the fighting. It was therefore decided, right at the outset, to concentrate the new models at a secure base well away from the front line where they could be assembled and test flown. It was decided that Seville-Tablada was the most suitable on account of its size, the availability of decent accommodation and the relatively peaceful conditions which reigned in Andalusia.

It seems probable that the first machines arrived at random and that the organization followed rather later. At first, there were an He 50G, two Hs 123s, and one, or probably two, examples of the pre-series Ju 87A-0, and definitely two prototypes of the Bf 109, which arrived during the month of November; looking at the available evidence, it appears that they were the V3 and V4, fitted with Junkers Jumo 210a engines.

Considering the traditional German reputation for orderliness and efficiency, it is perhaps difficult to appreciate that those same people can be muddled and confused. This was certainly the case with those who had responsibility for the prototypes sent to Seville and only one thing is clear: these needed testing. The military technicians and the engine specialists detached from Junkers between them assembled their most precious new acquisition, namely the Messerschmitt Bf 109V3. Shortly afterwards, it was realised that there were no pilots for it. One of the pilots from 3.J/88, *Unteroffizier* Erwin Kley, was therefore assigned to the task. Then it was decided that one of the "old hares" who had arrived earlier in Spain would be better and the choice fell upon Hannes Trautloft. A colorful character, Trautloft had gained several victories in Spain, among them the first German aerial combat victory since the Great War; he was also the first German pilot to have been shot down since then. On 9 December 1936, he was ordered to report to Tablada but he was then with 4.J/88 at Vitoria in the north of the country and the bad weather prevented movement by air. He therefore set off by road.

When he arrived at Tablada on the eleventh, Kley had already, under orders, carried out the first test flight. Surprised by the unpleasant habit of the Bf 109 to swing to the left on takeoff, he had over-compensated, fortunately surviving the subsequent crash. But the aircraft needed major repairs and the V4 was still not fully assembled. Trautloft therefore had to wait until 14 December before he could make the first flight of a Messerschmitt Bf 109 in Spain. If the first flight was uneventful, it was not the case with those following: defective water pumps, unreliable undercarriage locks, erratic carburettors, tail-wheel locking mechanisms which broke and above all, engine overheating, conspired to cause a number of emergency landings, such as that on 2 January 1937, and imposed long periods of immobility on the ground. It was not until 14 January that Trautloft felt confident enough in his mount for it to be transferred to the Madrid front for all operational trials short of actual combat. In the meantime a third prototype had arrived, the V5, as well as a first prototype of the He 112 (the V4) and the structure of the test unit had been defined. On the twentieth, VJ/88 was officially formed at Tablada. The Bf 109V3 previously crashed by Kley was also probably ready to fly again by that date.

*Versuchsstaffel 88*, or VJ/88, was to have only a short existence. This was only to be expected in a unit which did not have a command structure in the accepted sense and where the pilots were in the service of the civilian engineers who were dealing with leading-edge technology. Also, once the initial tests of the aircraft were completed they were then passed

This anonymous Heinkel He 112, finished in overall RLM grey 02, may be the V9 shortly after its arrival in Spain and before it received the code 8-2 for testing by Harro Harder.

on for several weeks of operational evaluation, shared between the three front-line units. In this way, Trautloft and the V4 were assigned to 4.J/88; the greater part of their time, however, was passed with 3.J/88 in the north. It is difficult to accept the theory that each of the prototypes was sent back to Germany for repairs and/or modifications and then returned on account of the length of time involved in transport by sea which would have certainly restricted their use with the operational units.

The third stage involved the training of the pilots in formation tactics. For this it was necessary to recruit pilots already established within the operational units. 2.J/88 and, above all, 4.J/88 were both imposed upon, the latter supplying the majority of the pilots to the test unit: Knüppel, Rehahn, Strümpell, von Gilsa, von Bothmer, Gödecke, and Mratzek. The former contributed Pingel, Boddem, Heilmayer, and Schlaffer, while for their part 1.J/88 gave up the services of *Unteroffizier* Buhl and *Unteroffizier* Haarbach. On 31 January 1937, Staff Order No 45 launched VJ/88 into action. It began badly when, on 2 February, *Leutnant* Rehahn was killed in 6-2, which was none other than the Bf 109V3 earlier crashed by Kley and returned to flying condition. Some reports indicate that while on a flight to one of the *Staffeln* for a period of operational testing he had badly stowed his personal effects behind his seat and his laundry had jammed the controls.

The unit then consisted of the three prototype Bf 109s, five pre-series Hs 123s with the codes 24-1 to 24-5, and the He 112V4, coded 5-1. This last was piloted by *Oberleutnant* Günther "Fips" Radusch, and the biplanes were led by *Leutnant* Heinrich "Rubio" Brücker, the other pilots being *Feldwebel* Hillmann, from 2.J/88, and *Unteroffizier* Hermann Beurer (of 1.J/88), *Unteroffizier* Emil Rückert, and *Unteroffizier* August Wilmsen. Noteworthy already by its absence was the single He 50, but also noteworthy was the presence of one or more Ju 87A-0s which had arrived in November.

By 2 March, VJ/88 was a unit of fifty-nine men, of whom sixteen were civilian specialists from the firms of Junkers, Messerschmitt, Henschel, and Jumo; from the RLM came a certain Joachim von Richthofen, brother of *Oberst* Richthofen, Chief of Staff of the Legion and technical director of the ministry. The pilots already assigned were Knüppel, Strümpell, von Gilsa, Radusch, Winterer, Gödecke, and Mratzek. Pingel arrived on the fifth and Heilmayer on the sixth. On 10 March, the RLM engineer Rudolf Herrmann joined the unit. Before the end of the month, still more pilots arrived: Schlaffer, Boddem, Buhl, and Haarbach. By the twenty-seventh, the number of civilians present had been greatly reduced to three engine specialists from Junkers, three fitters from Messerschmitt, and two executives from the RLM.

Thirteen of the first-production Messerschmitt Bf 109Bs were hastily readied and shipped to Spain. So hastily in fact, that there was no time to wait for the availability of the twin-bladed variable-pitch metal VDM-Hamilton propellers specified and the Messerschmitts consequently entered service with fixed-pitch wooden propellers of the types already used by the prototypes. As a consequence their performance was somewhat degraded but the aircraft remained revolutionary. Each of the Bf 109s was allocated to a specific pilot in order of seniority. 6-1 to 6-13 (less 6-2, which had already been lost) were issued in this order: Knüppel, Strümpell, von Gilsa, von Bothmer, Schlaffer, Pingel, Heilmayer, Gödecke, Mratzek, Buhl, Boddem, and Haarbach. Numbers 6-14, 6-15 and 6-16 remained in reserve. Winterer was already missing from the roster and never arrived at the unit as he had been captured on 25 February before he could try out the Bf 109.

VJ/88 was soon to disappear, the Messerschmitts being absorbed, pilots as well, by Franzl Lützow's 2.J/88 which was in action over the northern front from the first days in April. The five Hs 123s for their part, were formed into an experimental "mini unit" called Stuka 88, while the He 112 skimmed over the fronts in order to prove its immense capabilities (not the least of which was its cannon, capable of destroying T-26 tanks) in the hands of Radusch, Balthasar, and then Schulz, until it was written off in an accident in July 1937.

This is the Messerschmitt Bf 109 V3 as flown by Hannes Trautloft, who has had the green heart emblem applied to it as a reminder of his origins in the "green heart" of Germany. The aircraft has a large wooden propeller and appears to be still in a natural metal finish.

This is the Heinkel He 112 V4 at Tablada being run up prior to a flight, although it should not have been left with the engine running wih nobody in the cockpit. Wilhelm Balthasar made a name for himself by his exploits with this machine.

This is one of the Heinkel He 112B-0s sold to the Spanish. Its immaculate condition suggests that it has just been delivered and flown by a civilian Heinkel pilot who wears a natty trilby. In November 1938 a batch of seventeen B-0 (ex-Japanese order, eventually cancelled) aircraft got to Spain to be assembled in León. They were finally delivered to the Spanish 5-G-5 group. Its tally was not particularly remarkable: one victory, one aircraft lost in combat, and two lost in accidents during the civil war. The type later shot down an American P-38 during World War II.

# Stab/88

## Storks and Typhoons

In spite of the official archives mentioning only four *Taifun*s sent to Spain, it is now certain that there were at least five aircraft (some experts speak of seven). This one had to crash-land in open space, but it was apparently done by the book, engine stopped. Note the Messerschmitt badge under the windscreen, special to this particular aircraft.

Hidden among the famous olive groves around the Legion's mega-base at La Cenia, the first two Storchs are ready for flight.

Four of the new Fieseler Fi 156 Storchs arrived in Spain in late 1936. Delivered to Stab/88, they were not used for observation as was their main duty at the beginning of World War II, but mostly as hacks, used very often by the Legion's surgeon. This is 46-1, apparently repainted in the field.

The first Storch suffered a definitive crash in early 1939 in a landing that seems to have been much too short. It appears that these early aircraft were delivered in overall grey but were later repainted in the field.

An unidentified Storch under the shade of an olive tree in La Cenia at the end of 1938.

Waiting for a flight are the Storch's usual pilot and a Legion surgeon.

Another picture of 46-1 after its crash with its port wing folded back. Note the white wingtip and cross.

In order to replace 46-1, lost in the crash shown above, a fifth aircraft was sent to Spain. All four surviving Storchs were later put to use by the Spanish Air Ministry for photographic duties.

This is the third Fi 156 to reach Spain, 46-3, painted in dark green with the striking white wingtips and rudder. The first two aircraft (46-1 and 46-2) were Fi 156B-0s, with the Werk Nrs. 618 and 619, respectively. Three others, all C-1s, are shown in the production records as Werk Nrs 638, 640, and 647 and were all delivered to an unknown destination in July 1938. Possibly these are the ones that went to Spain.

Another shot of the Legion's surgeon and the Storch and its pilot. Note the white wing crosses do not go across the moving surfaces.

All the Bf 108s in Spain officially belonged to Stab/88, but it was not at all uncommon to have one detached for some days or weeks to the Stab section of J or K/88. This is 44-3 sitting on a featureless Spanish plain.

Most *Taifun*s in Spain were painted overall RLM grey with only the classic Nationalist markings, such as 44-4 shown here, except for 44-2 which had a personal insignia in the center of the fuselage black disc and a stylized vertical bomb on the tail fin.

This is another view of Bf 108 44-4 and a companion, well covered against the heat of the sun and dwarfed by a nearby Ju 52. This wears the badge of 3.K/88. The location is apparently La Cenia.

44-5 came to grief in a landing accident and the cameraman was on hand to record its recovery. In this view it can be seen that the engine was stopped at impact. The occupants' personal equipment is piled on the wing.

The crash team have removed the starboard wing preparatory to hauling the fuselage onto the back of the truck. Many Bf 108s seem to have retained a natural metal finish to the canopy framing.

After disassembling the wings, the salvage team has lifted the whole aircraft on a medium truck. There are at least groundcrewmen working on the operation.

Ready for return to the workshops. The truck appears to be an early Opel Blitz.

Among the first types of German aircraft to reach Spain officially, the Junkers W34 was retained as a light transport and hack aircraft, until more specialized tasks required its unglamorous services. This one seems to be 43-1 during the last weeks of 1936; it has received no kind of camouflage yet and has remained in RLM grey.

# They Also Served

## Weather Services and Aerial Taxis

The absence of any additional equipment suggests that this Junkers W34, registered 43-3, was only used for duties in its original role: transport—in fact, for the Spanish General Queipo de Llano.

This aircraft sporting a splinter camouflage is 43-2, used for weather forecasting (and by the navigation school) as shown by the big goniometer antenna and the relative anemometer mounted on a long support on the right flank. It was flown in March 1937 by two civilian specialists, Dr. Schulze-Eckhart and Dr. Schulz, here in front of the engine.

The other side of 43-3 shows that a decorative black area was painted over the newly applied splinter robe and engine cowling, as was typical of DLH aircraft at the time.

43-4, on the other hand, appears to still be in the original light grey in which most Junkers aircraft of the 1930s flew, and part of a name can be made out under the tarpaulin.

This RLM grey W34, 43-5, is in use as a navigation trainer/weather aircraft.

Proof that seven Junkers W34s served in Spain. This one is finished in what looks like Spanish-applied camouflage, but no other details are known.

30-65 and 30-66 are two of the three Klemm L.32s allegedly delivered to the Legion Condor as liaison aircraft. Both are in silver finish with dark blue trim, although there are differences between the two, notably the fin and rudders.

Little is known of the third Klemm delivered to Spain; certainly no photo is known to exist. D-EJZK would not seem to be a Legion Condor aircraft, but it is a Klemm 35B. Seen at Seville-Tablada, in late 1938, could it have been the third Klemm?

Among the many civilian transport aircraft that allowed a constant communication with the fatherland was this metal Junkers 60 of Lufthansa, registered D-UFAL and christened *Jaguar*.

A group of Legionnaires in front of a most unusual truck. Could this be the photographic section of the Legion Condor and their mobile dark room?

Quite a number of Legion Condor members were killed in traffic accidents in Spain. A combination of bad roads and cheap wine probably helped, but this picture puts a new slant on the saying "waiting for an accident to happen."

In their off-duty moments, the men of the Legion probably enjoyed tinkering with cars as much as any other. In this case, the vehicle is an Italian Fiat-Ansaldo L3/35 tankette in service with an unidentified Nationalist tank unit.

# In Spanish Service

## Expatriates and Latecomers

A lineup of some of the Spanish He 112B-0s probably sometime in late 1938, shortly before they entered service with *Grupo 5-G-5*.

A camouflaged He 112, probably during World War II.

Spanish officers by Messerschmitt Bf 109, 6-56, which carries the famous emblem of *Grupo 5-G-5* on its fin. Note the gust lock clamping the fin and rudder.

A carefully posed picture of Legion Condor pilots and late Bf 109E-3s, probably shortly before handover to the Spaniards at the end of the war.

Some *Rayos* survived the war to soldier on in the Ejército del Aire, like this natural metal machine seen in the early 1940s.

*Comandante Rambaud* was 27-3, ex-*Pedro 3*, transferred from VB/88 to A/88 in October 1937, and to 8-G-27 in August 1938. It is seen here during the offensive against Catalonia. Note the open crew access hatch and the propeller tip markings.

This picture shows a group of Nationalist airmen gathered around a Heinkel He 111B-1, which is marked with the boozy airman badge of 10-G-25.

A front view of a late-series He 111B-1 showing some useful underside detail. It has yellow spinners and red/yellow/red propeller blade tips. The type remained the primary Spanish bomber for many years after the war. Long enough in fact to fight the Battle of Britain all over again, in Spain.

The Bücker Bü 131 Jungmann began in Spain a long career that would bring it into the 1980s. It was mainly used in the primary flying school. Here is one of the very first delivered, 33-2. It was so successful in Spain that CASA built another 530 or so under license.

The splendid Bücker Bü 133 Jungmeister was also provided to Nationalist flying schools but reserved, most logically, for the aerobatic phase of the course. Twenty were delivered in 1937, numbered 35-1 to 35-20. The uniforms of these Spanish pilots, each of whom is a different rank, suggest that this is a postwar picture.

Twenty-one Gotha 145s were delivered to the Spanish Nationalist flying school at Gallur, to replace the unsatisfactory Polish PWS 10 for the second phase of the curriculum in El Copero and Jérez de la Frontera. The Spanish built another twenty-five under license.

An aircraft which crops up frequently in the background of pictures of the Legion Condor is the Douglas DC-2 42-1, the sole example of its type in Nationalist service. Named *Capitan Vara de Rey* after the officer who prevented its escape to the Republicans by shooting up one of the engines (!), it was used as a personal transport by General Franco.

Despite the fact that the postwar Spanish air force eventually standardized on German aircraft, the large contribution made to the Nationalist victory made by the Italians should not be ignored. The Italians, too, handed over quantities of aircraft, including many Savoia Marchetti SM.81 bombers such as the one shown here. 21-52 wears the emblem of *Grupo 18-G-21*.

Probably the most potent Italian aircraft bequeathed to Franco's men was the Savoia Marchetti SM.79, a well-protected example of which, 28-10, is seen here. Sufficient quantities were left for the Spaniards to outfit four *Grupos* with the "Hunchback" (as the Italians called it).

# Captions to Color Artwork

1. Heinkel He 51B 2-23 of the first batch of such aircraft sent to Spain in 1936. Flown by Hannes Trautloft, it was finished in the overall very light RLM 63 (L40/52) and bore double black disc markings on the upperwing, and probably double chordwise black stripes also. Note the individual aircraft number was larger than the type number on the fuselage. Single black discs under the wings and the usual black and white rudder markings. It also carried the top hat emblem of the first 4.J/88 and was recorded early in 1938. The overall finish was still quite clean.
2. He 51B 2-47 was flown by Alfons Klein until his return to Germany on 2 March 1937. Evidence of increasing Republican opposition is shown by the way in which a green and/or brown mottle has been applied over the original RLM 63, although whether this was more for protection on the ground than in the air is unclear. The machine carried twin black disc Nationalist markings on the upperwings (which had been carefully painted around when the mottle was applied) as well as white St. Andrew's crosses. The lower wing tips were white. It suffered minor damage in a landing accident in August 1937 at Calahorra de Boedo, a victim of the He 51's sometimes unforgiving behavior on the ground.
3. He 51B 2-60 wearing the "Pik-As" emblem used by the first 4.J/88 in its later days. It is shown as it appeared in spring 1938 when it was being flown by *Leutnant* Kurt Müller at Calamocha, shortly before the aircraft was handed over to the Spaniards and probably finished in overall RLM 63 or 02 with irregular soft patches of 61 and 62 on the uppersurfaces. Usual Nationalist markings were carried.
4. He 51B 2-64, this one being flown by *Oberleutnant* Harro Harder, *Staffelkapitän* of 1.J/88 during the battle of Brunete in summer 1937. It wears similar camouflage and markings to 2-60 but with the addition of Harder's personal markings, a swastika on the fuselage disc, and also applied direct to the camouflage on the uper wing centre section. Harder also found the He 51 unforgiving when landing on soft ground.
5. One of the three Arado Ar 68Es sent to Spain, this is 9-3, intended for use as a twilight fighter. Illustrated as seen at La Cenia in late 1938, it wears the simplest markings on an overall 63 (L40/52), a color very similar to that used by later and much more effective night-fighters.
6. Heinkel He 51B 2-78 is that flown by Adolf Galland, *Staffelkapitän* of 3.J/88, who reveals his individuality by the large white Maltese cross on the fuselage, while the camouflage is very large blotches of 61 brown and 62 green. It is possible that the undersides were repainted a light blue over the original 63 light grey. The aircraft gradually acquired other markings—at first a small name "Limon" (?) under the port access door and later still the famous Mickey Mouse below the cabane struts.

7. Heinkel 51B 2-86 is *Heidi*, flown by *Feldwebel* Erich Kuhlmann of 4.J/88. It wears very similar camouflage to Galland's machine but with only a small name and a diving "marabu" bird marking under the portside cabane struts. For a time, this was the *Staffel* marking.
8. Heinkel He 51B 2-102 was probably the most individually marked aircraft of its type in Spain. Flown by the Legion's doctor, *Stabszart* Heinrich Neumann, who was a semi-civilian and who used the aircraft as a taxi in order to reach his patients. With the striking Red Cross, the good doctor's fervent motto, his wife's name plus the Mickey Mouse (introduced to 3.J/88 by Douglas Pitcairn), there was barely space for the heavy scumble of 61 and 62 applied over the original 63. Note that the spinner was red. Neumann returned to Germany in February 1938.
9. 5-1 is the Heinkel He 112 V4 as flown by the irrepressible Wilhelm Balthasar and "Fips" Radusch. It appears to be various shades of natural metal with the simple markings shown.
10. Strictly speaking not a part of the Legion, Heinkel He 112B 5-52 was just too elegant to leave out. It could be assumed that it would have been finished in RLM grey 02, but it appears far too light in photos, so it has been shown in RLM 63.
11. Messerschmitt Bf 109V4, coded 6-1, as damaged by Erwin Kley and flown by Hannes Trautloft. Finished in what appears to be a mixture of natural metal and RLM 63(?), the aircraft is marked with Trautloft's personal green heart emblem, a badge still used by the *Luftwaffe* today. Based at Tablada, Trautloft made the first flight by a Bf 109 in Spain in 6-1 on 12 December 1936.
12. Messerschmitt Bf 109B-1 6-4 was flown by *Leutnant* von Gilsa while with VJ/88 in March 1937. It is shown with the top hat marking of 2.J/88 and finished in overall RLM 02 grey.
13. Messerschmitt Bf 109B-1 6-10 in rather mysterious markings. It wears a basic finish of 63 or 02 uppersurfaces with 65 below and the top hat of 2.J/88. Flown regularly at one time Fritz Mratzek, it carries fourteen victory markings on the fin and the name *Altertum* in shadow-style lettering on the cowling. As only Mölders scored fourteen victories in Spain, but served with *3 Staffel*, it is felt that the aircraft may have been "bulled up" prior to handover to the Spaniards in 1939.
14. Messerschmitt Bf 109B 6-19 was one of the relatively rare machines in Spain to be finished in the two greens, RLM 70 and 71 on the uppersurfaces. Both the *Staffel* to which it belonged and the pilot remain unknown.
15. Bf 109B 6-38, of 1.J/88 was flown by Ernst Terry. The finish was very weathered and appears to be originally 70 and 71 with a mottle of 61 on the fuselage and patches on the wings. Undersides are 65. White spinner and black panel above the exhaust and similarly coloured wingroot walkways.
16. Bf 109D 6-56 of Walter Grabmann, *Kommandeur* of J/88. It now wears his initials, but had previously been used Gotthard Handrick, Grabmann's predecessor. It appears to overall 63 above, 65 below with black and white markings. It also wears the top hat of 2.J/88.
17. Bf 109D 6-79 is Werner Mölders's aircraft, finished in 63/65 with the usual markings. The spinner appears far too light in tone in monochrome photos to be black and is shown here as red, the *3 Staffel* color. The Mickey Mouse of 3.J/88 is carried on the fuselage, and the name *Luchs* may also be on the port side of the engine cowling.

# Captions to Color Artwork 377

18. Bf 109E-3 6-99 wears a similar finish to the above, but with a large black panel around the engine exhausts and down to the wingroot. It is typical of many of the later Bf 109s in Spain.
19. Bf 109E-3 6-107 *Mors-Mors!* Similar finish to above, but the aircraft is from 2.J/88. Spinner is therefore yellow, and top hat emblem is black and white. The unidentified pilot may have had Hamburg connections on account of the slogan on the port cowling. Whether the matching call *Hümel-Hümel* appeared on the starboard side is unknown.
20. Bf 109E-1 6-111 was the aircraft of Walter Ursinus, hence the nickname *Bärchen* and the top hat of 2.J/88. It also wears the nearly standard 63 uppers and 65 below. The spinner should be white.
21. Bf 109E-1 6-119 was flown by Siebelt Reents. Again 63/65 as above, with the "wooden-eye" badge of 1.J/88. Spinner also is white.
22. Bf 109E-3 6-123 of 3.J/88 was Hans Schmoller-Haldy's machine. Finish as 6-99, but with the additional personal beer mug emblem (known as "Cardinal Paff" apparently). Here the spinner was most probably grey.
23. Heinkel He 45B 15-20 was originally overall 63, but has acquired World War I–style polygonal patches of 61, 62 on the uppersurfaces. The low individual number suggests that the machine may belong to A/88. Wheel discs were probably black.
24. He 45B 15-21 (*Elli*) of A/88 is in overall worn 63 (or possibly 02) with unit playing card emblem on fin.
25. Messerschmitt Bf 108 44-5 of Stab/88 was almost certainly overall dark blue with the BFW logo in white under the windscreen. Most 108s in Spain seem to have retained natural metal canopy framing. Red/yellow/red tips to prop blades
26. Klemm Kl 32 30-65 was used by Stab/88 in overall silver with a dark blue cheat line and black markings.
27. Detail of the Klemm company logo on 30-65.
28. Heinkel He 46C 11-156 in overall 63 with black code markings probably belonged to one of the newly-formed Nationalist units, sometime in summer 1937. The meaning of the Roman "II" on the fin is not known.
29. He 46C 11-162 has an overall coat of 63 with what appears to be a fine green or brown mottle on the fuselage spine. It is presumably a sister ship to 11-156 above as it too has the Roman "II."
30. The *Teufel* emblem carried by Hs 123 24-5 from *Stukakette 88*.
31. Henschel Hs 123A 24-5 wears standard *Luftwaffe* 61/62/63 uppers with 65 below but with an odd style in numbers. Note no headrest on this early version. The red/white/black devil unit emblem was painted below the center section struts, apparently on both sides.
32. Henschel Hs 123A 24-13 was one of the later batches delivered to Spain and has the headrest. The camouflage pattern is *Luftwaffe* standard 61/62/63 with the later style bold numbers.
33. Junkers Ju 87A-0 29-2 was the first Stuka to be sent to Seville late in 1936. It is finished in *Luftwaffe* splinter camouflage in 61/62/63 above, 65 below. The spinner tip may at some time have been white. As the only clear photo of the aircraft is of the starboard side it is not totally confirmed that the umbrella emblem was carried on the port spat, but it seems probable.
34. Junkers Ju 87A-1 29-5 was from the second batch delivered and is shown as it looked in summer 1937. It wears one of the many variations of 61/62/63

splinter camouflage and the pig emblem on the port spat only. Rear of spinner is probably 63.
35. Junkers Ju 87B-1 29-8 of K/88 in October 1938. Camouflage is standard *Luftwaffe* finish of 70/71/65 with the pig emblem and the usual Nationalist markings.
36. Junkers W34hi 43-5 in use as a trainer and meteorological flight machine is overall 63 with a glossy black cowling.
37. Junkers W34hi 43-7 was probably overall 63 with patches of 61 and 62 on uppersurfaces with the usual Junkers black cowling.
38. Junkers Ju 60 D-UFAL was one of the less common types of the many DLH aircraft used as couriers between Berlin and Spain. It is overall in shades of natural metal with a black registration, logo, the name *Jaguar*, and the usual black/white swastika tail marking on a red band.
39. Heinkel He 70F 14-45 had probably been repainted in the field, probably in 61/62 with 65 below, with the more or less standard Nationalist markings.
40. Heinkel He 70F 14-47 was in overall 63 (or possibly "Lufthansa grey"), with a black fuselage marking. Lightning flash is same as grey, not white. The earlier *Luftwaffe* (?) fuselage marking had been over-painted in slightly lighter shade of grey. The beer mug marking, presumably in realistic colours, is that of the pilot, Hans Schmoller-Haldy, later a fighter pilot with 3.J/88.
41. Fieseler Fi 156B-0 46-1 was the first of two such types sent to Spain (note the style of exhausts, only found on the prototypes). Probably originally overall RLM 02 or RLM 63 with field-applied 65 undersides. Note there is no black disc background to the underwing cross; also the rudder appears to be grey instead of white. Note both Storch side views show the aircraft as if in flight with their undercarriage dangling.
42. Fieseler Fi 156C-1 46-5 was one of three delivered. Probably originally overall 02, but now has a field-applied top coat of 71 dark green, and the earlier registration underwing painted out with 63 or 65. Note no black disc background to underwing cross. Black wheel hubs.
43. Henschel Hs 126 19-3 newly painted in the field, with uppersurface polygons in 63 or 02 with patches of 61 and 62. Undersides are 65. There may have been an attemp to standardise on this type of pattern also seen on He 45s
44. Henschel Hs 126 19-7 is entirely in standard *Luftwaffe* 70/71 splinter uppers and 65 below. Note the coloured sighting lines on the fuselage. Basic Nationalist markings, probably with traces of a delivery code painted out under the wings.
45. Heinkel He 60E 60-3 shown after it had been passed over to the Spanish unit Grupo G-60 at Cadiz in 1937. Finished in overall 63 or 02 with silver floats, the underside of which are finished with dark grey or black anti-fouling paint. The name commemorates the first CO of the unit who was killed in a crash. The Popeye marking and the name appeared on both sides of the aircraft.
46. Popeye emblem on 60-3, probably a personal marking.
47. Heinkel He 60E 60-6 also after transfer to *Grupo G-60*, with that unit's emblem on the fin. Both this aircraft and 60-3 carried the white St. Andrew's crosses under and above the wings. Finish as 60-3.
48. The emblem of *Grupo G-60*.
49. Arado Ar 95 64-2 is shown in overall 63 but could be in 02 with basic Nationalist markings. A dull finish for a dull aeroplane.

# Captions to Color Artwork

50. Dornier Do 17F 27-14 (*Schnuckes*), flown by Martin Hering of A/88, who later served in III./KG 53 before being killed during the Battle of Britain as a reconnaissance pilot. Finish is standard *Luftwaffe* pattern 61/62/63 uppersurfaces, 65 below. A/88 devil emblem on outer cowling panels.
51. The personal emblem on 27-14. Colors are speculative.
52. Heinkel He 111C-0 D-ATYL (WNr 1833), was another fast courier aircraft linking Germany and Spain, probably used for top-ranking passengers. This was the last of only six C-0s built for Lufthansa and appears to be overall natural metal with white spinners and black lettering.
53. Heinkel He 111B-1 25-15 (*Pedro 15*) of 1.K/88. Apparently well known, this is the first time the complete markings carried by this aircraft have been shown. Overall finish is 63 (L40/52), with white tips to spinners. Inscription on nose and nickname *Holzauge* ("Clog") on fuselage all white. The well known "Peter" Scottie on the fin is in black and white on a fresh panel of paint. On the fuselage is the white eagle of 4.K/88.
54. Detail of the nose markings on 25-15.
55. Dornier Do 17F 27-16 *Mucki* of A/88 in which *Oberleutnant* Wolfgang Fach and his crew were shot down by flak over the Ebro on 5 August 1938. One man was killed. Finish is standard *Luftwaffe* pattern 61/62/63 upper surfaces, 65 below. Red and white personal emblem and spinners (?). Note A/88 unit emblem on outer faces of engine cowlings.
56. Detail of the personal emblem on 27-16.
57. Heinkel He 111B-1 25-9 (*Pedro 9*), of 1./K/88 is L40/52 light grey overall. Name *Pedro 9* in white on nose. The champagne bottle marking on the fuselage was carried by several other aircraft. It has been suggested that it may be the emblem of "5.K/88."
58. Detail of the witch personal marking on the tail of 25-9.
59. Heinkel He 111B-1 25-7 (*Pedro 7/Glitzer Mary*) of VB/88 in summer 1937. 61/62/63 uppers with 65 below. White name on nose, personal insignia on port fuselage. Red and yellow spinners.
60. Dornier Do 17F 27-25 of A/88, summer 1938. Camouflage is one of the many variations possible of the standard *Luftwaffe* pattern 61/62/63 upper surfaces, 65 below. Red and white personal emblem on nose and spinners(?). Note A/88 unit emblem on engine cowlings.
61. Detail of personal marking on 27-25.
62. The red/yellow comet with black "sunwheel" swastika emblem of 1.K/88.
63. Heinkel He 111B-1 (late series) 25-17 of 1.K/88, in early 1937. Overall finish of RLM 63 light grey, with a black chimney sweep personal marking on the port fin.
64. Heinkel He 111B (probably a B-2) 25-43 of K/88 at León. 61/62/63 uppers, 65 below.
65. Baron Münchausen emblem, carried on both sides of the fin of 25-43, slightly different each side.
66. Dornier Do 17P 27-28 of A/88. Standard *Luftwaffe* 70/71 splinter pattern upper surfaces, 65 below. Unit emblem on outer engine cowlings.
67. Heinkel He 111B-1 25-3 of VB/88 (*Pedro 1*), in early 1937. Overall finish of light grey, which was apparently at some later time given additional soft-edged bands of a darker color. The diving eagle insignia on the fuselage was used by VB/88 at this time and later by 4.K/88. White *Pedro 3* on both sides of nose.

68. Heinkel He 111B-1 25-4 (*Pedro 4/Castelo Branco*) ex-VB/88, now 1.K/88, late summer 1937. 61/62/63 uppers with 65 below. Champagne emblem of "5.K/88" (?) on fuselage disc. *Pedro 4* in white both sides of nose. Main colours of personal emblem on fin unknown, but most likely black and white with yellow (?) dress.
69. Junkers Ju 86D-1 26-3 of VB/88. Standard *Luftwaffe* 61/62/63 in pattern A2a on uppersurfaces. Carries the name *Fumo 3* in white on both sides of the nose.
70. Heinkel He 59B-2 71-1 of AS/88 at Pollensa in late 1938–early 1939. Overall RLM 02. AS/88 emblem on nose.
71. Heinkel He 59B-2 71-1 of AS/88 at Pollensa in 1937. Overall RLM 02. As above but with red/white pennant on fuselage.
72. AS/88 ace of spades emblem
73. Junkers Ju 52/3m 22-79 possibly a modified Lufthansa aircraft. Overall light grey with Nationalist markings.
74. Junkers Ju 52/3mg3e auxiliary bomber 22-86 of K/88. Finish appears to be a non-standard pattern of 61/62/63 uppers with 65 below. Pale blue cross on fuselage. Worn finish on wings. Usual Nationalist markings.
75. Eagle emblem of 2.K/88.
76. Junkers Ju 52/3mg3e 22-90 in a similar finish of 61/62/63 as 22-86 but with 2.K/88 black/white eagle badge. The aircraft was very clean and new-looking.
77. Personal emblem of Hans Schmoller-Haldy, He 70 (Dwg 40).
78. Ace of hearts emblem, He 45 15-21 (Dwg 24).
79. Top hat emblem of 2.J/88.
80. "Marabu" emblem of He 51, 2-86 (Dwg 7).
81. Mickey Mouse emblem of He 51 2-102 (Dwg 8) and also 2-78, Galland's aircraft later (Dwg 6).
82. Inscription on He 51 2-102 (Dwg 8).
83. Name on He 51 2-102 (Dwg 8).
84. Fuselage marking on He 51 2-102 (Dwg 8).
85. Ace of spades emblem of 4.J/88.
86. Emblem of Harro Harder, He 51 2-64, (Dwg 4).
87. Emblem of Adolf Galland, He 51 (Dwg 6).
88. Emblem of Walter Grabmann, Bf 109 (Dwg 16).
89. "Cross of sticks" emblem of 1.J/88 (later).
90. Mickey Mouse emblem of 3.J/88.
91. Personal emblem of Hans Schmoller-Haldy, Bf 109 (Dwg 22).
92. Devil emblem of A/88.
93. Emblem of Hannes Trautloft, Bf 109 (Dwg 11).
94. "Wooden eye" emblem of 1.J/88 (Bf 109).
95. Personal sweep emblem, He 111 (Dwg 63).
96. Champagne emblem, He 111 (Dwg 57, 68).
97. Emblem *Stukakette 88*, Ju 87 (early) (Dwg 33).
98. Emblem of *"Jolanthe" Stukakette*, Ju 87 (Dwg 34, 35).
99. Personal emblem of *Pedro 7*, He 111 (Dwg 59).
100. Personal emblem of *Pedro 15*, He 111 (Dwg 53).
101. Emblem of VB/88, He 111 (Dwg 53, 67).
102. Personal emblem of *Pedro 4*, He 111 (Dwg 68).

# Notes

1. Strictly speaking, when translated into English the name should be Condor Legion. In the interests of accuracy, all German unit titles have been retained in their original language, consequently the name is shown as Legion Condor throughout this book.
2. A peculiarly Spanish custom whereby army officers would declare themselves dictators and savior of the country. Franco had many predecessors.
3. An overseas organization for expatriate German Nazi supporters.
4. Literally District Group Leader, a minor rank in the NSDAP (Nazi Party) hierarchy.
5. A senior rank within the NSDAP, approximately the same as the governor of an American state.
6. The German counterintelligence organisation.
7. *Reichsluftfahrtministerium*, the German Air Ministry.
8. This was almost certainly nineteen-year-old Brian Douglas Griffin, who had only 130 hours of flying time and was believed to have been shot down by CR.32s. The state of aircraft recognition at the time could easily have led the He 51 to be mistaken for a Fiat CR. 32.
9. In fairness, it should be noted that overclaiming was rife on all sides, both in Spain and throughout World War II. Most were made in good faith, but the speed of air combat left little time for rivet counting.
10. The Republicans originally had three Furies, one of which was soon lost as the result of an accident; one was captured by the Nationalists in August 1936, and the third survived until early November, when it was seriously damaged but not before it had been used to score numerous victories in the hands of several of the best Republican pilots.
11. Heinz Guderian, the champion of armored warfare, whose brilliant handling of his panzers was the decisive element in the defeat of France in 1940.
12. Mikhail Tukhachevskiy, popular modernizer of the Soviet army and a prime mover in Soviet tank development. He was one of the first to be murdered in Stalin's purges.
13. In view of the semiclandestine nature of the foreign aid to both sides of the Civil War, it was the custom for many of the officers to use a *nom de guerre*, one of the best known being "General Douglas," the cover name of Yakov Smushkevich, commander of the Soviet forces in Spain. He later became yet another victim of the purges.
14. In the German air force, the captain of the aircraft was often an observer, not the pilot. This dated from the early days of World War I, when the pilot,

nicknamed "Franz" and usually an NCO, was regarded as a mere coachman. Observation on the other hand was a task usually undertaken by officers.
15. Literally "free hunt," i.e., roving patrols looking for targets of opportunity.
16. German torpedo development was a major scandal early in World War II. The admiral responsible was court-martialled.
17. Legion personnel normally spent nine months in Spain before being rotated home unless killed or wounded.
18. By March 1939, Hitler had already decided to invade Poland, and the RLM was clearly concerned to gain as much experience as possible before the main event.
19. A *Staffel* was the basic tactical unit of the *Luftwaffe*. Fighter units normally had a complement of twelve aircraft.
20. Literally "chain," alluding to the "follow my leader" style of attack adopted.
21. The biplane Polikarpov I-15 (I = *Istrebitely*, or fighter) was known variously as a Curtiss to the Nationalists on account of it being presumed to be of American origin or a Chato ("flat nose") to the Republicans because of its flat-fronted radial engine.
22. The Russian Polikarpov I-16 monoplane was probably the most advanced fighter in service anywhere until the advent of the Bf 109. It was known as Musha (Russian for "fly") or Mosca, the Spanish equivalent, on account of its small size and buzzing maneuverability. To the Legion and the Nationalists, it was more commonly the Boeing on the foolish assumption that it had American origins or the Rata ("Rat").
23. This was the incorporation of Austria into the Greater German Reich, an event which Hitler greatly feared might lead to war. In the event, the western powers did nothing.
24. Another indigenous Russian design assumed to be of U.S. origin, the Tupolev-designed SB-2 bomber was faster than the opposing Nationalist fighters when it first arrived in Spain. Known as the Martin bomber by the Francoists, it acquired the Russian girl's name Katiuska for uncertain reasons in service with the Republicans.
25. Veteran pilots were known as *Alte Hasen*—"Old Hares"—in the *Luftwaffe*. Presumably, old hares ran faster and survived.
26. Mickey Mouse fought on both sides in the Spanish Civil War and throughout World War II. Adolf Galland and his *Staffel* adopted such a unit emblem on their He 51s very early on. Galland continued to use a variant on all his later Bf 109s in World War II.
27. Until the advent of the I-16 and the Bf 109, the Fiat CR.32 was probably the best fighter on both sides in Spain. Unfortunately for the Italians, this success led them to retain the biplane layout for their fighters for too long, with disastrous results in the later conflict.
28. OTU stands for Operational Training Unit.
29. At this time, observers were the elite of the *Luftwaffe*, being trained as aircraft commanders and fully capable of taking over any other crew member's duties in an emergency.
30. The official term German term *Bordmechaniker*—literally, "onboard mechanic"—has been translated here as "flight engineer."

# Notes

31. As the Spanish war developed, the opportunity for training became ever more apparent to the *Luftwaffe* chiefs. With a new and larger conflict looming, full advantage was taken to give a combat blooding to as many *Luftwaffe* personnel as possible, hence the rapid turnover of personnel.
32. Captain.
33. 2nd Lieutenant.
34. Lieutenant.
35. Sergeant.
36. Later to become infamous when he bombed the British passenger liner *Empress of Britain* on 26 October 1940 while with 2.KG/40.
37. Although the Legion must take most of the responsibility for the Guernica bombing, it should be noted that Italian aircraft also took part in the operation.
38. The "Iron Ring" was the propagandist name given to the less than effective defenses around the city.
39. On account of their clandestine support for the Republicans, the French were allowed to examine captured German aircraft before these were passed on to the Russians. With fears of the impending war in their minds, both French and Russian technical experts were keenly interested in any such aircraft. Several types were tested and their strengths and weaknesses were thus known well before 1940.
40. A formation of three aircraft. A *Rotte* was a pair, and two pairs made a *Schwarm*.
41. The flight of three aircraft flown by the headquarters staff.
42. Literally "dive bomber aircraft" and applicable to any such aircraft, although usually taken to mean the Ju 87.
43. Experimental Fighter Group.
44. A specialist unit devoted to testing equipment and developing new tactics and operating procedures.
45. Note how many of the aircrew were junior NCOs; in the *Luftwaffe*, responsibility for aircraft was frequently given to much lower ranks than in the RAF or USAAF, for example.
46. Six Douglas DC-2s reached Spain before and during the civil war and were used by both sides. One was captured by the Nationalists early on and used as a personal transport, numbered 42-1, by General Franco. The one noted here as destroyed was c/n 1257. No other details of its identity are known for certain.

And so the Legion Condor flew into history, but in the end, it was the men that counted.

The crew of a Heinkel He 111E of 2.K/88 prepare for their next mission. They are wearing a mixture of *Luftwaffe* summer- and winter-weight flying suits, but it can be cold above Spain.

# Stackpole Military History Series

*Real battles. Real soldiers. Real stories.*

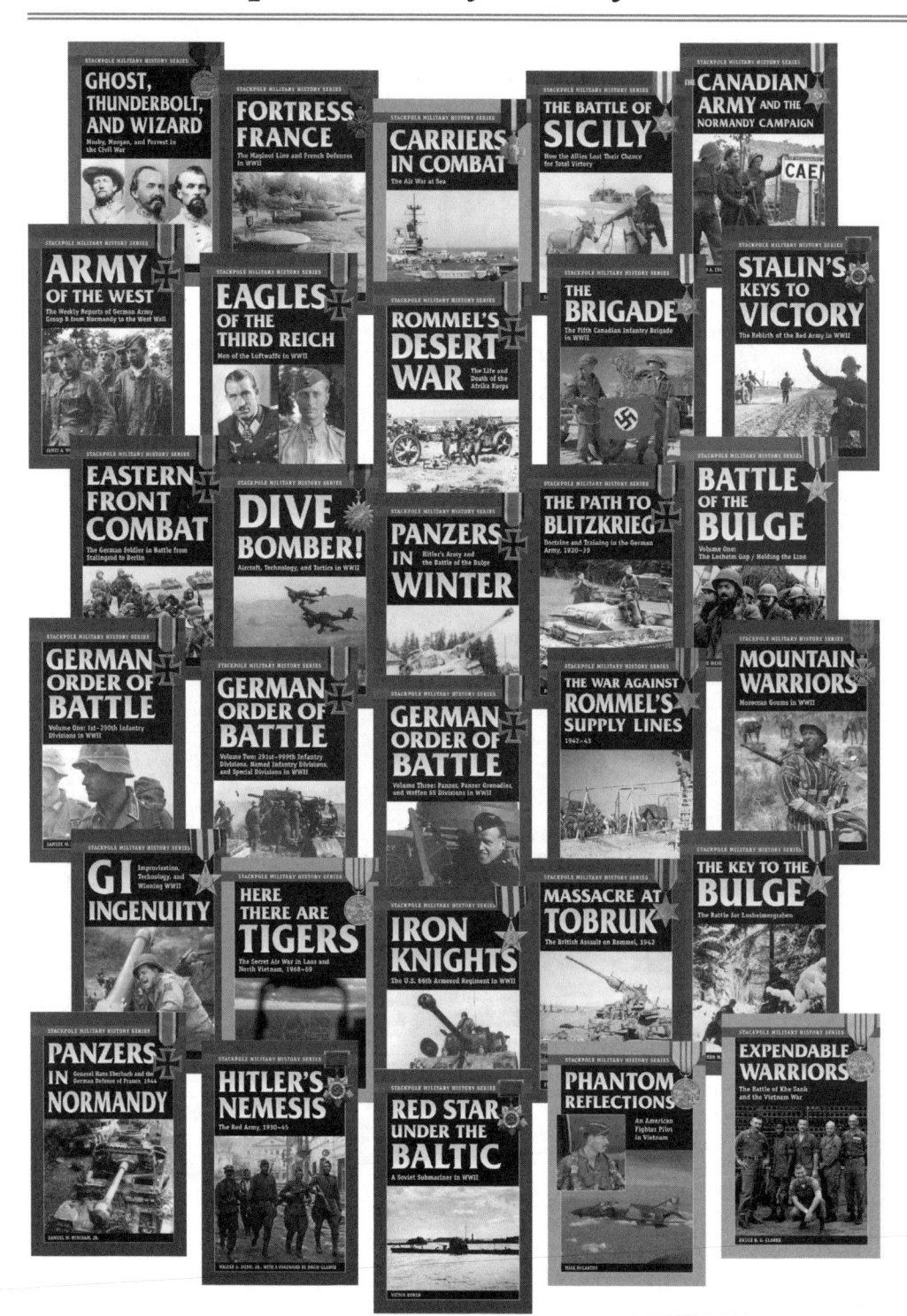

# Stackpole Military History Series

# *Real battles. Real soldiers. Real stories.*

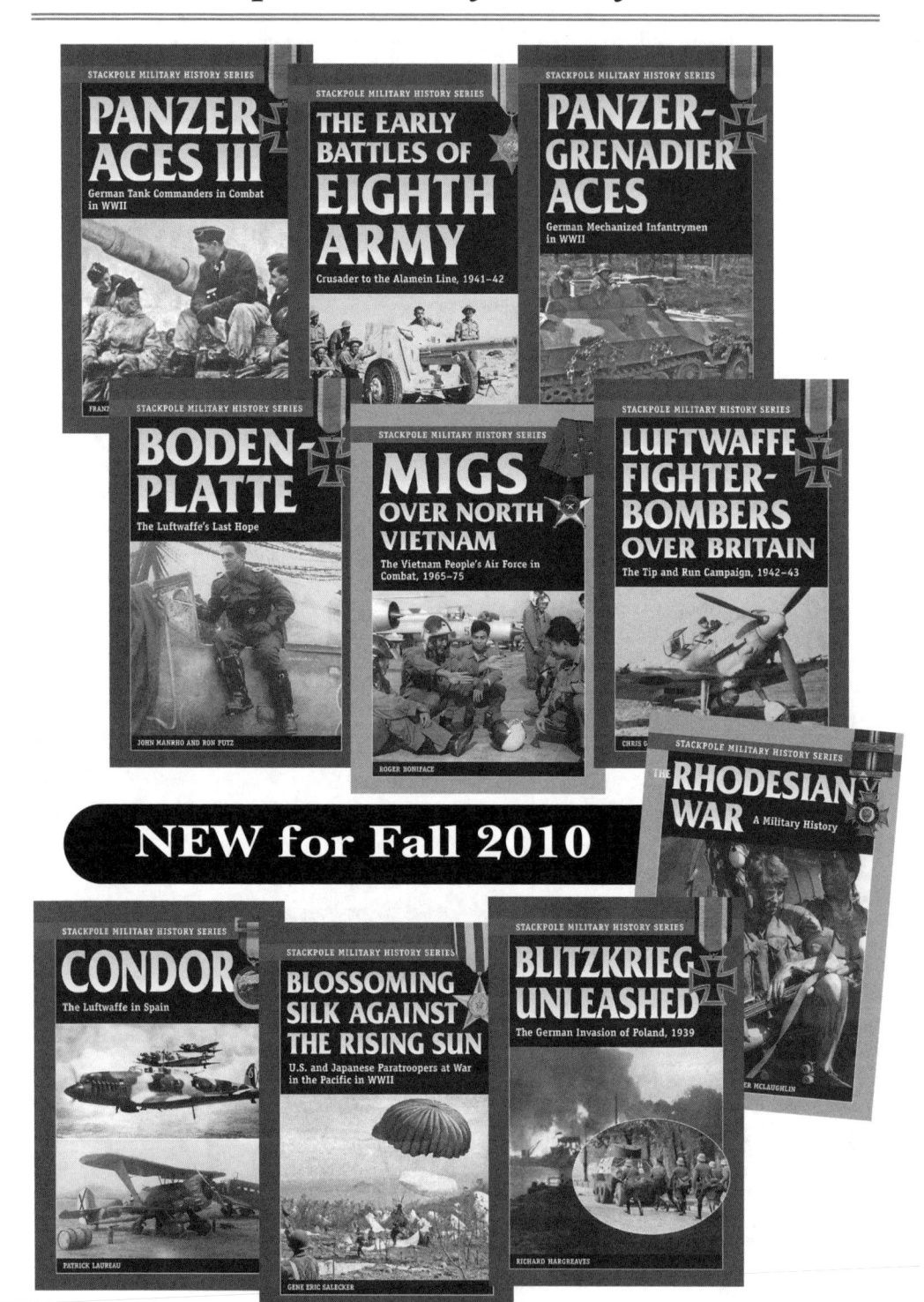

# Stackpole Military History Series

## NEW for Fall 2010

- **PANZER ACES III**: German Tank Commanders in Combat in WWII
- **THE EARLY BATTLES OF EIGHTH ARMY**: Crusader to the Alamein Line, 1941–42
- **PANZER-GRENADIER ACES**: German Mechanized Infantrymen in WWII
- **BODENPLATTE**: The Luftwaffe's Last Hope — John Manrho and Ron Putz
- **MIGS OVER NORTH VIETNAM**: The Vietnam People's Air Force in Combat, 1965–75 — Roger Boniface
- **LUFTWAFFE FIGHTER-BOMBERS OVER BRITAIN**: The Tip and Run Campaign, 1942–43
- **THE RHODESIAN WAR**: A Military History
- **CONDOR**: The Luftwaffe in Spain — Patrick Laureau
- **BLOSSOMING SILK AGAINST THE RISING SUN**: U.S. and Japanese Paratroopers at War in the Pacific in WWII — Gene Eric Salecker
- **BLITZKRIEG UNLEASHED**: The German Invasion of Poland, 1939 — Richard Hargreaves

# *Stackpole Military History Series*

## LUFTWAFFE ACES
### GERMAN COMBAT PILOTS OF WORLD WAR II

*Franz Kurowski,*
*translated by David Johnston*

Whether providing close-support for the blitzkrieg, bombing enemy cities and industrial centers, or attacking Allied fighters and bombers during both day and night, the Luftwaffe played a critical role in World War II and saw some of the most harrowing combat of the war. Franz Kurowski puts readers in the cockpit with seven of Germany's deadliest and most successful pilots.

*$21.95 • Paperback • 6 x 9 • 400 pages • 73 b/w photos*

**WWW.STACKPOLEBOOKS.COM**
**1-800-732-3669**

*Also available from Stackpole Books*

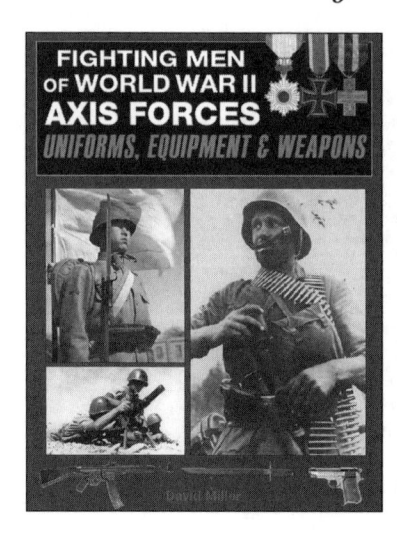

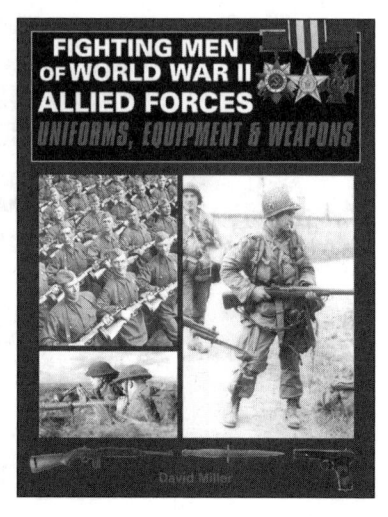

# FIGHTING MEN OF WORLD WAR II
## VOLUME 1: AXIS FORCES
## VOLUME 2: ALLIED FORCES
*David Miller*

These comprehensive volumes present a full-color look at Axis and Allied soldiers in World War II, covering their weapons, equipment, clothing, rations, and more. The Axis volume includes Germany, Italy, and Japan while the Allied volume presents troops from the United States, Great Britain, and the Soviet Union. These books create a vivid picture of the daily life and battle conditions of the fighting men of the Second World War.

$49.95 • Hardcover • 9 x 12 • 384 pages • 600 color illustrations

**WWW.STACKPOLEBOOKS.COM**
**1-800-732-3669**